THE QUEST FOR TIMBUCTOO

Brian Gardner

THE QUEST
for TIMBUCTOO

READERS UNION
CASSELL
London 1969

This RU edition was produced in 1969 for sale to its members only by Readers Union Ltd, at 10-13 Bedford Street, London WC2, and at Letchworth Garden City, Herts. Full details of membership may be obtained from our London address.

Originally published by Cassell & Co Ltd, London. Reprinted for Readers Union by The Hollen Street Press at Slough.

In Africa (a quarter of the world)
Men's skins are black, their hair is crisp and curled;
And somewhere there, unknown to public view,
A mighty city lies, called Timbuctoo.

—W. M. THACKERAY (1829)

Author's Note

THE narrative is arranged so as to allow the travellers considerable freedom to tell their own stories; owing to the nature of their experiences they themselves cannot be rivalled—particularly in the immediacy of their letters and journals—in communicating tensions, distress, and flavour. Some of this primary material has been published by specialized societies in recent years; a great deal of work has been done recently, and is being done, on the history of the exploration of North and West Africa. There are occasional gaps, and there it has been useful to go to unpublished sources. But as it seemed both pretentious and unnecessary to give documentation for all quotations, I have confined such documentation to the previously unpublished material, thereby avoiding a plethora of footnotes.

It would seem that a misunderstanding has caused some of the letters of Heinrich Barth from Timbuctoo to have remained undiscovered for so long. Barth wrote in his *Travels* that a large packet of letters he had despatched to Europe had never arrived—which was by no means surprising. This has naturally been accepted ever since. In fact, these letters reached Tripoli on June 20, 1857; they arrived in London in August, three and a half years after they had been sent. Barth's book was already written; the first volumes were in print. A correction was not made. Most of the 'lost' letters have been all the time in the Foreign Office files; they are now at the Public Record Office; some of the unofficial letters eventually came to the Manuscripts Department of the British Museum together with other material. It is remarkable that after a century virtually all Barth's voluminous correspondence from Africa remains unpublished, for on many occasions it complements his book. His Timbuctoo letters are quoted for the first time. Unpublished material concerning the singular international incident over the loss of Laing's papers also comes from the Public Record Office.

Some of the material was written on scraps of paper, thousands of miles from the nearest outposts, often in extreme danger and in near-impossible conditions. Therefore, where it seemed sensible to do so, I have sought some uniformity in the modern style with extracts that have been long published, at the expense of the fashions of long ago—with their abbreviations and punctuation no longer in use, their flamboyant use of capital letters, etc.—thus obviating the use of the condescending and irritating *sic*. This has effected only a detail here and there, and does not of course apply to previously unpublished material; the book is, I hope, the more easily readable. I have followed the convention of using the word Tuareg for singular and plural, although strictly the singular should be Targui or Tarqui (I notice that writers far more experienced than I in this field have had their difficulties here). 'Kingdoms' and Sultanates of West Africa up till the late nineteenth century, and their courts, should not be thought of in the light of European institutions: a confusion which was a source of misunderstanding about the nature of the interior of Africa for over three hundred years, and one to which many writers who should have known better added.

As well as the Public Record Office and the British Museum, mentioned above, I acknowledge with gratitude assistance from the Historical Manuscripts Commission, the London Library, the National Register of Archives for Scotland, and the Royal Society, which holds some of the Laing material.

B. G.

Contents

Illustrations

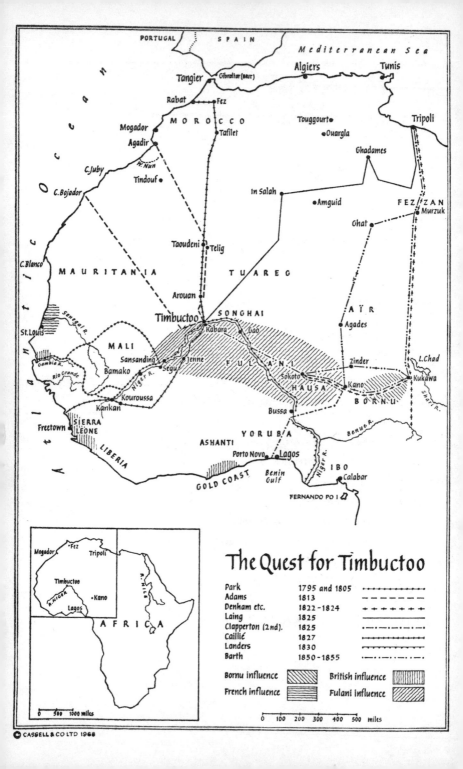

1 . *Prologue*

OR centuries Timbuctoo had been for Western man little more than an idea. It was not a place like other places, firmly implanted at a spot on the map. Not one person even knew exactly where it was. But that it was a great metropolis few had any doubt—the greatest in all Africa—and that its roofs were made of gold was widely agreed; the fact that it was believed to be the centre of a great culture, perhaps with answers to the problems of a puzzled age, and that it was the repository of priceless manuscripts of untold wisdom, made its attainment all the more attractive—even imperative; and the fact that its whereabouts were so uncertain, its inhabitants so mysterious, and that to reach it was said to be impossible, made it an irresistible challenge.

Few people at the beginning of the nineteenth century had not heard of Timbuctoo; but none had been there. The Arabs of the desert, however, had been going to and from the place for centuries. There was therefore nothing curious, it seemed, about the young Arab, who set out from a settlement on the Niger on April 20, 1828, at half-past three in the afternoon, for Timbuctoo.

The young Arab was with a large caravan, with which there were many slaves. It was, like most other days in those parts, hot, dusty and dry. As the great column snaked away from the river and penetrated the desert, the landscape became naked and barren. Soon the sand became fine and loose; progress was difficult and slow. Many of the slaves were travelling on foot, and each step further was a wretched labour for weary bodies. As all concentrated on the forward move there was little conversation, and there were few sounds apart from the gentle grunts and moans of men and beasts.

Men thought on their own affairs, and only once did anyone take much notice of the light-faced young Arab. A lone Tuareg marauder on a superb horse had attached himself to

1

the edge of the caravan like some fussy butterfly. He pranced about eyeing the young man narrowly. Several times he asked about him. Each time he was told that it was merely a poor traveller, and of no account.

The young Arab showed little concern, although he might well have done so: for he was not an Arab at all, but a Frenchman, despite his clothing and appearance; and a revelation of this fact would certainly have resulted in his death.

The caravan continued beside the lengthening shadows moving over the light-coloured sand. It was not until the vast, red sun was dipping towards the horizon that Timbuctoo was sighted in a slight dip below. The Frenchman contained his emotions with difficulty, for he had come far and risked life itself.

'I now saw this capital of the Sudan,' he wrote, 'to reach which had so long been the object of my wishes. On entering this mysterious city, which is an object of curiosity and research to the civilized nations of Europe, I experienced an indescribable satisfaction. I never before felt a similar emotion and my transport was extreme. I was obliged, however, to restrain my feelings, and to God alone did I confide my joy.'

He was not quite the first explorer of modern times to reach Timbuctoo—another had beaten him there by several months, and an American sailor had once been there as well—but he was to be the first explorer to return from it; it was to be nearly a quarter of a century before the next white man succeeded in breaking the challenge. Four men; three of them were to die young as a result of their dedication to the desert and 'the metropolis with the roofs of gold'. The American was first—but few ever believed him. Then came a Briton, a Frenchman and a German: in each one the characteristics of his nation were brought extraordinarily to the task. The Briton was of such superb but mindless courage that it was later to be asked whether he was 'afflicted with suicidal tendencies, for he ignored the most rudimentary precautions by travelling alone and undisguised'. The same source wrote of the Frenchman being 'filled with a romantic sense of adventure, mingled with patriotism, and determined to succeed not only to satisfy his own pride, but for the glory of France'. The expedition of the German, on the other hand, was 'prepared methodically and minutely in order that the results should give the maximum of value to science'.

The achievements of these men were to reveal not only the inherited qualities of nations, but also that men will believe not what is undoubtedly true but rather what they want to believe is true. No one knows exactly when it all began—probably some time in the Middle Ages—nor can they be certain as to when such misconceptions will end. . . .

2 . *The Legend*

SINCE the fourteenth century, Timbuctoo had haunted the imaginations of men. Children knew of it as the essence of mystery. In many languages it figured in phrases synonymous with distance and remoteness beyond experience.

The Sahara was the most inhospitable area in the world apart from the two poles themselves. Few men who entered it ever returned to Europe; those who did so told almost incoherent stories of madness through thirst, unspeakable cruelties of mirages, a fierce and terrible sun, and a vast, limitless ocean of sand.

At its broadest the Sahara was, in fact, about 3,200 miles from east to west: its extent from north to south about 1,400 miles: an area about the size of Europe minus Scandinavia. The greater part of it was apparently endless sand-dunes, continuing for hundreds of miles without feature or human life. The early method of crossing these wastes was in a caravan of camels: southwards with cheap goods from Europe: north with gold-dust, produce of West Africa and, mainly, slaves. Even this was by no means reliable; caravans which were sometimes thousands strong, disappeared over the sands never to be heard of again. To enter this area was in itself an act of extreme courage. Wells and oases were sometimes hundreds of miles apart, and the only way of travel was from one to the next one, which could involve detours of more than twice the distance for long journeys. Often, the wells were dry. No European even knew where the wells were. The ways between them were littered with skeletons and bones of both animals and humans.

To the north and north-west, this most-feared desert in the world was only halted by the Mediterranean shore, the almost impenetrable Atlas mountains, or the huge breakers of the Atlantic. To the east it stretched as far as the Nile itself, on the far side of the continent. But to the south it was bordered by a belt of tropical bush and jungle, of which equally little was known. The reputation of this steaming, damp, sultry area was almost as fearsome as that of the desert itself. It was the home of mysterious and seemingly incurable diseases: diseases about which at that time of primitive medicine little was known, and which often proved fatal. It was an area which came to be known as The White Man's Grave.

Somewhere beyond that dreaded desert, somewhere behind that belt of dank, swampy, disease-ridden bush, lay a great city—a place of learning, culture, sophistication, and above all of fabulous wealth. It seemed incredible that this could be so, but few doubted that it was true. And the only way to get to it was across the desert or through the incurable disease. . . .

That was the legend of Timbuctoo. But how had the legend come about?

*

In the Middle Ages the name 'Timbuctoo' was already known outside Africa. Arabs from the East had been settling south and west of the Sahara—in the area known as 'Negroland'—since the tenth century and before. Even the Romans, in their desert adventures, had penetrated to Negroland once—in the march of Julius Maternus, about AD 70. The Romans had built a border on the edge of the Sahara—hundreds of miles of continuous manned wall or ditch in the wilderness—which had lasted till at least AD 400, but the advanced forts beyond it had been deep into the desert and almost a third of the way to Timbuctoo.

In 1324 the vast and wealthy caravan of Mansa Musa, Emperor of Mali, had crossed the desert from West Africa to Cairo on a pilgrimage to Mecca. The merchants of Cairo had been astounded by the display of wealth, and particularly by the quantity of gold. It was perhaps the greatest caravan in history. It was said that much of it had been assembled at Timbuctoo. By the time this astonishment had spread to Europe it had gained in wonderment rather than lost. In 1353 a great Arab traveller, Ibn Batuta, visited Timbuctoo; on his return he described the wealth and gold of Mali, of which

Timbuctoo was an important centre. Thus began the connection of Timbuctoo and the idea of opulence and great wealth.

Although little further information arrived in Europe for nearly two hundred years, the legend refused to die.

Portuguese merchants were trading with caravans on the west and the north-west coasts of Africa. They already dominated the gold mines of the Ghana coast (Christopher Columbus was in their service there) and—before the arrival of the French—the Senegal coast; records show that they made contact with 'the kingdom of Timbuctoo'.* A Portuguese chronicler, Pina, said that his countrymen had settled in Senegal because of the king's 'conviction that the Senegal river, penetrating far into the interior, flowed from the city of Timbuctoo . . . where are the richest traders and markets of gold in the world, from which all Barbary from east to west up to Jerusalem is supplied and provided.'

John II and John III of Portugal had visions of ships transporting gold direct from Timbuctoo to Lisbon. An official attempt to reach the city was made in 1565. On March 1565, Diogo Carreiro wrote to King Sebastian, John III's successor:

I have pacified all chief kings here, and in the name of your highness I was liberal in distributing gifts among them. I have heard all about the river, and the road to Timbuctoo is generally clear, and—God willing—when this reaches your highness I shall have arrived there and be on my way back.

In his attempts to buy goodwill, and in his lonely fortitude, Carreiro set the style that was to be echoed by Europeans on the same quest for more than three centuries.

Practically nothing definite or new was learnt about Timbuctoo in the fifteenth century. But all the while a mysterious and bountiful supply of gold came from out of the desert into Europe, and few had any doubt as to where it had come from. Gold and Timbuctoo had become inseparable in men's thoughts; and so it was for over five hundred years.

In the middle of the sixteenth century a Moor born in Grenada published the first full account of the place, which he claimed to have visited. His book was widely discussed, not

*See Chart at end of this book, page 197.

only in the Spanish Court but in many other countries; it was translated into English. Leo Africanus had, in fact, been to Timbuctoo some years before, in 1526, in a diplomatic expedition on behalf of the Sherif of Fez. The news he brought back was the most detailed the world had heard of Timbuctoo. He said the town was close to a branch of the Niger, on which river it had its own port—called Cabra (i.e. Kabara).

There is a most stately temple to be seen . . . and a princely palace. . . . Here are many shops of artificers, and merchants, and especially of such as weave linen and cotton cloth. And hither do the Barbary merchants bring cloth of Europe. The inhabitants, and especially strangers there residing, are exeedingly rich, insomuch that the king that now is, married both his daughters unto two rich merchants.

. . . The coin of Timbuctoo is of gold. . . . The inhabitants are people of a gentle and cheerful disposition, and spend a great part of the night in singing and dancing; they keep a great store of men and women slaves.

It was exactly what Europe had longed to hear. He wrote of lavish, even fastastic, hospitality. 'The rich King of Timbuctoo hath many plates and sceptres of gold, some of which weigh 1,300 pounds. He keeps a magnificent and well-furnished court.' It seemed to be confirmation at last of the great desert metropolis where the supply of gold—the essential stuff of wealth—was inexhaustible.

When Leo Africanus wrote also of 'cottages built of chalk, and covered with thatch' it went unheeded.

After Leo Africanus, it became known in Europe that the Sultan of Morocco, tempted beyond endurance by the tales of Timbuctoo, had sent an army south to take the place. His army, under a Moor of Spanish origin, consisted of five thousand mounted men, two thousand infantry (many of them Spanish and Turkish renegades), artillery especially imported from England, and nine thousand supply camels and horses: the largest military force ever to cross the desert. Those who survived the four-months' march fought a Negro army on March 13, 1591. The Negroes had not seen firearms before and were massacred. The remaining Moors entered Timbuctoo unopposed. (Their rule did not last long, owing to lack of communication with Morocco. Cut off from home, they interbred, but their descendants, almost indistinguishable from Negroes, ruled the territory and the Songhai natives for much of the next three hundred years.*) The great military expedition furnished little information on Timbuctoo for those who waited impatiently in Morocco and Europe. But slaves, gold, ebony and spices came back to the Sultan in sufficient quantities not to weaken the legend—even to strengthen it.

The agents in Morocco of European merchants reported almost incredible wealth, all coming, it seemed, from Timbuctoo—for there it was that the caravans set out across the desert. In 1594, Laurence Madoc reported to his London firm the arrival at Marrakesh of thirty mules laden with gold. A month later he wrote of 'such an infinite treasure as I never heard of. It appears that they have more gold than any other part of the world beside. The king of Morocco is likely to be the greatest prince in the world for money, if he keeps this country'. In 1599 Jasper Thomson reported to London the arrival at Marrakesh of a 'great store of pepper, unicorns' horns . . . great quantity of eunuchs, dwarfs, and women and men slaves, besides fifteen virgins', and thirty camels laden with unrefined gold. He valued the caravan at £600,000, an enormous sum at the time.

The Elizabethan adventurers looked west rather than south. But a poet, George Chapman, prompted and urged the Queen's adventurers with the reminder that:

> Deep in the lion-haunted inland lies
> A mystic city, goal of high emprise.

In 1618 a company was formed in London for the express purpose of contacting and establishing commerce with the gold trade of Timbuctoo. Two expeditions were sent quickly out: the first ended in the massacre of all its members some 250 miles up the Gambia River.

The second expedition of the company was that of Richard Jobson, 'To advance the Golden Trade'. Jobson sailed up the

*Although the Moors accepted the loss of Timbuctoo in the seventeenth century, Mohammad V of Morocco based his claim to the town, as recently as 1958, on this campaign.

Gambia thinking it was the Niger, and expected to see the golden city around every corner. He brought back little confirmation.

But the city was now written about as 'an African Eldorado'. Of the background to this company, it was written:

The most flattering reports had reached Europe of the gold trade carried on at Timbuctoo; despatches were even received from Morocco representing its treasures as surpassing those of Mexico and Peru. The roofs of the houses were represented to be covered with plates of gold, that the bottoms of the rivers glistened with the precious metal, and the mountains had only to be excavated to yield a profusion of the metallic treasure.

Interest in the great city refused to die, and inquisitiveness was nearly always supported by greed. But Timbuctoo was known to be a place also of enviable learning. The university there was thought to be one of the great centres of Mohammedan culture; not only that, it was written that 'We shall one day correct the texts of our Greek and Latin classics by the manuscripts which are preserved there'. Moreover, the slave trade had drawn Englishmen and others to the Guinea coast, where forts and trading stations had been established; contact with the interior, and the rumours of the great city that lay within, increased.

The actual wealth of Timbuctoo was invariably given in loving detail—but the position of the place in the African Continent remained as vague as it had been in the fourteenth century.

About 1670 Paul Imbert, a French sailor, was shipwrecked on the west coast of Africa. He was taken by Arabs, who sold him as a slave to a Portuguese in the service of the Sultan. Imbert's master was sent on a mission to Timbuctoo by the Sultan, and it seems he took Imbert with him owing to the sailor's familiarity with quadrant and compass. From Timbuctoo the unfortunate slave tried to send news of himself to Europe. He died in captivity. Imbert's report of the city did not reach Europe; and the vague news of him only increased the mystery about the place.

*

In the eighteenth century several explorers and adventurers delved into the Sahara, few of them to return. Predictably, it was Dean Swift who, early on, sliced at the pretensions of scholars who drew maps of an area about which practically nothing had been learnt for centuries:

> Geographers, on Afric maps
> With savage drawings fill their gaps,
> And o'er unhabitable downs
> Draw elephants for want of towns.

By then the quest was ostensibly as much for the great Niger River as for the mysterious city, but it was the latter which continued to grip the imaginations of men. Three approaches were considered possible to reach the area in which the city was known to be: from the north or east, which meant traversing the desert; or from the west coast, through thick and unexplored forest, the unhealthiness of which was notorious. Several Frenchmen and a Swede had attempted to penetrate from the west, but with little success. The British, therefore, began to look hopefully at the north coast and the desert.

John Ledyard, an American born at Groton, Connecticut, was the most remarkable of the adventurers who set out for Timbuctoo at the end of the eighteenth century. He was a friend of Jefferson. He had sailed with Captain Cook in the South Seas, and had helped to bury him. Ledyard had then got the idea of walking around the world. He started from Hamburg and got as far as Siberia. But he had omitted to get permission from the Queen of Russia, and was deported. 'Little attentive to difference of rank,' one admiring Englishman wrote, 'he seemed to consider all men his equals.' In London, he visited the Secretary of the Association for the Promotion of the Discovery of Africa. It had been founded only two weeks before, ostensibly for scientific and humanitarian (investigating slavery) purposes, but commerce had an obvious interest in its success.

The Secretary spread out a map on the table. It was suggested that Ledyard might visit the interior. When could he leave? 'Tomorrow morning.' He was to attempt a crossing of the desert from Egypt, but his real objective was Timbuctoo. John Ledyard died in Cairo before beginning his attempt.

The African Association was not disillusioned; for it had procured in London the services of two Moors, Shabeni and Ben Ali. These men claimed to have been in Timbuctoo, and for a consideration they gave their accounts of the place, in 1789 and 1790 respectively. They described a fantastic centre of wealth and trade, with any amount of gold. The great king had hundreds of beautiful slave-girls, a bodyguard of 5,000 men, 600 horses in his stables, and had offenders bastinadoed to death. 'They play at chess and draughts, and are very expert at those games . . . they have tumblers, jugglers, and ventriloquists whose voice appears to come from under their armpits . . . [and] dances of different kinds, some of which are very indecent.'

This, and a report from the British Consul at Tangier, led the Secretary of the Association to refer to 'the luxurious city of Timbuctoo'. Ben Ali was engaged to lead a mission to the city, but he disappeared in the streets of London—after receiving some payments.

Daniel Houghton was the first man actually to be commissioned to find Timbuctoo: on July 5, 1790. An impoverished Irishman, little is known of him except the details of his Army career, in which he rose to the rank of Major, and his jovial disposition. Having been chased by creditors for many years, he married a wealthy lady, only to see her riches taken away by the persistent creditors. Shortly after this disappointment, he applied for the job of going to Timbuctoo, and was accepted. He was over fifty years old. He landed on the Guinea coast and proceeded west. He wrote to his wife:

I shall soon be leaving this [the Gambia River] for Timbuctoo, where I hope to be in one month. The king will send some of his people with me, for I assure you I am greatly caressed here, on account of my coming to make a settlement in their country, which will enrich them all by trade, and I hope myself too. I am afraid I shall have no opportunities of writing to you after I leave this till I return to the river; so do not be uneasy if my silence appears long. I am now out of all danger; the king assures me I can travel to Timbuctoo with only a stick in my hand; no one will molest me.

The last communication from him after leaving Gambia was: 'Major Houghton's compliments—Is in good health on his way to Timbuctoo, [but] robbed of all his goods.' There was no date and the place-name was indecipherable. It was the last the world ever heard from Daniel Houghton.*

Frederick Hornemann, a brave young German academic, sent by the Association to report on Timbuctoo and other matters, died on the banks of the Niger at the age of twenty-eight, the first European to have crossed the Sahara since Roman times, and the first ever to have done so from east to west. He never saw Timbuctoo, but he wrote of it to London: 'It certainly is the most remarkable and principal town in the interior of Africa.' Hardly a man who approached the great desert at this time, in what was to become known as 'the Timbuctoo Rush', returned. There seemed no chance of getting through alive. And then, at last, some success.

*

The African Association, which had financed Ledyard, and Houghton's ill-fated expedition to Timbuctoo, was now looking for a successor. English commerce was anxious to discover whether a rich potential market existed in the area, and whether the Niger was a waterway leading to it. The Association found its man in the person of a tough, ambitious Scottish ship's doctor. His name was Mungo Park. He successfully applied for the job, and in 1795 he penetrated from the Guinea coast as Houghton had done. His commission stated that he was to visit 'particularly Timbuctoo'.

Park set out from Pisania, a small trading station two hundred miles up the Gambia River, with two attendants: a Negro servant and a slave-boy. He had provisions for two days, beads and tobacco for bartering, a compass and pocket sextant, a thermometer, some firearms and an umbrella. He had no experience of exploration whatever. Thus provided, he set out for one of the least hospitable areas in the world.

After three days the first local king he met begged him to return as most of the natives of the interior had never seen a white man before. But Mungo Park continued—slowly but inexorably travelling eastward. For safety the little party travelled at night; only the howling of wild beasts broke the

*After reports of his death, Mrs. Houghton addressed the Association from a debtor's prison. She was awarded a pension, and the education of her sons.

silence as they went forward in moonlight. Having been robbed of nearly all his possessions, Park reached the Mali area—mainly Moslem country—and set forth into the desert. At this time his servant refused to continue, and Park was left with the black boy in a hostile and unknown country.

Inevitably, he was taken prisoner. His captors were a large band of Moors. They 'obliged me to unbutton my waistcoat and display the whiteness of my skin—they even counted my toes and fingers'. He was treated with casual brutality, but one incident—which he recorded with characteristic verve— lightened his sufferings:

A party [of Moorish women] came into my hut and gave me plainly to understand that the object of their visit was to ascertain by actual inspection, whether the rite of circumcision extended to the Nazarenes as well as the followers of Mohamet. The reader will easily judge my surprise at this unexpected declaration; and in order to avoid the proposed scrutiny, I thought it best to treat the business jocularly. I observed to them that it was not customary to give ocular demonstrations in such cases before so many beautiful women; but that if all of them would retire, except the young lady to whom I pointed (selecting the youngest and handsomest), I would satisfy her curiosity. The ladies enjoyed the jest and went away laughing heartily.

As well as crude wit, Mungo Park was possessed of hard, formidable and ruthless ambition. His iron will to succeed was perhaps greater than that of any other African explorer. Escaping at night from the hut in which the Moors had detained him, he continued alone. He was now in rags, and continually beset with misfortunes and hardships that would have broken any ordinary man. On the edge of starvation, he suffered the agony of thirst under a pitiless sun. He lay on the sand to die; there was a downfall of rain and he was able to find nourishment by wringing and sucking his tattered clothing. Three weeks after his escape he sighted the Niger 'glittering to the morning sun, as broad as the Thames at Westminster, and flowing slowly to the *east-ward*'.

The fact that the river flowed eastwards at this point only made the problem worse: did it curl round and enter the Atlantic after all, did it curl south and join with the Congo (as Park himself was inclined to believe), did it cross Africa and join with the Nile, or did it continue to the east and end in some vast lake or inland sea? These were the four views about which the geographical and academic world were divided. According to the natives to whom Park spoke it ran 'to the world's end'.

Park attempted to follow the course of the river for some hundreds of miles and to reach Timbuctoo. At length he was forced to give up.

Worn down by sickness, exhausted by hunger and fatigue, half-naked, and without any article of value by which I might get provisions, clothes or lodging, I felt I should sacrifice my life to no purpose, for my discoveries would perish with me.

After nearly two thousand miles of travelling he reached the coast and returned to London—via the West Indies, on an American slaver. He had been away for three years. The report of his journey, which was soon published, made him famous. It was the most detailed and informative description of the Niger area that had ever appeared, and it was written in a popular vein.

Park called Timbuctoo 'the great object of my search'. Although he had not visited Timbuctoo, he had inquired about it, and the information he had gained was far from disappointing: 'The present King of Timbuctoo is reported to possess immense riches. His wives and concubines are said to be clothed in silk, and the chief officers of state live in considerable splendour.'

Of all the West African explorers, only Mungo Park achieved posterity's favour: a not entirely just verdict, for others were to return with valuable information, but none with such a gift for popular exposition. He married and settled down as a country doctor in Scotland. He was famous; the father of four children; a family friend of Walter Scott. He adored his wife, Ailie ('my sweet wife, you are everything that I could desire, and wherever we go you may be sure of one thing, that I shall always love you'). But in 1805 he was invited—this time by the Government—to lead an official expedition: to determine finally the exit of the Niger, and to visit the towns on its banks.

It was to be a most elaborate expedition. An early intention was that it should be entirely military in nature, the objective being the capture of Timbuctoo. This idea gave way to less bellicose objectives, and the importance of discovering the termination of the Niger. Cost—about £60,000, a very large sum. A pension of £100 a year was to be provided for his wife should he not return. And Park himself was given the immediate rank and pay of a Captain in the Army. His brother-in-law, also a doctor (with rank of Lieutenant), was to be second-in-command. Park had already turned down offers to explore Australia, and extracted from the Government 'the most solemn promise that in case of my success I shall be put into a comfortable situation at my return'.

Forty-four Europeans, with native bearers and guides, set off into the unknown in Park's expedition. Before long most of them must have regretted it bitterly. Owing to governmental delay, they were obliged to march through the forest belt in the rainy season, which made every mile a sodden misery. The soldiers, in their tight red coats, dropped behind in the torrential rain; one by one they were left behind in remote villages, wasting with disease, never to be heard from or seen again. Park would not stop for anyone, and when, at nightfall, he stopped at a village to barter with the chief, as much as half of his column was stretched for miles behind him, lying feverish and exhausted or wandering aimlessly. The expedition had become an ill-disciplined rabble. Nearly everyone in the expedition had become a useless burden to Park, not least the brother-in-law, who had to be carried for many weeks until his death. The new second-in-command, an Army Lieutenant named Martyn, was seldom sober: 'Whitbread's beer is nothing to what we get at this place, as I feel by my head this morning, having been drinking all night with a Moor, and ended by giving him an excellent thrashing.'

Charges of inhumanity against Park ignore contrary evidence noted briefly in the Journal, which he somehow found energy to write up at the end of each weary day. Sixteen times he crossed one stream with sick and exhausted soldiers on his back (which left him 'somewhat fatigued'). His cheery dispatches describing everything as flourishing, when everywhere death and disaster surrounded him, were more likely to reassure his wife than to display callousness (for he had already arranged that the authorities should not reveal any set-backs to the newspapers, for the same reason). Evidence that he kept the medicinal stores for his own use is flimsy (he had more experience of the climate than the others, and was very likely more hardy). We know that he walked so that a sick soldier could have his mount. But by the time he reached the Niger again, after nearly four months' desperate travelling, only eleven Europeans survived, and most of them were in the mortal grip of disease.

It was ten years since Park had seen the Niger. This time he was determined to navigate it to its mouth, no matter what the cost to himself and his remaining companions. His reputation and security would then be certain.

With the only one of the remaining redcoats who could stand, he joined together two half-rotten canoes and prepared a forty-foot craft for the great journey, wherever it might take them—the Congo, the Nile, the inland sea, or the Atlantic. For this task four carpenters had been brought out from England, but only one remained, and he was dying. It took the two men eighteen days to complete; when they had done so, Park hoisted the Union Jack and the survivors of the once formidable-looking expedition pushed off into the river: they now amounted to Park himself, four Europeans (one of them mad), three slaves and a guide. Before leaving, Park had sent his Journal back to the Gambia, with news of his departure down the river. 'I shall set sail to the East, with the fixed resolution to discover the termination of the Niger or perish in the attempt. I have heard nothing that I can depend on respecting the remote course of this mighty stream.'

For more than five years there was silence. Then news of the craft came back, for the guide—suspiciously, perhaps—had alone survived. Park had decided to stay afloat, avoid all business with the natives, and to continue to the end. When approached by native boats, he had fired on them, causing many deaths. Only near Timbuctoo had he entered into communication with the natives—to report on the city being part of his commission—but there, too, he had fired into a crowd of Tuareg when they had appeared hostile. And so, as he had progressed down the Niger, Mungo Park had left destruction and bitterness behind him. According to one source, Park seems to have fired on practically everyone he sighted. Whether true or not, the natives certainly believed this to be the case. This was to have the most tragic results for later exploration to Timbuctoo. It may well be that Park's normal goodwill towards the Africans had deserted him, in his weak and tense condition, when he had known that he was almost at the end of his work; he dared let nothing stop him after already having sacrificed so many lives. At length he had been attacked in a narrows, near Busa, by a strong force of avenging Tuareg—almost an army according to one account. Clasping to him one of the soldiers who could not swim, he had disappeared into the swirling waters of the river on which he had travelled for over 1,200 miles.* Thus not one of Park's forty-four Europeans returned. He had travelled further on the river than probably any other human had done before, in a simple boat. Nothing like it was achieved again on the Upper Niger till French naval craft made the journey in 1896. He was thirty-four years old, and only four hundred miles from the sea.

*

Mungo Park's energetic—almost frenzied—efforts to reveal the secrets of the West African interior did nothing to sate the public's curiosity regarding Timbuctoo, and in particular its great wealth. The place was more frequently mentioned than ever before. In 1809 James G. Jackson, an English merchant resident in Morocco, wrote a book which included 'An Accurate and Interesting Account of Timbuctoo, the Great Emporium of Central Africa'.†

He was the first to record the fate of the disastrous 1805 caravan, of which all two thousand persons died of thirst when a watering-place was found dried up.

Jackson described Timbuctoo, from the many reports he had heard of the place, as twelve miles in circumference. He

---

*The usual account, based on Isaaco and Lander. It has been questioned by, among others, Stanhope White, who was District Officer in the area after the Second World War. Park's wife refused to accept his death, and believed he was living in captivity.

†The book was re-issued in 1814 and 1820, a measure of its success.

also confirmed that it was a considerable slave-trading centre. Timbuctoo—inaccessible, remote, private—had become an important slave-collecting centre. As the slave trade westwards, to the boats for the West Indies, decreased, so grew the trade east and north—destined for Cairo, Constantinople, Arabia and Morocco.* Plantation labour became less valuable, harem ornaments more so. An essential element for all caravans trekking north across the desert were some hundreds of Negro girls to make each caravan economically worth while. Jackson was able to give a rare and important account of this:

The slaves are more or less valuable in Barbary, according to their beauty and symmetry of person, and also according to their age and the country from which they are procured. A young girl of Houssa, of exquisite beauty, was once sold at Morocco, whilst I was there, for four hundred ducats [about £72 in the value of the time], whilst the average price of slaves is about one hundred, so much depends on the fancy, or the imagination, of the purchaser. The slaves are treated very differently from the unhappy victims who used to be transported from the coast of Guinea, and our settlements on the Gambia, to the West India islands. . . . But the Moors make an infamous traffic of them, by purchasing and afterwards intermarrying them, for the purposes of propagation and of sale, when they are placed in the public market-place and there turned about and examined in order to ascertain their value.

The eunuchs which the Emperer and princes keep to superintend their respective hereems are for the most part procured from the Sudan; these creatures have shrill, effeminate voices; they are emasculated in a peculiar manner, and sometimes in such a way as not to be incapacited from cohabiting with women.

It must have been from the slave traders, with whom he appears to have been on intimate terms, that Jackson was able to give his description of Timbuctoo; and of the late ruler of the place who

possessed an immense quantity of gold . . . it is said that the massive bolts in his different palaces were of pure gold, as well as the utensils of his kitchen. The climate of Timbuctoo is much

---

*Legal participation in the slave-trade was abolished by Denmark in 1802, U.S. in 1808, Britain in 1808, Sweden in 1813, Netherlands in 1814, France in 1818 (partially in 1791), Spain in 1820, and Portugal in 1836. Illegal West Coast slaving continued till after 1850.

extolled as being salutary and extremely invigorating, insomuch that it is impossible for the sexes to exist without intermarriage; accordingly it is said there is no man of the age of eighteen who has not his wives or concubines . . . it is even a disgrace for a man who has reached the age of puberty to be unmarried. The natives, and those who have resided there any considerable time, have an elegance and suavity of manner . . . it should appear that the banks of the Nile from Timbuctoo to the 20th degree of east longitude are as populous as those of any river in China.

If this was indeed true, the economic advantage to any nation gaining influence over the area was obvious. Such a great market would be priceless. In England, particularly, excitement and curiosity about Timbuctoo were aroused still further. Two more expeditions departed on the quest—both unsuccessful.

In France, as well as in England and Germany, the desire to reach Timbuctoo first was becoming an obsession among many courageous and honourable men. For Timbuctoo, as was well known, was a place of almost unthinkable riches and glamour. That was the legend. But what was the truth? Four years after Jackson's book, which had added such awe to the reputation of the world's most wonderful city, a man appeared who claimed at long last to have actually been there: and to know the truth.

3 . *The American*

BENJAMIN ROSE was a twenty-five-year-old
sailor. He was born at Hudson, New York
State, where his father was a sail-maker and his
mother a coloured woman. He was the first person ever to
give a full and long account of Timbuctoo—who had himself
been there.

Rose first appears in historical record on October 6, 1813,
at the home of the British Consul at Mogador, in Morocco.
He spoke in Arabic and broken English, but insisted that he
was an American citizen who had been kept as a slave by
Moors and Negroes for three years. At this time he gave his
name as Benjamin Rose. The British Consul, Joseph Dupuis,
wrote of him: 'Like most other Christians after a long captivity and severe treatment among the Arabs, he appeared on
his first arrival exceedingly stupid and insensible; and he
scarcely spoke to anyone.'

All Rose wanted in life, it seemed, was to return to the
United States as soon as possible. That was not easy—as
Britain and the United States were at war.* After nearly
seven months at Mogador, during which time he was able
to recuperate from his experiences, Rose was sent north, to
the American Consul-General, James Simpson, at Tangier.
After a few days he was moved on to Cadiz, where it was
hoped he would find an American ship. Plagued by misfor-
tune, the unfortunate sailor missed the ship by two days.
Eventually he joined the crew of a Welsh brig at Gibraltar—
the war having now ended—from which he was discharged at
Holyhead owing to sickness. From there he begged his way
to London. Sleeping on the streets, he was accidentally discovered by a man who had seen him in Cadiz and who had
been told that he had seen Timbuctoo. This man took the

---

*The Anglo-American War, 1812–14, of which it has been said: 'Its cause
was removed before it began and the fighting took place after it had finished.'

gaunt and starving American to the offices of the Africa Committee.*

The sailor had become 'Robert Adams'—by which name he has been referred to ever since, and by which he became known to history. The Committee checked on the details of his story from Mogador and found them to be true. The Africa Committee—not to be confused with the African Association above, which financed exploration—were interested in the possibilities of trade with Timbuctoo. They listened to the poor and wretched sailor who called himself Robert Adams both enthralled and suspicious. A certain S. Cock was commissioned to interview Adams at length and to write a full report. Bearing in mind the curious circumstances in which the man had been brought before them, and the fact that 'they considered how widely his account of Timbuctoo differed from the notions generally entertained of the magnificence of that city, and of its civilization and of its inhabitants', the Committee were dubious as to the worth of Adams's revelations. S. Cock, however, approached his task with commendable dedication. Adams was anxious to leave and board a ship for America. He feared a renewal of hostilities between England and his own country, of which rumours were circulating, but he was persuaded to remain for the few weeks only that the report would take. Cock, meanwhile, made the sailor's situation more comfortable; he equipped him with decent clothes, of which he stood peculiarly in need. He was also supplied with a trifle in money 'as an earnest of the future recompense which was promised to him, provided he would attend every day until the whole of his story should be taken down'.

*

Adams said that he had sailed from New York on June 17, 1810, on the ship *Charles*: 280 tons, captain and nine crew. After discharging cargo at Gibraltar, the captain took the

*The Committee of the Company of Merchants Trading to Africa; it was closely associated with the Government, which had taken the responsibility of exploration from the African Association.

ship down the west coast of Africa on a 'trading' voyage. It was soon evident to those of the crew who had been in those seas before that the captain did not know where he was or where he was going. This opinion was reinforced when the craft struck a reef of rocks (probably near Cape Blanco). All managed to struggle ashore, but soon after daybreak they were surrounded by thirty or forty Moors. Captain and crew, having lost all firearms and weapons in the wreck, were taken prisoner. They were immediately stripped naked and their clothes taken from them (many other accounts reveal that this was the invariable practice of Moors when whites were taken prisoner). Exposed to a scorching sun, their skins became terribly burnt and blistered. The Yankee captain deteriorated rapidly. 'Partly from an obstinacy of disposition, and partly from the lassitude brought on by sickness and despair, he refused to do as desired; and whenever pressed to do so, used the most threatening looks, actions and words.' The captors shortly ended his misery forever.

The Moors, who had been engaged in fishing on the coast, departed for the interior of Mauritania after ten or twelve days. It seems that they were ignorant of the fact that to the north, in Morocco, Christian slaves fetched high prices to those anxious to procure their freedom—notably the British Consul at Mogador. It was thus most unfortunate for Adams that he had fallen to these particular Moors, as most others would have taken the sailors north immediately. The Moor band also had a French and a Portuguese slave.* The whole party now moved off south-west—to Timbuctoo, where the Moors no doubt hoped to sell their white slaves. *En route* the mate, most of the crew and the Frenchman were apparently sold to another band of Moors, who took them away to the north. Despite his bitter remonstrations, only Adams and the Portuguese were left.

They crossed the desert, according to Adams's reckoning, at the rate of from fifteen to twenty miles a day. Water-holes were sometimes so scarce that they were reduced to drinking the urine of camels. After about sixteen days the

---

*At the beginning of the nineteenth century there were hundreds, perhaps thousands, of European and American slaves in North Africa and Islam, most of them sailors.

most terrible part of this trek was over; they reached a hilly area with small trees.*

Soon after reaching the hilly and vegetated area, the party was surrounded by a large company of Negroes, who took the Moors and slaves prisoner. Fifteen of the Moors were beheaded and the remainder, with Adams and the Portuguese, were taken first to the Negroes' village and then to Timbuctoo, which they reached in desperate condition after a twenty-six days' march. This was, Cock claimed, in February, 1811, four months after the shipwreck of the *Charles*.†

Adams and the Portuguese were greeted at Timbuctoo with the greatest curiosity. During their stay of four months, they were treated as honoured guests rather than as slaves. While the remaining Moor captors were put into prison, the two whites lived at the 'king's' house and moved as they pleased. Adams, therefore, was able to inspect the city at greater ease than any non-African or non-Arab visitor until almost the twentieth century. This was ironic as, being an uneducated and simple man, he had no ideas about what to look for, even if he had been so inclined, and was not observant. Indeed, he was not in the least impressed at being in the 'Mysterious City' which was the object of so much curiosity to the Western world.

Despite some obvious efforts of Mr. Cock to prompt him otherwise, Adams's description of Timbuctoo was of a dull, filthy and exceedingly unattractive town. In contrast to the information brought back by Mungo Park on his first expedition, Adams specifically stated that he never saw any of the inhabitants wearing silks.

The town appeared to him 'to cover as much ground as Lisbon'. There was a broad river about two hundred yards to the south, with very little current, flowing to the south-west: the water there was rather brackish. About two miles further south, however, the river was less broad—about half a mile across.

---

*At the rate he described, Adams would have covered between 250 and 326 miles of sandy desert. As it seems he was travelling in a south-westerly direction somewhere between 18° and 15° of latitude and 5° and 10° of longitude, this would be a very fair estimate and a remarkable feat of memory.

†The dates concerning Timbuctoo arrived at by Cock were almost certainly incorrect.

The houses were extremely simple, with no furniture. They were built of sticks, clay and grass, with flat roofs.

Elephant hunts were great occasions. But the most remarkable animals in the vicinity were like large dogs or foxes that had pouches in their backs for carrying their prey. They fed on coconuts (which Adams mentioned several times in his account). About once a month a party of armed men marched out to procure slaves. The slaves which were brought back, after an absence of one week to a month, were of a different race to the people of Timbuctoo. These slaves were chiefly women and children.

He did not see any mosques there.

Adams passed his time as comfortably as he could.

For some time after their arrival, the Queen and her female attendants used to sit and look at Adams and his companion for hours together. She treated them with great kindness, and at the first interview offered them some bread baked under ashes. . . . For a considerable time after the arrival of Adams and his companion the people used to come in crowds to stare at them; and he afterwards understood that many persons came several day's journey on purpose. . . . Neither Adams nor the Portuguese boy were ever subjected to any restraint whilst they remained at Timbuctoo. . . . Adams could not hear that any white man but themselves had ever been seen in the place; and he believes, as well as from what he was told by the Moors, as from the uncommon curiosity which he excited, that they never had seen one before.

At length a party of Moors arrived in the town. They were, it seemed, well known there, and visited the place every year during the rainy season. They traded in tobacco. These Moors ransomed the two whites and their imprisoned countrymen, and ten days later they set off for the east, travelling along the northern bank of the river.

Adams's adventures were not over. After ten days the Moors veered away from the river to the north. Eventually they reached the desert once more. Adams was fortunate to survive another terrible desert-crossing, during which the beasts of burden were eaten and the urine of the camels drunk. Some of the Moors, unable to proceed, were left behind lying in the sand.

Adams mentioned passing through a village called 'Taudeny',

at which there were 'numerous beds of salt': a reference to the famous salt trade of North Africa, the source of which had long been a mystery in Europe.*

On the northern edge of the desert they came to a Moorish village of tents. Here the party recovered from the desert-crossing. After two weeks Adams—once again a slave—was put to work tending goats and sheep, with the Portuguese youth. This continued for ten or eleven months.

They suffered severely from exposure to the scorching sun, in a state of almost utter nakedness; and the miseries of their situation were aggravated by despair of ever being released from slavery. At length Adams, after much reflection on the miserable state in which he had been so long kept, and was likely to pass the remainder of his life, determined to remonstrate upon the subject.

His master, unexpectedly short of slaves, declined to take him to Mogador, as he had previously promised. Adams thereupon refused to care for the animals any longer, even though such action endangered his life. The following morning several young goats were found killed by foxes. Adams's punishment was to receive 'a severe beating' from a dozen Moors, principally women. The aftermath of this was his only sickness during three years of arduous slavery. Soon after this he came under a new master. This man had two wives, to one of whom Adams was given as a slave—no doubt as a special gift on account of his rarity as a Christian.

Some days after he had been so employed, the younger wife proposed to him that he should also take charge of her goats, for which she would pay him; and as there was no more trouble in tending two flocks than one, he readily consented. Having had charge of the two flocks for several days without receiving the promised additional reward, he at length remonstrated; and after some negotiation on the subject of his claim, the matter was

---

*This was one of the first mentions of the notorious salt mines of Taoudeni, founded in about 1600. The nature of these was unknown until the arrival of three French officers in 1906. It has since been noted that Adams's short description was utterly misleading. He wrote of 'excellent water', 'fertility' and 'trees', whereas the water at the mines is undrinkable and there is no vegetation whatever. Adams must have confused it in memory with some other oasis. He probably did not visit it, as the main caravans to Morocco did not go to the mines (there being no water) but to a well close by. Even today it is by no means easy to find two maps which give the same position for Taoudeni.

compromised by the young woman desiring him to go to rest in her tent. This was an arrangement which was afterwards continued on those nights which she did not pass with her husband. Things continued in this state for about six months, and as his work was light and he experienced nothing but kind treatment, his time passed pleasantly enough.

The discovery of this affair soon resulted in Adams's sale once again, for a consignment of blankets and dates.*

His new master took Adams to a settlement of villages further north, 'Wed-Noon', where he met other white slaves.† To his astonishment three of these slaves were the mate of the *Charles* and two of the crew. They had been there over a year and were the property of the sons of the local chief. The only white person there was a Frenchman, who had given up hope of escaping from the country and had turned Mohammedan; he had a wife and child, three slaves of his own, and 'gained a good living by the manufacture of gunpowder'. He told Adams that he had been wrecked on a vessel from Liverpool. Adams gave its name as the *Agezuma*.‡ From him Adams learnt that it was August, 1812: some eight months earlier than his own calculations. Among the Negro slaves that Adams met at Wadi-Nun was a woman who said she came from a place called Kanno, § a long way across the desert. She had seen white men before—'as white as the wall'—'in a large boat with two high sticks in it, with cloth upon them, and that they rowed this boat in a manner different from the custom of the Negroes, who use paddles: in stating this she made the motion of rowing with oars, so as to leave no doubt that she had seen a vessel in the European fashion manned by white people.'‖

---

*It was about this time that the British Consul, Dupuis, heard from one of his agents of 'a Christian slave in possession of an Arab who would doubtless be very glad to dispose of him, in consequence of the slave having been detected in an affair with his wife.'

†Wadi-Nun, about 110 miles south of Agadir. At one time this was an important caravan terminus, but it is now almost deserted. Today it forms the southern boundary of the Spanish territory of Ifni.

‡The Liverpool ship *Montezuma*, belonging to T. Koster & Co., was wrecked in November, 1810, on the West Coast of Africa.

§Adams's spelling; obviously Kano.

‖It is most unlikely that a woman of Kano would have seen Mungo Park on the Niger, some 280 miles away, but news of the Scotsman did spread over West Africa. Or was this the work of Cock?

Adams did not please his new master. On one occasion he was in irons for nearly five weeks. He was frequently beaten; and once almost killed. The mate died as a result of ill-treatment. The two other members of the crew of the *Charles* agreed to become Mohammedan in order to escape the brutality. Two days later Dupuis at last succeeded in contacting them, and relayed a promise that he could effect their release providing they were still Christian. (Dupuis's funds for the ransom of slaves were restricted to Christians.) On hearing this, one of the American sailors, who had renounced his religion, 'burst into a flood of tears'. About a month later an agent of Dupuis arrived at Wadi-Nun disguised as a trader. He paid for Adams and took him to Agadir, and then to Mogador.

*

Before Adams's story was published it was read by Dupuis, who corroborated everything in it concerning himself. Dupuis —and this seems to have been ignored by later writers—was himself of the highest reputation: a man who had devoted much of his life to freeing slaves, and who was one of the leading experts of his day on Morocco and the Sahara: not a man to be fooled by a simple and ignorant sailor. Dupuis completely satisfied himself as to the genuineness of Adams during the latter's stay of nearly seven months with him at Mogador. In his memorandum on the subject, he explained how he had frequently presented Adams to Sheiks and merchants who had visited Timbuctoo, 'who, after questioning Adams very closely respecting that city and its neighbourhood . . . [gave] their universal opinion that he must have been at the places he described'. Dupuis had earlier ransomed three other members of the *Charles*'s crew from slavery, and these had already supplied him with details of the shipwreck and the events immediately following it, which were virtually identical to the relevant part of Adams's own story. Later the two who had renounced Christianity were also brought away, and these also gave a similar version, although disclaiming having taken the Mohammedan faith.

Despite the backing of Dupuis, Adams's book was widely

dismissed as the work of an outrageous impostor, on the publication of its three editions—English, American and French. (The speed and energy with which all information regarding Africa was collected and studied, so that nothing, however slight, would be missed or unnecessarily duplicated, astonishes today.) It gave a description of Timbuctoo different from anything written on the subject before—a description, moreover, that was completely disappointing. Criticism was worst in America, where a savage notice appeared in the *North American Review*. Adams's own shipmates turned against him and contradicted his story. The American Consul at Cadiz revealed that the story told him by Adams was different from the one in the book. It was revealed that Adams was masquerading under a false name.

The only important writers of the age to accept Adams's story were Hugh Murray and, later on, R. Huish. Huish wrote: 'Adams may be said to have been the first traveller who ever reached the far-famed city of Timbuctoo . . . one of the most extraordinary travellers of modern times.'*

Explorers and writers who were to take up the challenge left by Mungo Park and others invariably dismissed the American as a worthless impostor. In 1830 Jomard, of the Geographical Society of Paris, published an apparently unanswerable indictment. Adams, the Society said, mentioned two mountains: no one had ever heard of mountains in this region before, and *subsequent* explorers—particularly the Frenchman Caillié—did not observe them. The city, said Adams, was as extensive as Lisbon: other writers gave the population as up to twelve thousand, whereas the population of Lisbon was over a quarter of a million. Adams said there were no mosques: it was certain that there were several. Caillié was to state that buildings were made of brick: Adams said they were made of clay and grass. Adams implied that the natives were illiterate: the French explorer was to discover the contrary. Adams said that many elephants were to be seen there: the Frenchman was to see none.

It was surprising that a learned body—and it was not

---

* In 1892 Sir Lambert Playfair and Robert Brown resurrected the affair, but only for demolition purposes. In 1962 a work of meticulous scholarship said: 'As far as Timbuctoo was concerned, he was probably an impostor.'

alone—should launch such a savage attack on a sailor who made no claims for himself as explorer or a contributor to knowledge. If Adams did not answer these charges—and he did not—it was no doubt because he never heard of them and was, in any case, illiterate. He had returned to the United States and had reverted to the obscurity from which he had so startlingly sprung in a London street. Years after Jomard had dealt with the sailor, Dr Heinrich Barth wrote that Adams's 'narrative does not reveal a single trait that can be identified'; this was from a man who was, and still is, regarded as one of the most scholarly and careful explorers ever to have landed in Africa. It is not surprising, therefore, that Adams has been remembered, if at all, as a footnote in treatises and books.

The dismissal of Adams has overlooked a number of factors. He was an uneducated and unsophisticated man who suddenly found himself the object of curious attention by any number of superior and haughty gentlemen who actually found him not only of interest, but even of some importance. It is not unreasonable to assume that he did not want entirely to disappoint them in the matter of curious animals, for instance, and let his imagination play here and there. But it has been quite wrong to examine Adams in the same way as, say, scientists or geographers subject each other's work to examination. This may explain the variations of detail in the story noticed by the American Consul at Cadiz. It is also difficult to imagine that a man such as Adams could have imagined Timbuctoo—and particularly so when much of what he said can now be proved correct.

He had to be assisted to tell his narrative, and any police-man or journalist, for instance, knows how difficult it can be to obtain a clear narrative from an inarticulate person. If, as was very probably the case, Mr Cock prompted Adams from time to time, it does not necessarily mean that Adams's book was all Cock.

The information contained in the narrative was drawn from Adams, not as a continuous and straightforward story, but in answer to the detached and often unconnected questions of the editor, or of any gentleman who happened to be present at his examinations; for he related scarcely anything without his attention being directed to the subject by a special

2*

inquiry. Timbuctoo being the point to which the curiosity and inquiries of all his examiners were mainly directed, his answers on that subject were thus swelled to the prominence which they possess in the narrative. This lack of expression and continual prompting by question is not the way of the romancer.

For instance it was known that coconuts did not grow so far from the sea. These were constantly mentioned, and publisher and editor were ridiculed. What was forgotten was that Adams had certainly never seen a coconut and very probably did not have an accurate idea as to what they were or looked like. Gourds, not dissimilar to coconuts, have always been in plentiful supply near Timbuctoo, and were used as vessels exactly as Adams described.

The nearest mountains south of Timbuctoo are not less than seventy-five miles away. It may be that Adams had *heard* of these, if not himself seen them, but decided to simplify his story. There are number of hills both sides of the river near Timbuctoo. Kabara itself is on a very obvious hill.

Adams described the city as being beside the river, whereas, because of Leo Africanus, and Mungo Park, it was known to be situated some miles to the north of the Niger.* This was the point at which all defence of Adams always fell— for he categorically stated that the river was very wide just beside the city, and flowing south-west although very sluggishly—whereas south-east would have been correct. Even the otherwise favourable Africa Committee, in its concluding remarks on the Adams affair, was bound to admit:

To the truth of this fact Adam's credit is completely pledged. On many other subjects it is possible that his Narrative might be considerably at variance with the truth, by a mere defect of memory or observation, and without justifying any imputations on his veracity; but it is evident that no such latitude can be allowed to him on the present occasion; and that his statement respecting the river, if not in substance true, must be knowingly and wilfully false.

What was not known then, and what has not been observed in this connection since, despite the observations of even the

---

*In fact both these writers indicated they had been much nearer to Timbuctoo by water than its river port some five miles away.

early explorers to reach the city, is that the Niger rises for some six months of the year sometimes to the edge of the city itself:* this flood water, in some of its channels, recedes again in a south-westerly direction. (Adams told Dupuis, when in Mogador, that the river he saw 'was steady, without any appearance of a strong current'.) During the dry season a dried-up river-bed lies immediately south of the town; in the flood time it sometimes becomes filled, thus making an island of the sandy waste between Timbuctoo and its port. The dates calculated by Cock for Adams's stay in Timbuctoo may be incorrect—unless exceptional climatic conditions prevailed in that year—which seems more probable than that the sailor went to the trouble of inventing a river which he did not see. Cock's dates must, of necessity, have been the wildest guesses. There is no reason at all, in fact, to doubt that Adams described exactly what he saw regarding the river outside the city.

There are other points in favour of the truth of Adams's story:

The many occasions when Adams described what later was proved true. For instance, despite prompting, he insisted that there were no walls or fortifications. By the time of Adams's alleged visit the walls of Timbuctoo—which were never dominant features in a medieval sense—were crumbling, and in places probably indistinct to a stranger.

Adams mentioned Jenne, correctly, as being a town of importance, direct contact with which could be made on the river. He also frequently referred to the Bambara, quite correctly, as an area, and the name of a nearby people.

His description of the houses and the building materials was extremely accurate.

It is clear from his account that Adams lived in the poor Negro quarter of Timbuctoo rather than that of the merchants. This would account for the lack of literacy (which he did not, in fact, completely deny), although he must have been singularly unobservant not to have noticed the mosques; but it is known from a later traveller that the mosques were seldom used by the inhabitants at the beginning of the nineteenth century. Cock said: 'It does not appear that they have any

---

*First detailed by Barth, apparently unaware that he was vindicating Adams.

public religion, as they have no house of worship, no priest, and as far as Adams could discover never meet together to pray.' Adams's failure to mention a mosque remains the strongest point against his genuineness.

It was not by any means impossible for there to have been elephant hunts, as Adams described, in the Timbuctoo area. His description of the pouched animal, however, was the one unmistakable case of romancing in the book; it may be thought remarkable that there were not more. Adams, however, did not claim to have seen this animal close-to himself.

Adams's description of the time taken between known places was uncannily accurate, as even the Geographical Society of Paris had to agree.

Much of Adams's experiences were spent in the company of some of the rest of the crew of the *Charles*. These all told the same details when interviewed by Dupuis, independently of Adams. Dupuis said that at this time Adams 'did not appear to attach any importance to the fact of his having been at Timbuctoo'. Why, then, should he make up one portion of his story only? The fact that his shipmates later denied him may well be due to the contrast between their later experiences and his. American critics of Adams, who based their case on these men, might well have noted that some of the crew were extremely embarrassed by their 'conversion' to Islam, which Adams had told in some detail. When they eventually arrived at Cadiz, they had difficulty in arousing sympathy there, and spent most of their time in jail; Adams, on the other hand, had lived in a gentleman's house.

Adams distinctly refused to give any idea as to the population of Timbuctoo. But he did say that he estimated a very large gathering, a high percentage of the people, at about two thousand. It is unlikely that he had any idea as to the true extent of Lisbon—a comparison obviously inspired by Cock. He said: 'As the houses are not built in streets, or with any regularity, its population, compared with that of European towns, is by no means in proportion to its size.' It is remarkable how Adams's denigrators ignored such evidence.

Those who met Adams, rather than those who only examined his story, were all convinced of his honesty—with one exception: the American Consul at Cadiz. Among them were some formidable men, the kind of persons who would have been likely to have had considerable and natural prejudice against a starving and penniless beggar found on the London streets. A distinguished and sceptical company, they included Lord Bathurst (Secretary for War and the Colonies), Sir Joseph Banks (the leading naturalist of the day, explorer, and President of the Royal Society), and several M.P.s and members of the Government. The Quartermaster-General, Major-General Sir Willoughby Gordon, was sufficiently impressed to write to Cock: 'The perusal of his statement, and the personal examination of Adams, have entirely satisfied me of the truth of his deposition. If he should be proved an impostor, he will be second only to Psalmanazar.'

Adams had been impressed into the British Navy, from which he had deserted. It was, therefore, a reasonable precaution to change his name while in England. Ironically enough, after the Africa Committee had finished with him he was provided with Government funds for his expenses and his passage home.

The Africa Committee ended the Adams book with a thoughtful resumé of the meaning of his report:

Notwithstanding, therefore, the alleged splendour of its court, polish of its inhabitants, and other symptoms of refinement which some modern accounts (or speculations), founded on native reports, have taught us to look for, we are disposed to receive the humbler descriptions of Adams as approaching with much greater probability the truth. And here, we may remark, the relative rank of Timbuctoo amongst the cities of central Africa, and its present importance with reference to European objects, appear to us to be considerably overrated. The description of Leo in the sixteenth century may, indeed, lend a colour to the brilliant anticipations in which some sanguine minds have indulged on the same subjects in the nineteenth . . . there is a great reason to believe that Timbuctoo has in reality declined of late, from the wealth and consequence which it appears formerly to have enjoyed.

When the storm broke around Adams, he was happily returned to his family after one of the most remarkable African adventures of modern history: one which he was very fortunate to have survived. The Africa Committee did nothing to defend him, nor did those famous names who had supported him. The public, and particularly business interests, were not prepared to believe that the desert metropolis existed only as a poor and utterly primitive slaving depot.

Future explorers all decried him. The conclusion is inescapable that the American was dismissed as a liar in case his experience and book should appear to belittle the later efforts of professional and expensive expeditions. For it can now be seen that Adams's book contained—as Dupuis suggested—a good deal of valuable information; remarkably so, coming as it did from a complete amateur; more information than any professional explorer had been able to collect, or more than many others would be able to for half a century. If this had been considered, it would have lessened the work—but also, of course, the importance—of those who followed.

The first white man to have been in Timbuctoo since 1670, and the first ever to have returned with up-to-date and accurate information, was dismissed as the purveyor of rubbish and for a hundred and fifty years has been forgotten.

*

Two years after Adams escaped from Africa there was another American shipwreck on the West Coast of Africa—the brig *Commerce*, captained by James Riley.

Riley was born in Middletown, Connecticut, in 1777. His father was a farmer, and Riley received a formal education for four years at the village school. He was widely travelled, could speak, read and write French and Spanish, understood a number of other languages, and had risen from ship's-boy to Master and part-owner of his own craft. He was, in fact, a man of substance—and, as compared with Adams, of eminent respectability. He left Hartford on May 6, 1815, for New Orleans and Gibraltar. The *Commerce* was wrecked on August 28.

Once ashore, Riley and his men were taken captive, stripped and put to work on the livestock—as Adams had been before; but the sufferings of Riley and the four sailors who remained with him were even more extreme. Naked and on foot, they were taken on the long and agonizing march across the desert. They did not, however, penetrate it deeply. The caravan was probably making for the slave assembly at Wadi-Nun, across what is now the Spanish Sahara (Rio de Oro).

We had no other drink than the camel's urine, which we caught in our hands as they voided it; its taste was bitter, but not salt, and it relieved our fainting spirits. We were forced to keep up with the drove, but in the course of the day found a handful of snails each, which we at night roasted and ate. Our feet, though not swollen, were extremely sore; our bodies and limbs were nearly deprived of skin and flesh, for we continually wasted away, and the little we had on our bones was dried hard and stuck fast to them. Hunger, that had preyed upon my companions to such a degree as to cause them to bite off the flesh from their arms, had not the same effect on me. I was forced in one instance to tie the arms of one of my men behind him in order to prevent his gnawing his own flesh; and in another instance, two of them having caught one of the boys, a lad about four years old, out of sight of the tents, were about dashing his brains out with a stone, for the purpose of devouring his flesh.

As masters suffered about as much as slaves on the desert-crossing, it is remarkable that even the demands of trade were able to insist on these appalling journeys. Adams recorded that on the journeys to and from Timbuctoo the way was littered with bones of men and camels, the water-holes being nearly all unreliable. Meeting an Arab merchant *en route*, Riley begged him to buy himself and his companions. He explained that he had a friend in Mogador who would pay highly for him—a man named 'Consul'.

They examined every bone to see if all was in its right place, with the same cautious circumspections that a jockey would use who was about buying a horse, while we, poor trembling wretches, strove with all possible care and anxiety to hide every fault and infirmity in us occasioned by our dreadful calamities and cruel sufferings.

The Arab, named Sidi Hamet, agreed to purchase them on the understanding that if the friend called Consul, at Mogador, did not wish to buy them after all—Riley's throat would be cut. They trekked away from the desert towards the coast; then northwards beside the shore. The country was easier and the Americans' condition more bearable, although they still progressed on foot.

Near Mogador, Sidi Hamet stopped the small caravan and Riley was instructed to write a letter. This he did with the aid of two scraps of paper, a reed and some staining liquid. Considering the circumstances of the writer, it was not an ill-expressed letter, and it—together with the noble reply which it induced—deserve a better fate than the total obscurity which rewarded them. Some exchanges which have survived from the history of Europeans in Africa are trivial in comparison. Riley's letter was addressed to the 'English, French, Spanish or American Consuls, or any Christian merchants in Mogador'.

Sir,

The brig *Commerce* from Gibraltar for America was wrecked on Cape Bojador, on August 28 last; myself and four of the crew are here nearly naked in Barbarian slavery; I conjure you by all the ties that bind man to man, by those of kindred blood, and everything which you hold most dear, and by as much as liberty is dearer than life, to advance the money required for our redemption, which is 920 dollars and two double-barrelled guns*. I can draw for any amount, the moment I am at liberty [on banks in London, Liverpool Lisbon and Gibraltar.] Should you not relieve me, my life must instantly pay the forfeit. I have a wife and five helpless children to deplore my death.

The reply came by messenger eight days later.

My dear and afflicted Sir,

I have this moment received your two notes, the contents of which, I hope, you will be perfectly assured have called forth my most sincere pity for your sufferings and those of your companions in captivity. By a Gibraltar paper I discover, under the arrivals from August 5 to 11, the name of your vessel, and that she was American, from which I conclude both you and your crew must be the subjects of the United States.

I can in some measure participate in the severe and dangerous sufferings and hardships you must have undergone; but, my dear Sir, console yourself, for, thanks be to God, I hope they will soon have a happy issue. I have agreed to pay the sum of 920 hard

---

*The Spanish dollar, or 'Maria Theresa', nominally equivalent to five English shillings: for more than a century the most acceptable currency in North Africa and in many parts of the interior: minted in London up to 1962. All references below are to this dollar.

dollars to Sidi Hamet on your safe arrival in this town, with your fellow sufferers. I have sent shoes and cloaks, which I have no doubt you will find very useful in preserving you from rain or cold on the road. I have also forwarded you some provisions and spirits, that you may enjoy a foretaste of returning liberty. I shall send off an express tomorrow to the United States' Consul-General at Tangier.

I trust there is no occasion for me to say how truly I commiserate and enter into all your misfortunes; when God grants me the pleasure to embrace you, it will be to me a day of true rejoicing. I beg you will ensure everyone with you of my truest regard—and with sentiments embittered by the thoughts of the miseries you have undergone, but with the most sanguine hope of a happy end to all your sufferings, I subscribe myself, with the greatest esteem, my dear Sir, your friend,

William Willshire

Riley's letter, in short, could not have been received at a more sympathetic house. Willshire was an Englishman resident in Mogador. Riley was, understandably, as moved as he was relieved to get this reply, 'from a perfect stranger, whose name I had never heard before, and from a place where there was not an individual creature that had ever before heard of my existence, and in one of the most barbarous regions of the habitable globe.' It was the end of his two months of slavery.

Arriving at Willshire's house, he had a mental collapse. For three days he went berserk, skulking in corners, ignorant of where he was, and terrified of the sight of every human being.

During his recovery, he took extensive notes of his experience. He also took the precaution of showing these to his fellow-survivors, thus giving them an opportunity of denial. At length he went to Tangier, where James Simpson accepted everything he said and offered every support for the book which Riley intended writing. On his return to America, he was received with great interest and, of course, with greater attention than Adams had been. He was taken to Washington, where he was interviewed by the Secretary of State, James Munroe.* He also met several members of Congress. As a result of this, James Simpson was given power to ransom

---

*President of the United States, 1817–25.

shipwrecked American sailors and to make every effort to do so. Riley's book showed him to be a man of real compassion as well as of fibre. It was published also in London soon after it appeared in America. It deserved the attention from posterity which it did not get.

The most interesting portion of the book to his contemporaries was a chapter describing in detail two journeys which Sidi Hamet had made to Timbuctoo. Riley had taken this down from Sidi Hamet in Mogador. It was an obvious pandering to public taste—for the fame of Timbuctoo was at its height—and as the word 'gold' appeared on almost every page it was not unacceptable.

Sidi Hamet told a story of a dreadful journey across the desert. The caravan consisted of over a thousand men and four thousand camels laden with merchandise. Three hundred men were suffocated in a sand-storm. Another hundred died on the way to the most vital of the water-holes; when this place was reached at last it was found dry. Furious digging and delirious arguments were no help. Camels were ordered to be slaughtered so that liquid could be squeezed from their guts and their blood drunk. This resulted in bitter disputes, and anarchy ensued; between two and three hundred men were killed in fighting. The survivors drank the blood of those who were killed. When the caravan reached Timbuctoo it consisted of twenty-one men and twelve camels. It was by no means the only terrible crossing of the ferocious and deadly sea of sand.

The city was described as being 'very rich as well as very large', with a population of about 215,000. It was 'strongly walled'; the four gates were heavily guarded at night.

But among Sidi Hamet's embellishments there were some interesting grains. He mentioned that a little river ran close to the town; it was dried up during his visit and water had to be carried from 'the great river south of the city', which flowed eastwards and which was about an hour's ride away by camel. If this was accepted—as it was by the Geographical Society of Paris—then here was a clue to the truth of Adams's story.

Secondly, Sidi Hamet described how there were two main quarters of Timbuctoo: one Muslim, the other Negro with only the poorest Arabs and Moors. The two quarters were kept separate, and there was little communion between the two. As Adams had clearly lived with Negroes, here also was information which made his apparently unbelievable information acceptable.

Thirdly, Riley gave a most remarkable account of the course of the Niger River, constructed from information gained from Sidi Hamet, but also from Moor merchants who visited Willshire's house. In this he gave a very fair description of the course of the river, with a correct version of the 'Niger Bend' which was still unaccepted by many of the greatest experts on the matter. He concluded that the river turned right round, flowed westwards, instead of east as it did at Timbuctoo, and ended in the Atlantic.

If the geographers of the day had paid as much attention to the Captain of the *Commerce* as they had to the theories of Mungo Park and others, they could have saved themselves a good deal of trouble and the lives of some others. Most authorities were critical, even indignant. But on the publication of Riley's account another geographer—Hugh Murray— was added to Adams's supporters. He pointed out that the mud dwellings of Timbuctoo which had been mentioned were only what Leo Africanus had said long before: that Leo's account, because of his talk of gold, had been much exaggerated. He commented on the importance of Riley's assertion that Moslems and pagans lived separately at Timbuctoo, and the relevance of this to Adams's book.

Riley's book always received a good deal of critical comment despite the respectability, as compared to Adams, of its author. But it received the important support of De Witt Clinton, Governor of New York State. The Governor also supported the publication of a book by Captain Judah Paddock, of Hudson. Paddock had been shipwrecked in 1800, had been captured soon after, and sold into slavery with his crew. They had joined two English youths, also in slavery. His bloodthirsty and gruesome account of his sufferings corroborated much of what Riley had said.

Captain Riley also offered some advice on how Timbuctoo could be successfully reached by a white man:

A plain and very simple method for reaching Timbuctoo in safety and returning again; to accomplish this journey, the traveller, after being duly qualified, has only to become a slave by his own consent, and a secret understanding with his hired master; being bargained away by the Consul to one of the principal merchants trading in that city in the yearly caravans, and who might be induced to enter into the project for an ample remuneration.

In other words, to go in disguise. Oddly enough, few had thought of this before. To become a slave, to degrade oneself, was not an attractive idea to many explorers, even if the prize were Timbuctoo itself: especially not to Englishmen, for whom such subterfuge would rob them of half the satisfaction of the achievement;* and to some it would even savour of dishonourable practice. And, of course, it would be better to die in the sands than that. But not all those who wished to get to Timbuctoo were Englishmen. . . .

*

Antonio Piloti, a Spaniard, had arrived in Morocco while Adams was still in slavery. He had assumed Moorish dress, learnt the language and had joined the guards of the Emperor. He intended to get to Timbuctoo in his official capacity as an Imperial Guard of Morocco. Piloti, hearing of French interest, offered his services to the French Consul, who supported him and approached the government in Paris. The Consul continued to encourage him as he believed that Piloti, travelling as a Moor in a caravan of Moors, had every chance of success. The Geographical Society of Paris took an interest in him and arrangements were being made to send scientific instruments to Piloti when he suddenly found himself innocently involved in political intrigue in the imperial court. Suspicions about his activities had been aroused; he was wrongly suspected to be plotting with the party which was opposed to the Emperor. Before he could escape to the Consul, Antonio Piloti was beheaded.

*

---

*But such reluctance was not in evidence in the hero-worship accorded Sir Richard Burton after his entry to Mecca in 1853. Burton himself did much work in West Africa, not a little of it inaccurate.

While the books of Adams and Riley were being discussed in the drawing-rooms of London, Boston and Paris, one of the most extraordinary characters in the history of African exploration had arrived on the West Coast of Africa.

René Caillié was the son of a baker at Mauzé, where he had been born in 1800. His father was convicted for a petty theft, and died in prison, when Caillié was seven. His mother dying very soon after, Caillié and his sister came under the care of an uncle. He received a little education at the village school. His only desire was to travel. As a young boy he had read travel books with precocious fascination.

I already felt an ambition to signalize myself by some important discovery. . . . The map of Africa, in which I scarcely saw any but countries marked as desert or unknown, excited my attention more than any other. In short, this predeliction grew into a passion for which I renounced everything: I ceased to join in the sports and amusements of my comrades; I shut myself up on Sundays to read all the books of travels that I was able to procure.

Despite the efforts of his uncle to dissuade him, Caillié boarded a brig bound for Senegal. He was sixteen years old. Senegal was the French section of the West Coast, and from there all French efforts to gain influence in West Africa radiated. The chief settlements were St. Louis and Dakar. Rivalry with the British—who had settlements further south at the mouth of the Gambia River and at Sierra Leone—was intense. The British were also taking a great interest in the coast further south still, at the Gold Coast and the Benin Bight (or Lagos). Young Caillié, ardently patriotic, was inspired by the glory of France.

Caillié landed in the steaming and suffocating little settlement of St. Louis. He was soon penniless. But already he had decided that he must penetrate the interior. He reached the Gambia and begged to be allowed to join a mission, under Major William Gray, which was setting out for Timbuctoo 'by the most convenient road' (as Gray had told the African Association).* He was refused and was sent off to the West Indies. But he was soon back in West Africa. He reached

---

*This was the remnants of the Peddie Mission of 1816, mentioned at the beginning of the next chapter.

Gray's expedition when it was 250 miles from the coast and struggled back with it when that inept and futile attempt to proceed was given up. In the same year a French expedition, under G. Mollien, entered the interior, under the auspices of the French Government. One of the objects was to gain information about Timbuctoo; Mollien gained little, but returned a wiser man: 'The climate is the enemy most to be dreaded in the countries which I have visited.'

Wherever he went Caillié seems to have found people to listen to him. The English particularly always seem to have had ready sympathy for the slim, boyish youth with the good manners and the ridiculous story about wanting to become an explorer. He always got on best with men considerably older than himself. The only love of his life so far was his lame sister, Céleste, whom he adored, and for whose sake he was desperate to make himself famous. Caillié was not averse to accepting such charity and patronage as came his way. Although only an impoverished youth, he became friendly with the two most important men on the coast: the French Governor of the Senegal and the British Governor of Sierra Leone. He was the mascot of the West Coast. And he had more charm than that of any other ten people there. But even his charm could not help him at this time and he had to return to France to find employment.

Caillié was further inspired by Mungo Park's book, which he read avidly. He had no particular scientific notion of exploration. He wished only to discover for its own sake—to achieve some great feat for his sister and for France. It was obvious to Caillié what he had to do. He must return soon to the West Coast, and then he must go to Timbuctoo.

4 . *The Briton*

IN LONDON the cartographers and geographers were still as bemused and frustrated as ever. The efforts of Ledyard, Houghton, and Mungo Park had resulted in the deaths of the explorers in every case, but not in any substantial information. The African Association was to some extent discredited. This was not entirely fair. It had, for instance, sent Frederick Hornemann to study at the University of Gottingen, at its own expense, before his departure. This was in marked contrast to the Government's ponderous expedition of soldiers under Mungo Park. What no one in London really appreciated was the task which these explorers, and those who followed them, undertook.

European travellers had no knowledge of tropical medicine: mosquito bites were considered no more than a minor irritant: ill health of white men in Africa was considered due to the 'bad air': nothing was considered wrong in drinking water found in static ponds, apart from its filthy taste and its green or brown appearance: there was no special equipment, food or training. Some men entered the desert in the clothes they would have worn if entering their clubs in St. James'. To cross the desert, therefore, meant the inevitable contraction of disease and almost certain early death, there being no known cures for the diseases. Negroes dared not make the crossing; even Arab caravaners, with the knowledge of centuries at their disposal, considered four or five crossings a life achievement, the death-rate being so high. On the far side of the desert were little-known lands and a city of unknown greatness and wealth. To discover this city while in the throes of unchecked and untended disease was not all, for suspicious people had to be placated.

There were three great 'kingdoms' south of the desert: Bornu; the remaining Hausa area ruled by the Fulanie, who had conquered it in about 1804, together with other possessions of the Fulani, who had their capital at Sokoto; and the

Yorubas.* In the desert itself power was divided between the rapacious and fanatically religious Moors from Mauritania, Morocco and Algeria, who held the wealth, and the wandering Tuareg, fierce and proud, whom all feared. The part of all this area which lay adjacent to the desert was the Western Sudan.†

And, to return with the information, the implacable desert had to be re-crossed once more. That all this had hardly ever been achieved by a European, except perhaps a Roman, is not surprising. It was a feat of almost impossible physical stamina.

Along the north coast was territory nominally belonging to the decaying Ottoman Empire, but virtually independent. Here it was that the British and French even co-operated, in 1819, in a mission to abolish piracy on the Barbary Coast.‡ On the West Coast, small European settlements, often based on freed slaves, made tentative efforts at colonization. It was not an ignoble period in Africa, especially when compared to the various imperialisms of the end of the century.

The men who were attempting to penetrate the interior were a splendid advertisement to posterity of their age. Incompetent adventurers and indifferent scholars, they sweated across the sands for months, their city suits and barrack-square uniforms disintegrating into rags; struggling to learn unfamiliar languages; eating food which was obnoxious to them; writing their letters with restrained and formal courtesy while surrounded by potential assassins, knowing that they would not be delivered for many months or years, if they were delivered at all; praising God for his mercies, for men believed in their religion without reservation; giving their animals to exhausted slaves while they walked; doing what they could from their own puny knowledge to comfort the many terribly ill or maltreated natives who came to them; and all without hardly one sentence of complaint or self-pity from any of them. The British among

*Corresponding to today's Chad, Northern Nigeria, and the coast from the Niger to Togoland.

†Not to be confused with the Sudan, south of Egypt.

‡Barbary was a general term for Africa north of the desert: inhabited mainly by Berbers.

these, were not, for the most part, London dare-devils or favourites at the Horse Guards: from them applications were few. They were mostly impecunious and obscure junior officers of the Royal Navy and the Army who came from modest backgrounds, and who were anxious to further careers faltering through lack of money, privilege or patronage.

The next expeditions sent out by the British Government illustrated these characteristics to the full: all very different men—but each one brave, loyal, uncomplaining, gentle-mannered and doomed.

In 1816 the Government sent two large expeditions from the coast to solve the Niger mystery: one from as far south as the Congo, the other under Major Peddie from the Guinea coast. Both ended in tragedy without any addition to knowledge, about a hundred Englishmen dying on them. It seemed that the West Coast entry, despite the qualified success of Park's first expedition, was too murderous to hold out any chance of real success. The experts and theorists in London began to consider once more the route from the north, across the Sahara into the unknown, which had been favoured, with such unfortunate results, by the African Association some twenty years before. Also, in 1816, a naval commander was sent to Tripoli from Malta to investigate. He reported: 'I think this ought to be the chosen route, because practicable, into the very heart of the most benighted quarter of the globe.' He told London that caravans left Tripoli for Timbuctoo annually. (This was, in fact, erroneous, the frequency being unpredictable and probably less.) Within six months plans to send a mission to Timbuctoo from Tripoli were being considered. Lord Bathurst, the Secretary for War, was extremely favourable: 'Lord Bathurst is . . . most anxious to forward the project entertained . . . of proceeding to Timbuctoo.'

It was enough. Bathurst was a powerful man. For, since 1801, colonial affairs had come under the brief of the Secretary for War.*

*Third Earl Bathurst (1762–1834). The capital of Gambia is named after him. As nearly all official exploration was conducted by naval or army officers, who had to apply for permission through the Admiralty or the War Office, he had charge of two of the three authorities involved. The Colonial Office sponsored the expeditions.

Yet another Scottish doctor, Joseph Ritchie, was engaged to cross the Sahara. He was twenty-five years old; an admirer of John Keats, of whom he predicted: 'If I am not mistaken, is to be the great poetical luminary of the age to come.' With him were to go a naval captain, G. F. Lyon, and J. Belford, a shipwright (the Niger, or the mysterious lake into which it was said to flow, being the objective). Lyon was one of the most intelligent men ever to attempt the crossing. It was probably his suggestion that they should go in a kind of half-disguise, as mercenaries who had been converted to Islam, thus adding to the controversy of their day as to whether disguise was acceptable for a British explorer.

The expedition was ill-provided and essential funds for bribing and paying tribute to sheiks on the way were missing owing to Treasury indifference. Ritchie and Lyon did not get on. They reached the important trading centre of Murzuk, some 480 miles south of Tripoli, where Ritchie died of fever. Lyon went on, and only give up through lack of funds—not having enough money to feed himself and his horse. At Zuila, about seventy-five miles east of Murzuk, he turned back. Belford had long been incapable through sickness.

They joined a slave caravan to take them on the way north once more. Most of the slaves were women and girls. Like all those who were to follow him for nearly half a century, Lyon was dominated by the presence of slavery and the slave trade and horrified by its spectacle. He was appalled by what he saw of the slavers and their methods. He constantly did all he could to ease the sufferings of the girls, and must have often endangered his life in doing so. One fourteen-year-old girl was lashed to a camel:

> She told me in the morning that the fatigue of the day would kill her, and that I was the only person, with the exception of her companions, who had treated her kindly since she was taken from her mother.

Lyon walked while dying slaves rode on his camel.

> None of the slave-owners ever marched without their whips, which were in constant use. [One] was so frequently flogging his poor slaves that I was frequently obliged to disarm him. . . . When the poor sufferer dies, the master suspects there must have been

something 'wrong inside' and regrets not having liberally applied the usual remedy of burning the belly with a red-hot iron.

The picture of the young Royal Navy officer thus rebuking the fierce slave-trader, in whose power he was, is intriguing. At last Lyon sighted civilization again. He solemnly sang 'Rule Britannia'—'as loud as I could roar'.*

The greatest achievement of the Ritchie expedition was that two-thirds of its whites returned alive. Its scientific value was very little. It was inspired amateurishness—at which the British were just beginning to believe they were so good; professionally it was almost useless. Lyon did state, however, that the Niger 'by one route or another' joined up with the Nile. In his report he insisted on his correctness in travelling in disguise.

I am confident that it would never be possible for any man to pass through Africa unless in every respect he qualified himself to appear as a Mohammedan; and should I myself return to that country, I would not be accompanied by anyone who would refuse to observe these precautions.

It was not unreasonable advice, and based on the experience of an explorer who had actually lived to give it. But in London it went unheeded.

The Niger mystery remained. Where did the river go? What was the wealth of the land south of the Sahara? What was the importance of Timbuctoo? Another expedition must be sent across the desert to bring back the answers.

*

The government continued for a time to follow the sensible policy of sending small parties rather than one explorer alone —at least one of them could be expected to return with the vital information for which all Europe and America was so greedy.

Two years after Lyon and Belford returned to Tripoli,

*In 1823 Lyon suggested to the Admiralty that he should join a caravan for Timbuctoo at Tripoli. 'If the government will give him £1,000 he will ask for nothing more.' He was turned down, and he never returned to the desert. But later he did some exploration of the Arctic. Going blind, he died aged 37.

another party of explorers set out from the same city. As explorers, they were no more experienced than the Ritchie expedition had been—that is to say, not experienced at all. But they were provided with one all-important advantage—a great deal of money.

They were: Walter Oudney, a serious Royal Navy doctor from Edinburgh; his friend, Hugh Clapperton, the tenth child of a Dumfriesshire doctor, a brawny, professional adventurer and ladies' man, with a gift for sketching, who had been impressed into the Navy; and Dixon Denham, a socialite Army Major who had fought at Waterloo. Denham had already offered to mount a mission to Timbuctoo on his own, but the offer had been declined. Of these three, Clapperton was destined to be the most important explorer. He possessed an unusually amiable disposition, but was not without his ambitions. It was said that 'He had a noble figure. He was six feet high and broad chested'. Also in the expedition were two Jewish attendants and a shipwright named William Hillman, of whose part in the expedition little is known.

Denham joined the others at Murzuk. He said, proudly: 'We were the first English travellers who had determined to travel in our real character as Britons and Christians and to wear our English dress: the buttons on our waistcoats and our watches caused the greatest astonishment.'

By the time they left Murzuk they had already gone down with fever. All except Denham nearly died of it. They were sick men before they even entered on the main crossing of the desert. A hundred years later they would have been considered invalids who would not have been allowed out of hospital to cross the road, let alone the Sahara Desert. As Denham, with typical under-statement, put it, their condition was 'ill-calculated for undertaking a long and tedious journey'. For three months they advanced over the billowy sand-dunes with their caravan of camels and attendants. What impressed them most were the numbers of skeletons that lay about in the wastes of the desert. Denham's entries became crisp and succinct as the agony wore on week after week: 'Desert as yesterday. High sandhills.'

On February 4, 1823, they sighted water: a vast shimmering expanse of it, 'glowing with the golden rays of the sun'.

This was Lake Chad. They were the first Europeans ever to see it except possibly for unknown Roman legionaries centuries before. It was eleven months since they had ridden out of Tripoli. Was this the repository of the Niger?

To their relief, they were cordially received by the local king, whose astonishment at their arrival equalled almost their own exhaustion. It seemed that trade was not only possible with these people—they actually wanted it. Many questions were asked about Europe and the way of life there. The only difficulty seemed to be the question of slavery. This would have to be abolished—the expedition said—before full trade relations could be set up.

While Denham took part in a slaving war, Oudney and Clapperton went west towards Timbuctoo.

Their reports were received with great pleasure in London —after a month's crossing of the desert by two messengers (only one being expected to survive the trek). A relief was sent out to join them. All that is known of him is that his name was Ernest Toole, that within two months of his arrival at Lake Chad he was dead, and that he was 'in every sense a most amiable and promising young officer'.

Oudney, obviously dying, insisted on carrying on. One morning, after being dressed by Clapperton, he died while trying to mount his camel. Continuing on his lonely way, Clapperton eventually reached Kano. 'Arrayed in what was left of my naval uniform, I made myself as smart as circumstances would permit.' Here Clapperton tried to recuperate for a month, in a hut beside a stagnant swamp that acted as an open sewer. In one of his few phrases of complaint, Clapperton wrote of 'an abominable stench'. His condition was improved, however, by the safe arrival of three bottles of port from Denham. Clapperton also managed to visit Sokoto, six hundred miles from Timbuctoo, the furthest he could stretch from his base at Chad. When he tried to get permission to continue west towards the Niger, the Sultan refused. On his return towards Lake Chad he was met by Denham at Kukawa, who had come to look for him. Denham wrote:

It was nearly eight months since we had separated. . . . I went immediately to the hut where he was lodged, but so satisfied was I that the sunburnt, sickly person that lay extended on the floor, rolled in a dark-blue shirt, was not my companion, that I was about to leave the place when he convinced me of my error by calling me by my name.

But relations between the men were not really friendly. Clapperton had done rather more than his fair share of the expedition; and Denham was inclined tactlessly to take too much credit for success to himself. Denham never really got over his disappointment at not being able to go direct to Timbuctoo. Also, he took his position as leader too seriously, as though they were in a barracks at home. Worst of all, accusations by the Africans that Clapperton was having a homosexual affair with one of the Arab attendants, were fully reported by Denham to Bathurst. Clapperton, protesting his innocence convincingly, was furious. For some time, the two men were not on speaking terms.

They returned to Tripoli, nearly three years after they had left it. They had travelled throughout as British officers and Christians; that they, and the shipwright Hillman, had survived was one of the most remarkable and unlikely achievements in the history of African exploration. Moreover, they had returned with real and useful additions to knowledge at last—even though the crucial problems remained unsolved. They had information about the interior of which practically nothing had been heard since Leo Africanus in the sixteenth century. But despite the length and scope of their agonizing years in the wilderness, they had not discovered the mouth of the Niger nor its source. They had not been to Timbuctoo; of the city, and its rumoured wealth and architectural glories, they had little to report; but Clapperton mentioned it as a source of gold. (Its position on their map was over three hundred miles to the south-west from its true position.)

But soon attention was being held by yet another expedition; one that would, it was hoped, answer the most intriguing question of African exploration and that would satisfy at last an important item in the great quest for knowledge that was the obsession of the age. The only object of the new British expedition was to reach Timbuctoo —and to return.

*

The news that Clapperton and Denham had returned to Tripoli spread through the communications—dependent on the ships that sailed the sea lanes—and at every port the news was received and sent away inland to be greeted by those interested in African exploration, of whom there were many, with relief. One of the first to hear was Major Gordon Laing, who was in Malta: a slightly built Scotsman with fine features and dark, curly hair, with deep recessions at the temples.

Of all the great travellers in Africa, Alexander Gordon Laing is perhaps the least known. It is a fate he has not deserved, for although his discoveries were not major, his greatest journey was one of the most prodigious undertaken in the nineteenth century.

He was born in Edinburgh in 1794, and it seemed that he was destined for an academic career. His father was a well-known Edinburgh headmaster; his grandfather was a famous Scottish educationalist. Laing himself entered Edinburgh University at the age of thirteen. The Professor of Latin, Alexander Christison, considered him his star pupil. When he left university he became a schoolmaster—first at Newcastle and then at Edinburgh. It was a brilliant start to his career. Of all the travellers to undertake the quest for Timbuctoo before the mid-nineteenth century, Laing was the best educated. But his adventurous spirit, and probably his ambition, rebelled against the life he was entering. With the aid of his uncle, who was a Colonel, he obtained a commission in an unfashionable but cheap West Indies regiment of infantry. He was seventeen.

Laing impressed his senior officers with his efficiency, but it is likely that he found the regimental duties of a junior officer frustrating and irksome. Also his usefulness was limited by the ill health which plagued him all his life. We know that he spent a year and a half back in Scotland on half-pay owing to ill health. When he rejoined the 2nd West India Regiment it was stationed in Sierra Leone, a colony intended for freed slaves.

Freetown, the capital of the colony, was one of the few centres on the coast with any pretensions. Efforts had been made to lay the foundations of a European town; there were a church and a few modest public buildings. Laing, sickly but ambitious, was an important addition to the life of the place, where most white men had no other ambition but to survive the climate and one day return home. Between 1822 and 1830 about 1,400 Europeans died in Freetown out of a white population of less than 2,000. Not surprisingly, drunkenness was almost universal.

The only interest most people had in the 'White Man's Grave' was trade and exploration. Laing quickly tried to get himself involved in the latter. He consistently denied—perhaps rather too often—that his major motivation was personal ambition.

Not long after his arrival Laing wrote to his commanding officer: 'I have had for many years a strong desire to penetrate into the interior of Africa—and that desire has been greatly increased by my arrival on the Coast.' Without further ado he suggested that he should strike inland and make an attempt on Timbuctoo. Apparently oblivious of his own inexperience, and of the fate of others who had gone off in the same direction for the past fifty years, he said he would do so without drawing on any official funds apart from one or two essential items of equipment. His request was turned down, although it did get as far as Lord Bathurst in London.

Timbuctoo was the most irresistible word connected with Africa. It was the one which insisted on clinging to the public's imagination. And, so far as Laing was aware, no white man had ever been there. For the time being he dropped Timbuctoo from his requests, but it was always in his mind.

In 1821, when he had been on the West Coast for two years, he was still only a lieutenant in his regiment. It was decided that an exploratory mission should be sent into the interior to discover the effects of the abolition of the slave-trade on the natives, and their willingness to trade. Laing, after his previous badgering, was the obvious man to lead it.

At last he had begun. Within the same year he made two more expeditions into unexplored territory.

Laing did not care for the people among whom he travelled. He found them 'depraved, licentious, indolent and avaricious'.

Laing was an exceedingly impatient man, but he was not without compassion, and he recognized that these people had been depraved by the slave trade.

The considerate reader will judge of the degree in which their character is to be attributed to the long prevalence, in their country, of that detestable trade, which strikes at the root of industry, destroys the bonds of social order, and even extinguishes the most powerful natural feelings.

Laing was horrified to be offered on two occasions, by mothers, child slaves for thirty shillings each. When he refused, he was abused 'as being one of those white men who prevented the slave-trade and injured the prosperity of their country'.

Laing's travels in West Africa were mostly of local interest, and were not of great scientific value, but there was one piece of information which he seized on; he recognized that with it he had a chance to gain serious attention at last. The Niger River had long been considered to rise in the area of Mount Soma. Laing returned with the latitude and longitude of the mountain and, more important, its height. This convinced Laing of the correctness of the least popular of the theories about the Niger: that it swung right round and flowed into the Atlantic. He explained:

I have considered that a knowledge of the height of the Niger's source would be of the utmost importance; for that point being once gained, we could to a certainty determine where that river could not finish its course, and consequently save much trouble and expense in future research. . . .

The question of the Niger uniting with the Nile must therefore be for ever at rest—the elevation of its source not being sufficient to carry it half the distance. . . . I stated this fact in order to prevent, if possible, any further missions being sent on foot for the purpose of exploring the Niger from Northern Africa, and that his Lordship* might be enabled to judge of the propriety of recalling the mission under Major Denham . . . as it is now very clear that nothing in the way of discovery can be effected from that quarter, and that the attempt is only attended with expense, disappointment and perhaps the loss of valuable lives.

*Lord Bathurst.

3

It was self-confident—even impertinent—but there was no doubt that it was also relevant. And its message was clear: the West Coast approach to the Niger and Timbuctoo should be favoured once more and that the next attempt should be by Captain Laing. Again he wrote for permission to solve the secrets of the interior—'without regard to emolument or expectation of reward.'

Meanwhile, however, war with the Ashantis broke out in the Gold Coast. Laing was sent there, and acquitted himself well in the fighting. On the way there he was in command at Mesurado (now Monrovia) when a settlement of liberated American slaves were saved from annihilation by the natives. But once again, as in the West Indies, his health broke down. Laing was chosen as the officer to return to London in order to report the situation personally to Lord Bathurst.

Laing was not popular with all his fellow officers, which may account for their surprising leniency regarding his ill health. In West Africa sickness was too commonplace to allow every sick officer to be sent home. Laing was determined, opinionated, proud, touchy and ambitious. He edited a newspaper in Sierra Leone which, according to the acting Governor, was 'filled with the most fulsome panegyrics upon himself in prose and rhyme'. He was very concerned about his rank.

When he arrived in London, he was not slow to point out that he considered his services in West Africa entitled him to the rank of major.

Laing was now utterly determined to get permission for his projected journey to Timbuctoo. If he did not do so soon, he knew it would be too late, for the race to Timbuctoo was reaching its climax.

*

While Laing had been occupied with the—to him irrelevant—Ashanti troubles, others had been free to concentrate on Timbuctoo. And while Clapperton was struggling hopefully towards it from Chad and the East, an Italian explorer, Giovanni Battista Belzoni, was making an attempt from the West Coast.

Belzoni was primarily an explorer of Egyptian antiquities. He had begun life as a circus showman in England, Spain and Portugal. He was described by one who knew him as 'Possessed of great bodily strength. His manners and deportment were marked by great suavity and mildness. He was brave, ardent, and persevering in pursuit of his objects'. He became an inventor, and went to Egypt in an attempt to sell his idea of a hydraulic machine. The British Consul promptly recognized his talents and put Belzoni to work on the removal of the enormous Rameses II head for the British Museum.

Belzoni then interested himself in Egyptian archaeology and did important work, not least at Abu Simbel. He was the first to penetrate into the second pyramid of Giza. He then went to England, where he published an account of his excavations.

In London, he decided that to be the first man to reach Timbuctoo would be a suitable climax to his extraordinary career.

He was landed by a Royal Navy vessel at Benin, and prepared to depart into the interior with a native guide. He was dressed in Moorish clothes. His plan was to proceed to the Hausa country (i.e. into Nigeria) and then ask for directions to Timbuctoo—which was not known at Benin. Before leaving, he gave each of the crew of the brig a present, and they gave him three loud cheers as he left the ship and walked away. Belzoni, six and a half feet tall and immensely broad, turned and cried: 'God bless you, my fine fellows, and send you a happy sight of your country and friends!' After about ten miles he was struck down with dysentery, and died eight days later.* His last words concerned the huge amethyst ring he wore, 'which he seemed particularly desirous should be delivered to his wife, with the assurance that he died in the fullest affection for her, as he found himself too weak to write his last wishes and adieus'.

A few weeks after Belzoni's death, René Caillié, now a clerk in the wine business at Bordeaux, was making plans to return to Senegal. Caillié was still obsessed with one idea. He

---

*G. B. Belzoni: born 1778, at Padua, Italy. Showman, engineer and archaeologist. Died December 3, 1823, at Gwato, Nigeria.

was not much interested in exploration. He was not concerned with the direction of the Niger or the whereabouts of its mouth.

He wanted simply to be the first white man to reach Timbuctoo.

*

It was in August, 1824, that Captain Gordon Laing arrived in London: probably aware of Belzoni's fate, certainly unaware of the fanatical young Frenchman, and thoroughly alarmed as to whether Clapperton might not reach Timbuctoo after all.

August was holiday-time in the capital. Offices were half-empty, officials away in the country. Laing was told to come back later. As he was determined not to return to Africa until his expedition to Timbuctoo had been granted, he wisely applied for an extension of leave—thus infuriating his commanding officer still further. At home in Edinburgh, he was restless and intense. He trained himself in hardiness for the expedition and the trials which he was certain were coming. To his mother's consternation, he slept on the hard floorboards rather than in his bed, displaying, perhaps, as much of the masochistic streak present in many explorers as of foresight; he practised writing with the left hand.

He returned to London from Scotland early in October. The headquarters of the Army were at the Horse Guards, and Laing became a familiar figure there. His memoranda, letters and interviews bombarded all those around Lord Bathurst, and even the Secretary of State himself. His extension of leave was granted; so, eventually, was his promotion to Major (but 'in Africa only'—which was of very little satisfaction to him).

The preoccupation of Lord Bathurst with Timbuctoo was considerable. The trouble was that he was more than ever convinced of the North Coast being a better point of departure for Timbuctoo than the West Coast; whereas Laing, of course, was committed to the West Coast. Bathurst's argument was that it was known that Moslems had travelled south from the Barbary Coast for centuries, while no traffic from the West Coast to Timbuctoo had ever been discovered: what Arabs and Moors could do, he said, Europeans could do also. The problem of being a Christian could be overcome by bribes and tact. To this Laing replied:

I would prefer penetrating from Sierra Leone for various reasons. Firstly because, having already travelled a considerable distance in that quarter, I am personally acquainted with many of the most powerful Chiefs who command the road to Timbuctoo, and who have all of them and severally made repeated promises to me of facilitating my journey to that capital; secondly, because I am sufficiently versed in the Mandingo language to make my way through the country without an interpreter; and thirdly because the commercial advantages which I have already obtained for one of our African settlements by prosecuting that route might be greatly extended at the same time that the subject of discovery was in progress. After reaching the capital city of Timbuctoo and endeavouring to effect a trading communication between it and the colony of Sierra Leone, my object would be to pass through the Kingdom of Houssa . . . and follow the Niger to its termination.

Lord Bathurst was not swayed by these arguments, which could certainly have been more impressive. The dialogue had by now continued for such a time, however, that Laing had cleverly made it almost certain that he would conduct the next expedition.

Another trouble was the cost. It was a time of financial difficulties for the Government, and every department was under great pressure to keep its expenditure to the absolute minimum. Laing was asked to prepare an estimate of the cost. As he knew nothing of the Barbary Coast or the Desert, this was almost certain to be misleading—a possibility which did not occur to the authorities. He considered, for instance, that two servants would cost him £30 each per annum, that camels would cost him £15 each, and that the subsistence for the five camels he said he would take would come to £10 each (including 'expenses at watering places'). For presents on the journey he said he would require £40 2s. (including 'One Common Watch, £3 3s.'). In all, Laing said he would require £640 10s. to set up the expedition if it started from the north; and he estimated that its annual expenditure would come to £173 7s. 6d.

As Lord Bathurst showed no signs of changing his opinion, discretion got the better of the Scotsman's obstinacy. He wrote that he would be ready 'to proceed to Tripoli at any time and by any conveyance Government may desire'. So it was settled. And everyone knew well that the northern route to Timbuctoo was one for which Laing had no qualifications whatever, going as it did through country and among people with which he was utterly unfamiliar.

In the same month that Laing had arrived in London, René Caillié, back in Africa, had gone to live with the Moors on the edge of the desert. Unknown to any of the explorers of the world, unheard of by all the learned societies in London, he intended to live with the Moors as one of themselves—eat, drink, sleep, wake and talk native. He was doing so for one reason only—to prepare himself for travelling in disguise to Timbuctoo.

Few men can ever have craved more for fame, with desperate and passionate longing, than did René Caillié and Gordon Laing.

In December, 1824, while Laing was in London and Caillié in West Africa, the Geographical Society of Paris announced a reward of 7,000 francs, plus many other subscriptions and a gold medal valued at 2,000 francs, for the first person to return with information about Timbuctoo. In all the prize was worth about 10,000 francs.* Subscribers to it included the French Ministry of Marine, the Ministry for Foreign Affairs and the Ministry of the Interior. The success of the Clapperton-Denham mission had not gone unnoticed in Paris, and the French were determined to make contact with the wealth of Timbuctoo before the British succeeded in doing so. The Society's announcement said:

The fortunate attempt of the English travellers who penetrated into Central Africa in 1823 has lately attracted the attention of Europe towards the interior of that continent . . . it was natural that the Geographical Society should direct its attention to this quarter also, pointing out as preferable the route already attempted by Mungo Park, and which touches upon the French establishments in the Senegal; with it, therefore, originated the idea of a subscrip-

*About £420 in the values of that time: perhaps £2,000 today, a good salary then being £250.

tion for the encouragement of travels to Timbuctoo. . . . France was the first country of Europe which formed permanent establishments on the Senegal, and her honour is interested in assisting those travellers who seek to penetrate into the interior of Africa, by the route approaching nearest to her settlements. Such an enterprise, if successful, would not be without profit to our commercial industry. . . . As the judge and dispenser of this reward, the Geographical Society will duly appreciate the merit, courage and the devotedness of travellers, as well as the real services they may have rendered to science. It does not expect from a single individual all the results which would require the concurrence of several observers and many years' peaceable residence in the country; but it demands precise information, such as may be expected from a man provided with instruments, and who is no stranger either to natural or mathematical science. . . . The Society demands a manuscript narrative, with a geographical map, founded upon celestial observations.

The announcement of this Prize had an immediate effect on plans for exploration in the Niger area, for it was not restricted to Frenchmen and demanded only that the exploration 'touched on' the Senegal, which might be stretched to include a large part of the West Coast. It would be wrong to suggest that Laing's preference for the West Coast was moved by the thought of this tempting sum, as he had already made his preference clear, but it must have caused him added bitterness at Lord Bathurst's insistence on the Barbary route.

Laing spent his last day in London going over the proofs of his book on his exploration of Sierra Leone, of which less than a third was in print.

On February 6, 1825, Gordon Laing sailed from Falmouth for Malta and Tripoli. With him were a faithful manservant, Jack le Bore, who had been with him on his West African expeditions, and two West African boat-builders (Laing intended to sail down the Niger, as Park had done). His party was officially known as 'The Timbuctoo Mission'.

Laing had got his desire at last.

Not long before his departure it was discovered that Laing had forgotten to add a medicine-chest to the detailed list of items and expenses he would require. One was hastily bought for £29 11s. 2d. And then it was discovered that he had forgotten stationery on which to write the reports that were

—were they not?—the very object of the Timbuctoo Mission. And forgotten the quills with which to write the reports. . . .

*

It was three months before Laing reached Tripoli. He had suffered another of his recurrent liver attacks in Malta and this had held him back. Waiting for him there was the British Consul, Hanmer Warrington.

Warrington was one of that remarkable band of Consuls in the Mediterranean, particularly at Tripoli and Tunis, who served their country in the first half of the nineteenth century. Winning over their local rulers by a mixture of charm, personality and bland bullying, they kept Britain powerful in the area, with occasional support from the Royal Navy and the Marines.

Warrington was a man of some mystery. Nothing is known of his family, his background or his childhood. He himself said that he joined the Army at the age of sixteen, rising to the rank of Lieutenant-Colonel, and that he served in the Peninsular Wars. In 1814 he appears at Tripoli as Consul-General.

At Tripoli, as elsewhere on the African coast, there was intense rivalry between the British and the French. Both Consuls intrigued for influence. Warrington entered into this with such gusto that he earned the admiring respect of his opposite number. It was a document of this French rival, discovered in 1928, that first revealed that Warrington had married an illegitimate daughter of King George IV, born when the latter had been Prince Regent. Warrington, it seems, was therefore subject to a certain amount of patronage.

Warrington had a lovely daughter—Emma—for whom, one can imagine, life at Tripoli was a lonely and wretched affair.

The previous expeditions which had gone south from Tripoli had all spoken of Warrington in the highest terms and with obvious sincerity. He was clearly a personable character, although testy when roused, and was genuinely interested in exploration; the efficiency of his contributions to the expeditions was less certain. That he had considerable influence over the Pasha—the hereditary ruler of Tripoli—is clear from the fact that he once rushed into the latter's court, shouted at him that he was a rascal, threatened him with a whip, and entertained him to a more than convivial dinner the next day. The Pasha's policy with French and British, inevitably, was to play the one off against the other: he thereby turned rivalry into a bitterness which was to last in that area for many years. By the time Laing arrived at Tripoli the French were again in the ascendant. The Pasha had been forced to give up all his British-subject slaves—a matter about which he was extremely disagreeable. Moreover, shortly before Laing's arrival a new French Consul had arrived. He was a man with a greater knowledge of Arab affairs and life than Warrington (who seems to have had no experience whatever of consular matters or the Moslem world until his appointment). The new French Consul, Baron Rousseau, quickly made a close friendship with the Pasha's French-educated prime minister, Hassuna D'Ghies; and he kept the closest watch on the arrangements for the Timbuctoo Mission.

Warrington was impulsive: an incorrigible optimist. Before the Oudney, Denham, Clapperton expedition, he had told London 'the road from Tripoli [to Chad] was as open as that from London to Edinburgh'.

One of the first things Warrington told Laing was that Clapperton might be making another expedition. But that this time he would go from the West Coast! He would probably reach Timbuctoo. And it was Warrington himself, as he blithely told Laing, who had suggested this in a letter to Lord Bathurst. If this was so, Laing's entire trip might be a waste of time.

There were also rumours of an official French expedition, from Derna, that was going to attempt the journey to Timbuctoo. The British Vice-Consul in Benghazi had reported its arrival to Warrington.*

Laing, after all his efforts, lasting several years, was exceedingly depressed. He hastened to prepare his departure, but maintained a disregard for competition unseemly in a serious explorer. He wrote in a letter of his distaste for

---

*The rumour appears to have been ill-founded.
3*

running a race with Captain Clapperton, whose only objective seems to be to forestall me in discovery. Should he succeed in reaching Timbuctoo, which I doubt much, I shall have much pleasure in meeting him.

There was no mistaking the challenge.

Clapperton had first heard of Laing and his Mission from Warrington when he had returned to Tripoli with Denham. It seems that Warrington had been instructed to obtain any information from Clapperton that might be useful to Laing, and that Clapperton had been most reluctant to supply it. Foolishly, Warrington—who had a high opinion of both men —told Laing about this.

Laing must have thought it unlikely that Clapperton could be back in Africa in less than six months; but he did not delay.

*

Warrington was alarmed at Laing's appearance. He seemed wan and sickly. He looked more ready for a long spell of recuperation than for one of the most difficult and dangerous journeys in the world. He even tried to insist that Laing should take a doctor with him, but Laing dismissed the idea. He intended to be the only white man on the Timbuctoo Mission. Warrington, still worried, wrote to London:

He is both gentlemanly and clever, and certainly appears most zealous in the cause he has undertaken, although I much fear the delicate state of his health will not carry him through his arduous task—I have strongly recommended him to apply himself, or to allow me, to make application to the Government of Malta for a Surgeon to accompany him.

In the same letter he complained that the Pasha was expecting payment if he were to help Laing, and that he had not been satisfied with payments at the time of the Denham and Clapperton expedition.

At the moment the Pasha was professing disinterested conduct, a glance of his eye and the rubbing together of his thumb and finger gave strong indications that he expected something more substantial between them.

In fact, the expedition would cost much more than Laing had indicated in London. This, and the attitude of the Pasha, were now the only factors detaining Laing. His health, he insisted, was much better. Typically, he had not been wasting his time, and had busied himself taking lessons in rudimentary Arabic. He wrote to Lord Bathurst supporting Warrington's letter, pleading with him openly, as he had not done before, to give his approval to the extra cash being drawn on Malta. He reminded him that 'the French Government is jealous of our success and desirous of being beforehand with us in reaching Timbuctoo'.

No answer came from London. Surely Lord Bathurst would be disturbed at the thought of a French expedition reaching Timbuctoo first? After the expense of the previous, unsuccessful, missions to make contact with the great city, it would indeed be galling to reach it now only to be greeted there by the French. If the extra funds were made available, Laing assured Lord Bathurst in his last letter to him before departure, then all would be well: 'I consider protection and safety will be as fully ensured to me as if I were merely on a tour through the secure districts of my ever-blessed and happy country.' When Bathurst's reply eventually came, it showed that he was infuriated at the extra expense. But by then Laing had gone into the desert. . . .

*

Laing was able to pass much of the time with Warrington's lovely daughter Emma. The latter was no doubt delighted at the unexpectedly long stay in Tripoli of the intense and brave young Scotsman, whose visits to her father's house relieved the relentless monotony of her life.

Laing had already written to a friend in London asking for

a handsome little cabinet of mineralogical specimens, such a one as will suit a lady of taste and refinement. . . . I am much interested in the young lady in question.

Interest rapidly developed into love. Laing had always been, as he said, 'passionately fond of the fair sex'. But it was at this moment of his life, of all times, that he first fell in love.

With only a few days to go before the departure which the Pasha had at last arranged, he proposed to Emma Warrington. The delighted and adoring young woman accepted.

Warrington was astounded. Knowing something of his character, we may also assume he was apoplectic. When he predictably forbade the marriage, there is some evidence to suggest that Laing threatened suicide. What is certain is that there was a clash of violent and electric intensity between these two excitable but formidable men. The atmosphere for Laing's departure could not have been more extraordinary. Laing left the Consul's house and set up camp just outside Tripoli, in readiness for departure. Warrington and Laing, apparently not on speaking terms, engaged in a frank correspondence. Warrington wrote to Lord Bathurst:

I must allow a more wild, enthusiastic and romantic attachment never before existed and consequently every remonstrance, every argument and every feeling of disapprobation was resorted to by me to prevent even an engagement under the existing circumstances the disadvantages so evidently appearing to attach to my daughter.

After a voluminous correspondence, I found my wishes, exertions entreaties and displeasures quite futile and of no avail.

It had been the custom for British Consuls to conduct the marriage service themselves; but whether or not it was more than a custom, Warrington was uncertain. Nevertheless, this doomed couple persuaded him to marry them.

Uneasy as to the legality of the affair, Warrington would not allow the marriage to be consummated. From the moment of the service he arranged that his daughter should never leave the sight of either himself or of Mrs Warrington. The couple, therefore, had a prim audience to all their meetings. Not content with this, Warrington wrote a letter to Bathurst in which he seems to try to absolve himself from any blame in case he had done wrong. He did not, however, forget to inform George IV of the marriage—as the King could be expected to have a private interest in it.

This unhappy victory of propriety over gentleness was Laing's last experience of civilization.

Laing made 'a solemn promise to my dear Emma that melancholy night never again to part from her when it should please God to restore us to each other'. He gave her a miniature of himself, in a locket, which she was to wear around her neck. Emma gave him a miniature golden bird.

He was married on July 14. The quarrel with Warrington was broken off and, of necessity, cordial relations were hurriedly re-established. On July 16 he left Tripoli for the Sahara Desert, the unknown, and for Timbuctoo. He had with him the small caravan which he had been obliged to get the Pasha to assemble (there being no regular annual caravan for Timbuctoo as he, and London, had previously believed); also Jack le Bore, his servant; Rogers and Harris, the West African boatbuilders; and an interpreter. He had with him also impressive credentials. A note of credit:

We, His Britannic Majesty's Consul-General to the Regency of Tripoli hereby authorize the bearer Major Laing to draw on us for any money which he may require during his journey into the interior of Africa.

This was supported by similar notes from the Pasha and from the Pasha's chief minister. There was also a letter to 'The Sultan of the Kingdom and Territory of Timbuctoo'.

My great and revered master the King of England wishing. . . the most friendly intercourse with every great and good sovereign, sends the bearer of this, an Englishman, Major Laing, to express his most sincere and friendly sentiments to your Highness. . . . The King of England is very anxious to know where the great river which passes your kingdom proceeds, and he particularly wishes that your Highness would allow the bearer to trace this river. . . .

One could not tell how His Highness, the Sultan of Timbuctoo, ruler of the greatest and most-sought-after city in Africa, would react; but the sentiments were well-expressed and honestly meant. It was not much, but Warrington, Lord Bathurst and the Government could do nothing more for Gordon Laing. The camels of his caravan stalked slowly away into the scrub-land south of Tripoli, the Mediterranean glistening behind them, towards the sandy horizon.

Almost impossibly, against all odds, the pale officer in the hopelessly unfashionable regiment had begun the journey of which he had dreamed so long and with which he intended to escape from obscurity at last. He was supremely confident.

No matter about Clapperton, the French, or anyone else—he would get there first:

I shall do more than has ever been done before, and shall show myself to be what I have ever considered myself, a man of enterprise and genius.

*

Four weeks earlier, in June, Clapperton and Denham had returned to London. There Clapperton must certainly have heard of the Prize of 10,000 francs of the Geographical Society of Paris—if he had not already heard of it from Warrington in Tripoli. In Denham's chambers at Albany, they worked fast on the account of their travels to Chad and Kano, which they hoped would assure their fame. But Denham soon found that most of the work was to be done by himself. Clapperton travelled up to Scotland to see his family; he seemed restless and unable to concentrate. He spent much time closeted with Lord Bathurst.

Bathurst managed to wring from Clapperton a letter, for Laing's guidance, giving various hints on how best to get on with the Sheikhs and how to survive in the desert. It seems clear that the Colonial and War Secretary did all he could to eliminate personal rivalry from the quest for Timbuctoo. This letter was immediately sent out to Tripoli with instructions for Warrington to forward it to Laing.

Clapperton's exploit in reaching Kano had made him the most celebrated and important explorer of West Africa since Mungo Park. He was very much in favour in Whitehall, and Lord Bathurst was delighted with him. Unlike Laing, who had made such a nuisance of himself but who had as yet done next to nothing, Clapperton had brought great credit to the Secretary of State's policy of African exploration with a view to territory and trade. With remarkably little resistance, in view of the contrary experience of Laing, he agreed that Clapperton should go to West Africa and travel from that direction—as Warrington had already suggested in his letter. It was what Laing had always wanted to do himself.

Lord Bathurst's instructions were that Clapperton should first go to the town of Sokoto. 'You will also, during your

stay in Central Africa, endeavour to visit the city of Timbuctoo, provided you shall not have heard that Major Laing
had already accomplished that object.' Whether Clapperton,
who was to penetrate far south of the Senegal, would qualify
for the French Prize must have been questionable.

Two months after his arrival in England from Tripoli,
Hugh Clapperton set out again for Africa. Such devotion to
the cause of exploration had never been known before. Mungo
Park had needed years to recuperate before he returned to
the wilderness. With Clapperton were to go two doctors, and
Captain Pearce, R.N., Richard Lander, and two black servants. Lander was a manservant from Cornwall, aged twenty-
one, whom Clapperton, promoted Commander in the Royal
Navy, had engaged in London. Richard Lander, of whom
more will be heard, was described as 'very short and fair', but
of 'great muscular strength and iron constitution'. They embarked at Portsmouth on August 27, 1825: 'a light breeze
springing up from the north-east, the vessel got under way
and made sail, the shores of England gradually lessening
from our view.'

Through the time that Laing had wasted at Tripoli, and
the time that Clapperton had saved in London, the latter was
catching up on the former, fast.

*

Nearly all that is known of Laing's remarkable journey
is what is contained in his occasional letters. These were sent
back to Tripoli by courier as he progressed, but some of
them clearly have not survived or did not reach their destination. Sometimes a finely drawn sketch of a native, illustrating
a custom of dress, or a neatly prepared map, would accompany the letters. They say little of the rigours of his progress
and mull more and more on the character of Clapperton, on
the greed of the natives, on the promotion for which Laing
always longed despite all distractions, and on 'my dear, dear
Emma'. Even when the difficulties of writing and concentra-
tion are borne in mind, and the trying circumstances, the
letters do reveal a lack of balance. The underlying frenzy of
Laing's earlier life seems to have become more evident under

this special strain. The confidence is thinner, sometimes mere bravado. But all the time there is evident fierce courage, sensitivity, intelligence, and a stubborn determination to battle with all the many trials which came his way. But Laing was not a stoical man and he suffered both mental as well as physical agonies while struggling to fulfil his self-imposed destiny. As Laing became further and further distant and communication became a matter of months rather than weeks, so the breaks become longer, the letters shorter and the link connecting him with Tripoli and safety more and more tenuous.

There was a local war in the hinterland behind Tripoli and this had necessitated a change in the route. The way was now to go through the important oasis of Ghadames. There a guide was waiting to take Laing on to Timbuctoo; this man, Hatita, was an impoverished Tuareg Sheikh who had met Lyon and had later helped Denham and Clapperton. He was the only certain friend the British had in all the Sahara, and Laing did not want to miss him by travelling another way. However this change of plan made another humble, even degrading, letter necessary to the increasingly irascible Lord Bathurst.

The route to Ghadames had not been taken by a European since Roman times. To get there at all was a considerable achievement, as it was known to be a large place of great interest and importance. Although it was less than three hundred miles south-west of Tripoli, Laing's caravan had to travel a detour of over twice that distance in order to avoid the fighting. This route was seldom used even by the natives, and Laing was almost certainly the first European ever to have been along it.

As Laing's chief assistant and guide, the Pasha had introduced him to a Sheikh called Babani. This man claimed to have been in and out of Timbuctoo for thirty years. Babani said he knew the road from Ghadames to Timbuctoo well. His value was so obvious that Laing hired him for 2,500 dollars (with contrite apologies to Lord Bathurst). Babani considered the entire journey would take about thirteen weeks. This prompted Laing to write: 'I expect about the middle of November will see me in the far-famed capital of Central Africa.'

Laing soon discovered that the choice of route was not at all like 'the road to Edinburgh'.

I have for the sake of convenience, as well as to avoid observation in passing through a strange country, adopted the Turkish costume, as have also my three attendants . . . our dresses are of the simplest and humblest kind in order not to create jealousy: and lest it should ever be supposed that we attempt to pass ourselves for what we really are not, it is my intention to read prayers to my three attendants always on Sunday, on which day we shall appear dressed as Englishmen*.

If Laing wore Turkish clothes to avoid too much attention, it did not succeed, as he made no other efforts to hide his religion and race and was plagued by inquisitive onlookers at every oasis.

Laing was increasingly pestered by demands for money. The chiefs of villages hinted that if more was not forth coming, robbery or death might lie in wait on the road ahead.

He insisted I should go no further if I did not pay . . . he said as I must go a journey of six days without water I must hire some camels from his people—this I accordingly did—but I must say this *friendly* [chief] has made me pay for them. . . . At one time people would lag behind on pretext of their camels being lame, at another they would cut down the loads, let them fall in the road and there leave them, threatening to maltreat Roger, Harris or Jack, whomsoever I left in charge. As night came on they commenced irregular firing as we marched along, and as their shot whistled over our heads, several times caused an alarm, it being so dark that we were uncertain whether we were attacked or not. Pray say nothing to Emma about the detention I have met with, as it will only cause her to fret and to suppose that I may be much longer on the journey than I expected—which will not be the case, for Babani assures me that although he is quite a stranger on this road, he knows every foot of ground between Timbuctoo and Ghadames, and that we shall meet with no stoppage there. Bye the bye, I have suffered a good deal from intermittent fever. . . .

---

*Laing's letters given here and below were mostly to Warrington; others were to his family in Edinburgh, to two friends in London, and to the Under Secretary of State at the Colonial Office. Extracts are not in strict order. (Public Record Office and Royal Society.)

A Regiment Majority is my right, and I should have got it had I gone to the Gold Coast; if they refuse that at the Horse Guards (which I know they will), let them give me the local rank of Lt.-Colonal when I reach Timbuctoo. I shall be very dissatisfied indeed if this is not done, not that I care so much about the rank, but because I shall not otherwise be able to divest myself of the feeling of being ill-used. Excuse all this—I write with the paper on my knees by a glimmering lamp seated upon *Alma mater*.

It was in a letter from Warrington that he heard, later, of Clapperton's speedy departure from London, and of his sailing for West Africa. Warrington innocently suggested that Laing would probably meet him in the interior; on several occasions he repeated this, apparently in efforts to cheer up Laing. He even imagined them returning together to Tripoli. These messages, of course, had the reverse effect. Laing became increasingly alarmed and obsessed about Clapperton. He had now received the memorandum which Clapperton had been ordered by Bathurst to write for his guidance.

I care little for any information that Clapperton could comunicate, and you were right in saying you did not think that I should wait for it. I smile at the idea of his reaching Timbuctoo before me. How can he expect it. Has he not already had the power? Has he not thrown away the chance? Clapperton reminds me much of Mr. Martyn, who accompanied Park, remarkably fond of country wine and beer. . . . He amuses me by saying you should not eat or drink before a Turk. Four bottles of port wine before dinner whenever he could get it—I am not suprised Mr. C. should not wish to drink before them; such sort of potations would not command respect in any country, much less in a Mohammedan, where the inhabitants are by religion abstemious.

I have received the information communicated by him to the Colonial Office. It is worth nothing, and has been evidently wrung from him.

"I must wear a plain Turkish dress", just as "I must be kind and patient with the natives". Tis not my nature to be otherwise. "I must not take observations secretly." The sun does not shine in sly corners. "I must not speak disrespectfully of the women." I wonder how he found this out—I might have been a century in Africa and never have made such a discovery. "I must not meddle with the females of the country." Prodigious! "I must have presents to give away." We need not ghosts to rise from their graves to tell us this.

Not content with these outbursts of wounded pride, Laing, now nearing Ghadames after three weeks' travelling, sent a huffy official receipt to the Colonial Office:

I have the honour to acknowledge your letter of the 7th June, transmitting a copy of the opinions and suggestions which Lt. Clapperton has been called upon to furnish for my guidance, and which, I beg you will be pleased to aquaint His Lordship the Earl Bathurst, shall meet with the attention and consideration which is due to them—at the same time I beg to refer to my letter of the 10th Ulto, dated Wadey Ramel, from which it will be observed that their general tenor has been anticipated and acted upon by, Sir, Your most obedt., Very Humble Servt. A. Gordon Laing

The Timbuctoo Mission progressed slowly throughout August and September. There were more troubles with the local natives, but Babani remained optimistic. The explorer longed for the oasis, where he expected letters to be awaiting him from Tripoli. He sent off a request to Warrington:

As I shall remain only a few days at Ghadames, pray send off a courier with my dear Emma's picture the moment it is done. Don't wait for the packet*—the picture is worth to me a million packets.

After that: one note four days later, on a scrap of paper, giving his position. Then, for four weeks, silence.

*

Laing arrived at Ghadames exactly two months after leaving Tripoli. He was still some 1,300 miles from Timbuctoo. But it was an exciting moment.

A large deputation met us about three miles from the town and accompanied us with acclamations expressive of the warmest welcome, and although we are not yet two hours in quarters, my house is filled with provisions of every description, and my attendants, my half-starved attendants, have at length satiated themselves upon the most substantial viands.

But after this initial pleasure Laing experienced the first of the two bitter disappointments with which Ghadames was to greet him. There were no letters waiting for him. His loneliness and his sense of isolation were almost unbearable.

*i.e. from London, via Malta.

I now with eagerness take up my pen to make the most solicitous enquiries regarding your welfare, that of Mrs. Warrington and the whole family; respecting which I am indeed most anxious, a period of six weeks having elapsed since I have had any tidings from Tripoli—during my long journey through Fezzan and across the desert, during privations and exposure to a degree of heat, which I am inclined to believe few European constitutions could stand, I consoled myself with the hope that on my arrival at Ghadames I should hear tidings of my dearest, most beloved Emma; that I should be made happy in the knowledge that the only object I prize in this world was well—alas, how cruelly I have been disappointed.

For Heaven sake, my dear Consul, do endeavour to let me hear occasionally from Tripoli. If I can only know that my Emma is well, I will answer for my successful completion of this journey, but if I am left to conjecture and despondency the state of my mind may prove much more prejudicial to the state of my health than the climate of Africa.

The road has been for the most part a complete desert, and for the last three days we ran very short of water, and entirely so of provisions.

It was typical of Laing that the lack of letters were more important, and a worse hardship, than the fact—which he referred to again elsewhere—that for nearly a week the caravan had been without any food whatever.

The heat has been almost intolerable; since I left you the thermometer at noon standing not infrequently at 120 degrees Fahrenheit, which was the more severely felt in consequence of the cold which often-times prevailed in the mornings.

Laing spent five weeks at Ghadames: about five times longer than he had intended. He found it disappointing. He sent back a full report on the place, but remained unexcited even by some Roman ruins he discovered. The technical problem of ascertaining by bearings the latitude and longitude of the place, he found long and tiresome (and the results of his efforts were inaccurate). This may have been because he seems to have spent so much of his time in the town in morose contemplation and dejection. Clapperton would have been glad of the opportunity to relax; Mungo Park would have lost himself in preparations for continuing the journey. But Laing fretted and lost control of the caravan. Already he

had let himself become dominated by those who were meant
to be in his service. Knowing little or nothing of Moslem
customs, or of the conditions, until his arrival at Tripoli, he
had to learn as a novice while he progressed. This he was
very capable of doing. But the dangers of his position—a self-
confessed Christian travelling with a great deal of money and
desirable gifts—were apparent.

Hatita, the guide who had been contracted from Tripoli,
was at Ghadames as arranged. Having already received some
money, he now hesitated about joining with Laing. His dis-
inclination, Hatita said, was to do with Babani, who would
be able to guide Laing to Timbuctoo well enough. Babani,
meanwhile, had so impressed himself on Laing that the latter
believed he was the Governor of Ghadames, a 'circumstance I
was ignorant of till this morning'. (While Babani did live in
Ghadames, he was not its Governor, and in fact had no real
power there whatever.)

Laing's reaction to all trouble was to pay out a little more
from his dwindling treasury. The requests—or blackmail—
not surprisingly increased. While the days went on in
haggling about matters which Laing had naïvely imagined
had all been settled before departure from Tripoli, he busied
himself with doctoring the inhabitants.

I have gained great celebrity as a medico. I am now a graduate
of Ghadames College. That is to say I have taken the local rank of
Surgeon, which in this country would be of more service to me than
that of Major. Though I may not be able to do much good, I shall,
like the apothecary who had only two drawers in his shop, one for
Magnesia and the other for money, do little harm.

I have for about an hour been amusing myself with a number of
little children who have come out of curiosity to see the Christian—
I like the play of incipient man in all countries, and it is strange to
observe similitude which exists between Turk, Jew, Kaffir or
Christian before the effects of government or education are felt by
the mind.

I should be happy to depart tomorrow, there being apparently
little to interest me here, and as I expect to find little more till I
reach Timbuctoo, the country being so provokingly monotonous.

Laing's troubles were not decreased by the fact that his
interpreter was 'rarely successful'. About the three West

Africans he reported little, but as they spoke English (having been recruited in England) they must have been some comfort to him.

And still neither Hatita nor Babani seemed anxious to leave.

Laing was ceaselessly nagged by his love for Emma. Every day he wrote to her; when he despatched his courier, therefore, hers was easily the longest letter and the fullest envelope—a fact for which he apparently felt it necessary to apologize to Warrington.

When at last the letters from Tripoli for which he had longed so desperately arrived, time and distance had healed the wound he had received from Warrington; and as for the latter, afflicted it seems with guilt and remorse, there has never been a more loyal or proud father-in-law. Two couriers, one with the letters, the other with Emma's portrait, arrived the same day.

They did nothing to relieve the unfortunate Laing, now plagued by worries and imagination as much as by practical difficulties.

*

My heart throbs with sad pulsations on account of my dearest, most beloved Emma. You say she is well and happy, but I fear, I feel, she is not. Good God, where is the colour of her lovely cheek, where the vermilion of her dear lip? Tell me, has Mr. Herrador,* or has he not, made a faithful likeness? If he has, my Emma is ill, is melancholy, is unhappy—her sunken eye, her pale cheek and colourless lip haunt my imagination. Was I within a day's march of Timbuctoo, and to hear my dear Emma was ill, I would turn about and retrace my steps to Tripoli. What is Timbuctoo? What the Niger? What the world to me, without my Emma? Should anything befall my Emma, which God forbid, I no more wish to see the face of man; my course will be run—a few short days of misery and I should follow her to heaven.

I am agitated, but you will bear with me I hope—never since this terrestial ball was formed was there a man situated as I am—never, never, and may no man ever be so placed again—it requires rather more than the fortitude which falls to the general lot of mortals, to enable me to bear it—I must again entreat that you will 'Bear with my weakness, my brain is troubled'—I must lay down my pen awhile—oh that picture.

---

*The Spanish Consul-General at Tripoli, who had done the portrait.

Warrington, who had been fulfilling Laing's wishes in having the portrait made and sent out, must have been mortified by its unexpected effect. He no doubt dismissed the sunken eyes and the pallid face of his daughter as being no more than the ramblings of a love-sick man. He was himself having his own troubles with Emma, who was worried that if Laing was too often assured of her good health he would think she had less reason to pine for him:

Your dear wife Emma, you may believe me, is well and happy as it is her duty to be. So I am sure you will wish her to be so, and that you do not suppose she loves you the less because she is so. I have impressed that on her as much as possible, and cautioned her against representations which cause you to entertain a different belief. It is very natural she should wish to see you, and it is very probable she might resort to every argument to induce you to return; but for Heaven's sake do not let your powerful feelings operate on you so as to adopt a proceeding which you would for ever repent.

Emma has seen this letter.

Unlike Warrington, however, Laing would not have assumed that any illness of Emma's was simulated in order to accelerate her husband's return. From what little we know of her, she would have been more likely to bear the parting with fortitude. She herself was worried, not only about Laing's situation, but about his own health.

Some person has told Emma that I had fever, and she fancies I am ill although I say nothing. The slight fever I had was so trifling I did not think it necessary to say anything of it. At present I am as well in bodily health as I ever was, or ever wish to be, upon my honour I am, and you may assure her of it in the most positive manner.

It is clear that Warrington had become increasingly startled at having to deal with this man, excitable and neurotic as compared to the phlegmatic Denham and the dare-devil Clapperton. Laing had the self-absorption, the impatience of others, the certainty in himself, and the obsession to be recognized that occurs in so many outstanding men fired with wordly ambitions. While one can find some sympathy for Warrington in his strange position between these two lovers, there is no doubt that he could have handled the affair rather better. For he had not only been unable to soothe the sufferings of both of them, he had added to Laing's depression by unloading on him his own worries about the cost of the Mission and the letter he had now had from Lord Bathurst on the subject. He had also forwarded a letter from Bathurst to Laing.

Squatting in a mud-house a thousand miles from the nearest European, with no one with whom he could discuss his feelings, Laing perused the contentious reflections of the Secretary of State on the increasing costs of the Timbuctoo Mission. Laing was so full of bitterness at what he considered contempt for his sufferings and efforts that he considered abandoning the expedition and his ambition of being the first to reach Timbuctoo.

Had I thought it possible that such mean, such sordid, illiberal ideas could have existed in the fabric of Downing Street, I should have dropped the Mission after the first interview I had with the Pasha. Would to God I had; I might now be enjoying the happiness I hope I deserve, with my dearest Emma in England. Good Heavens; have I made such a sacrifice? Have I left all that is dear to me on earth to embark upon so thankless an enterprise? I never looked for, I never cared for, reward, and well they know *that* at Downing Street. I might have been a Regimental Major by resigning the mission. . . . I sacrificed both promotion and emoluments to serve the good cause of discovery, and ought to have been more liberally dealt with.

I am, however, satisfied of the correctness of my own conduct. I am so sensible that I merit commendation and not censure that I shall endeavour to care as little for their displeasure as I now feel I should for their praise. . . . I shall never, never let me execute what I may, apply for any reward. They cannot reward me for what I have suffered! I know His Lordship will think that the step of Lt.-Colonel will be a most ample reward. I would not accept of it.*

One of the subjects which had enraged Lord Bathurst was the suggestion that Laing should take with him a doctor.

You know well, my dear Consul, that I never desired a Surgeon, that I detested the idea of such a companion, and if His Lordship

*Warrington sent a somewhat unpleasing reply to this outburst, in which he praised Bathurst, explained the Secretary of State's difficulties, and absolved himself from all criticism of Whitehall. It did not reach Laing, and one can only hope that Warrington intended it for his file rather than for the explorer.

thinks that under any circumstances I should have required medical assistance to enable to proceed, he knows not my character or disposition. It is the mind that will bear Laing through. Should *it* fail me, what doctor could strengthen it? Really, this world is made up of such commonplace matter that it is painful for a purpose of mind to exist in it.

I have not yet determined whether I shall proceed or return to Tripoli.

Laing's interest in his rank did not dwindle as his other worries progressed: it gained in strength. Again and again he referred to it with indignation (although, in fact, the rank of Local Major was not ungenerous for an obscure officer of his comparatively short and limited military experience in an age when influence and money counted for much in the Army). He decided to make a strong application for a substantive Majority when he reached the next stage on his journey, which would be in the very heart of the depopulated and unexplored desert.

For Laing had managed to conquer the temptation to return, which had been so fortified by Lord Bathurst's ill-considered letter, and had resolved to go on to Timbuctoo. Although the question can never have been long in doubt, perhaps he was strengthened by a letter from Denham. This described the departure of Clapperton's expedition to the West Coast, and 'its liberal terms'.

I feel assured he will never go beyond Benin!—mark my words. He and his friend will arrive at the worst season of the year, the season which proved fatal to the enterprising Belzoni. . . . I cannot help expressing a hope that he may be prudent enough to return if he finds the bad effects of the climate lay hold of his constitution, which they undoubtedly will.

I had a long argument with myself last night, and I felt too keenly the triumph which my enemies (for I have my share of those miscreants who are jealous of the little reputation I have so hardly earned) would have over me. . . . Government may find fault if they please; let us go on with our labour with undiminished enthusiasm, and if we can not command, let us at least deserve commendation.

The enemies to whom Laing was referring were certain critics of his book on his West African travels. As has always been the custom with critics, men being what they are, they had laced their comments on Laing's material with only partially concealed personal attacks on himself; of this Laing had now heard.

When at last all was ready for departure, when the three West Africans had sufficiently recuperated from the famine of the last days of the preceding stage of the journey, when the camels had fattened, when Hatita and Babani had decided they could soak Laing's treasury no further, when Laing had written his final despatches from Ghadames—then Babani developed a boil on—in Laing's phrase, typical of the coy delicacy of the time—'his head's antipodes'. This meant that Babani was unable to ride on a camel, and the whole caravan had to delay while Laing attended the offending boil for two weeks.

Once more Laing's longing for Emma—and the personal reward which awaited him—voiced themselves in his stilted way to Warrington.

Should I return to Tripoli overland after having done everything that I intend performing, should circumstances of any kind bring about such an event—will you still consider it necessary to keep me to the promise which you have from me in writing (and which would be sacred was it merely verbal) or will you absolve me from it?* . . . Now, my Dear Consul, unless you will do this, or either accompany us to Malta or Leghorn, where the ceremony may be reperformed, I would not attempt to return by way of Tripoli; but, if compelled to recross the desert, would make my way either to Morocco or Tunis. . . . I therefore trust that you will understand me, that I ask for the sake of information and to prevent (what might at least be considered) an awkward dilemma hereafter.

The question was, at the time, somewhat academic. For Laing had long before decided to continue to the mouth of the Niger after he had examined Timbuctoo. For this reason he wrote more than once from Ghadames seeking assurances that a warship would be patrolling the coast in the Benin area (where he was confident the river existed). He had no wish, as he said, to dally on the shore for months waiting to be rescued. He suggested the ship should expect him from between six and nine months' time.

But there was always the danger of Clapperton getting there first.

---

*i.e. Laing's promise not to consummate the marriage.

Clapperton may as well have stayed at home if the termination of the Niger is his object. It is destined for me. It is due to me, and neither a Pearce nor a Clapperton can interfere with me. Only take care of my dearest Emma, and Timbuctoo shall be visited and the Niger explored within a very few months.

René Caillié, unheard of by Laing or Clapperton, was then living at a primitive Moorish village. He wished, he said, to learn everything about the Moslem faith, into which he wished to enter. As a Christian, albeit a potential convert, he was treated with every indignity that the primitive villagers could devise—and which Caillié seems almost to have enjoyed. He spent nine months at that place. When it was over, he could pass as an Arab.

*

While Laing was just about to leave Ghadames, his rival, Clapperton—still progressing with remarkable speed—was preparing to land on the West Coast of Africa. The disembarkation, at a small African village, was a dangerous affair owing to the surf. It was also, according to Lander, not without emotion:

There was something so moving in the pathetic spectacle of Englishmen parting under a strong persuasion, almost amounting to a conviction, of meeting no more in this world; in seeing the manly resolution and stubborn indifference of British officers combating with the tenderer and more amiable feelings of human nature, that I myself could with difficulty stifle my emotion; and to dispel the gloom which hung upon my mind, I bade the officers a hasty and respectful adieu and, shaking hands with many of the honest seamen on deck, I sprang into a canoe that lay alongside; and, as two of the natives were rowing it towards the shore, I took the opportunity of playing 'Over the Hills and Far Away' on a small bugle horn which I had brought with me.

Thus Clapperton, with his comparatively large party of Europeans, including two doctors, a merchant, and his own manservant, advanced hopefully into the dark continent—destined, they believed, for Kano, Sokoto and Timbuctoo.

*

While this activity, at which he could only guess, was proceeding on the West Coast, Gordon Laing was still as far from Timbuctoo as London is from Madrid. But not for long.

I am on the road to Timbuctoo. The camels are all loaded and only wait for me while I give you notice of the event. . . . I am off and, please God, shall sleep in the long-looked-after city in forty-two days more. . . . Endeavour, if possible, to let me hear from you and write to me at Sierra Leone immediately, by way of England. God bless you. As soon as I envelope this I am off.

The next oasis of size on the way to Timbuctoo was In Salah: as inaccessible a place as most in Africa. In Salah lay some five hundred miles south-west of Ghadames and was nearly half-way to Timbuctoo from Tripoli. Like some tiny ant crossing a meadow the length of which he was uncertain, Laing was dragged on by the lure of the great and mysterious city which lay so far ahead. He was now mixing with men who had themselves visited it. Did they not describe to him the nature of the place? If so, he kept such information to himself and out of his letters; but the tone of these suggest he was still as hypnotized by the uncertain glories of Timbuctoo as ever, and it seems likely that the Arabs thought it convenient to keep their knowledge to themselves. Or perhaps Laing—like so many others before and after him—preferred not to know.

The Timbuctoo Mission plodded on to the horizon across the loose, featureless sand; Laing, the three West Africans, the interpreter, Hatita, Babani and a few camel-drivers and attendants. Laing considered the West African sailors a burden rather than a help, as he had now wisely decided to use a native craft on the Niger, rather than one of European style, in order not to attract attention. The West Africans caused Laing a lot of concern due to their pestering native women, a dangerous occupation in the Moslem world. As for the two Sheikhs, they seem to have become more untrustworthy and disrespectful of Laing each day. Laing sometimes was left to unload his camels himself as the Sheikhs walked away, ignoring him.

The route itself was no less demanding than that prior to Ghadames. Laing was now entering a land where the rulers were marauding bands of suspicious and proud Tuareg; where feuds and wars continued for generations between Tuareg and Arab and the darker-skinned natives further south, between comparatively rich oasis and poor nomads; where foreigners were not always welcome and where Christians were distrusted at best and at worst hated. Babani had to order the caravan to zig-zag to avoid particularly hostile or notorious areas.

This is not exactly the way I ought to travel for the sum of four thousand dollars. I ought to have been placed beyond the reach of risk; and the Sheikh might have brought an escort of twenty men all the way for the sum of four hundred dollars, instead of which he only has with him two slaves to load and unload his camels, so that if attacked I have only my own people to depend upon.

All the presents which he showed me as intended for Tuat [to which area they were going] are merely the merchandise which he carries to dispose of at Timbuctoo. In granting the four thousand dollars, I had an idea that he would be put to very great expense, and that idea was entertained by me till very lately, but I have many conspiring reasons now for thinking otherwise. . . .

Apart from his continuing unease and the obvious extreme physical hardship, little more is known of this section of Laing's journey.

The Timbuctoo Mission arrived at In Salah on December 2, 1825, exactly one month after leaving Ghadames—having left Tripoli the previous July.

Five days later, on December 7, Clapperton, Pearce, Lander and the three other Englishmen of their party left the village at which they had established their expedition, after a farewell 'drinking revel' with the African chiefs. They struck out for the interior up the Lagos River.

*

Laing was greeted with even more amazement at In Salah than he had been at Ghadames.

Upwards of a thousand people of both sexes came out to meet me, and so surrounded my camel that I had much difficulty in proceeding. I have been in the habit of late of covering my face *à la mode* Tuareg, as a convenient protection against the sun, and as nothing but my eyes were yesterday visible the curiosity of the multitude was not gratified, and my poor attendants were beleaguered with a thousand questions. Is he white? Is his hair like a Turk's? Has he a beard? Can he fire a gun without a flint? alluding to my rifle, the fame of which has preceded me.

After being shown to a house, there was still no peace for Laing. He was surrounded by the inquisitive. A request was made for him to appear on the roof of the house so that he could be more generally seen; when he did so, he found about a hundred women assembled to gaze at him. In the end Laing had to nail up his door. Such was In Salah—a poor and simple place where a European had never been seen before.

In Salah was an important meeting place in the trade routes of the desert, being a junction of the routes Morocco–Cairo, Timbuctoo–Tunis, and Timbuctoo–Tripoli. The Timbuctoo journey, however, was little used as the gold supply had virtually ended, the slave route north had not yet substantially rivalled or replaced the old routes to the West Coast and Morocco, and the Tuareg plundered as they pleased. It was an area of anarchy, claimed by Tripoli, but terrorized by brigands and rival factions. Laing wrote in In Salah that 'communication from Timbuctoo, excepting by way of Morocco, is infrequent'. He was told that, owing to the influence of Babani, a large caravan, bound for Timbuctoo, had been waiting for their arrival. He later discovered the falsity of this; travellers had, in fact, been congregating at In Salah for some months waiting for the unrest in the desert to die down.

Laing, no doubt feeling the effects of the journey, the heat, the food and the water, made fewer inquiries at In Salah than at Ghadames; it was certainly of less interest. His calculations placed it 'exactly north of Timbuctoo'. This reveals that he was still almost totally ignorant of the position of the latter place—an ignorance based probably on Clapperton's wildly inaccurate positioning of the town.

There were no letters for him, and as the days went on none arrived. The only communication he'd had with Tripoli were the two couriers—with portrait and letters—who had arrived in Ghadames.

As always, Laing found little except trouble. A rumour

spread in the town that he was Mungo Park. The fame of that explorer, and of his deathly progress down the Niger, had spread even that far. There was in In Salah a man who had been shot in the cheek from Park's vessel, and who was ready to swear that Laing had been the commander of the craft.

When you consider that the great discrepancy in point of time (I being only thirty-one years of age and the expedition of Park having taken place twenty-one years ago) is a matter of no moment among people who do not trouble themselves with investigation, you will regret it as much as I do now, absurd and ridiculous as it may at first appear. . . . How imprudent; how unthinking; I may even say, how selfish it was in Park to attempt making discovery in this land at the expense of the blood of its inhabitants.

Laing was in fear of his life throughout his stay in In Salah. Had it not been for the intervention of an unusually hospitable Tuareg, he would almost certainly have lost his life: for the presence of this lonely and brash Christian, who could barely speak a few words of Arabic, in their midst, increasingly irritated the chief inhabitants.

Laing spent five weeks there before Babani would deign to move on, and he despatched a number of letters back to Tripoli; some he sent by courier, others by Hatita, for whom he had decided he had no more use.* Those that have survived tell a great deal of Laing's sense of isolation and the strength of his pet obsessions, which remained with him still: foremost among them was his 'dear Emma', and not far behind his promotion:

I have written and requested that [the Colonial Office] will interest itself about my promotion when my arrival at Timbuctoo is known. . . . It would be truly pleasing to me on emerging at the other side to find myself confirmed.

And, of course, there was always the nagging thought of Clapperton to bother him:

I am not yet in Timbuctoo but am gradually drawing near to it. . . . I shall not reach the great Capital before the middle or end of

---

*Those sent by courier eventually reached their destination, where they were preserved in the Consul's files and later were transferred with all correspondence to the Colonial Office, and later still were deposited in the Public Record Office, where they were only discovered in 1964.

January, but that signifies little. I shall do much more, and render my journey much more interesting, by proceeding quietly and coolly through the country than by running a race with Clapperton, whose only object seems to be to forestall me in discovery. Should he succeed in reaching Timbuctoo, which I doubt much, I shall have much pleasure in meeting him.

And still, after all he had already succeeded in doing, Laing was uneasy about the question of his expenses. Despite his fulminations on the subject from Ghadames, he now wrote a humble and pathetic letter on the subject to the Colonial Office. He seems to have thought that this might not sufficiently subdue Lord Bathurst, for two days later he followed it up with another, and even more contrite, letter to the Colonial Office.

I have also the honour to state that I have paid Sheikh Babani, under whose protection I travel to Timbúctoo, the sum of fifteen hundred dollars, which I can consider an ample reward both for his services and disbursements, which latter have not been great, and I have therefore to assure you that His Lordship shall hear no more on this, or any other subject connected with money, until the return of the Mission to England. I shall, however, regularly transmit to the Colonial, as well as to the Audit Office, quarterly statements . . . .

It is doubtful if any explorer engaged on such a desperate expedition, travelling through an area previously unknown to Western man, has ever been so troubled by matters which should have been left behind at his base long before. Clearly the angry letter from the Colonial Office—not the kind that should be sent to a man who was daily in danger of his life— had not lost its effect on Laing; but the bitterness seems to have given way to doubt. On Christmas Day, Laing wrote a dutiful letter to the Under Secretary:

And now, Sir, I shall most respectfully take my leave of you for the present year, and although it is not exactly customary in an official letter, yet, situated as I am in the midst of the bigotry of Mohammedanism. . . . I cannot permit it to pass over without impressing a desire that you will be pleased to assure His Lordship, the Earl Bathurst, with how much sincerity I wish His Lordship all the compliments and many happy returns of the season. . . .

Laing did not allow himself to be deterred by the likelihood that such seasonal greetings could hardly reach the Colonial Secretary before the end of April, in the unlikely event that they would even get as far as Tripoli.*

It was from In Salah, with its unbearable temperatures and perpetual danger, that Laing wrote the last of his letters from Africa to his home in Scotland. He wrote to his sister:

I am already possessed of much curious and valuable information, and feel confident that I shall realize the most sanguine expectations of my numerous friends. . . .My father used often to accuse me of want of common sense, but he little thought that I gloried in the accusation. 'Tis true, I never possessed any, nor ever shall. At a very early age I fell in with an observation of Helvetius which pleased me much and chimed in with my way of thinking to a tenth part of a second. 'A man of common sense is a man in whom indolence predominates: he is not endowed with activity of soul, which, in high stations, leads great minds to discover new springs by which they may set the world in motion, or to sow the seeds, from the growth of which they are enabled to produce future events.' I admit that common sense is more necessary for conducting the petty affairs of life than genius or enterprise, but the man who soars into the regions of speculation should never be hampered by it. Had I been gifted with that quality which the bulk of mankind consider so inestimable, I might now have been a jolly subaltern on half-pay, or perhaps an orthodox preacher in some country kirk. . . . I hope you have written to my dearest Emma, the most amiable girl that God ever created. She is, indeed, such a being as I had formed in my mind's eyes but had never before seen, and has just as much common sense as has fallen to the lot of your most worthy elder brother.

Above all, Laing was still tortured by loneliness and by the pangs of love. He wrote to Warrington:

I am not a little pleased when I look at the great improvement I am already making, and contemplate those I shall make, in the map of Africa. You must keep up the spirits of my dearest Emma and allow nothing to create the smallest alarm. If ever you should be six months after the receipt of this without hearing from me, a circumstance which I think by no means improbable . . . you must always consider me safe, for it is my destiny to be so, and perhaps you may see me before the Sheikh [Hatita] makes his appearance.

---

*At least one of Laing's letters did not reach Tripoli for two years.

4

I so much despair of hearing again from Tripoli that I no longer look back: my whole ideas, my thoughts, my prospects, are 'forward', for I cannot enjoy a moment of happiness till I return. Do not think I despond, or that my enthusiasm, which for a while lay dormant, is in the least abated; no, I am still the African traveller, and as eager as ever for discovery, though I lament every moment which my enthusiasm inclines me to devote to it. In former days I used to derive the greatest of earthly enjoyment from living alone: my thoughts took the most fascinating direction. . . . Times are changed. I am now almost afraid to trust myself with the full swing of thought, and for the first time in my life I express a wish that I had with me a *companion de voyage.* . . . I would have been proud and happy of a companion who would have united with me in saying: 'I have not travelled to Timbuctoo for the sake of any other reward than that which I shall derive from the consciousness of having achieved an enterprise which will rescue my name from oblivion.'

Laing's letters tell us practically nothing of the physical rigours of the Mission and of its day-to-day life. But they leave us in no doubt as to his feelings for Emma.

Do not, I pray you [in letters to the West Coast], omit to apprise me exactly of the state of health of my dearest Emma, whose image ever occupies my thoughts, is ever before my eyes. I feel in its full force the truly peculiar and delicate situation in which I have left her, and the bare idea is oftentimes nearly sufficient to drive me to distraction. My only consolation arises from the consciousness that it was necessary to the happiness of us both. If it pleases God to spare us for each other (and that it will so please Him I have implicit faith), I shall devote the remainder of my life to atone for the unhappiness I have occasioned her.

Further reports of disturbances on the route, and rumours of the capture of a caravan on its way to Timbuctoo, delayed departure from In Salah still longer. Although this time Laing would be travelling in a bigger party than hitherto—some forty-five persons—it was decided again that a detour would be made. At last the caravan, in which Laing's Timbuctoo Mission was a small part, left In Salah on January 9, 1826. Laing's ignorance of his position, and of the situation of Timbuctoo, was such that he believed they would reach Timbuctoo in about four weeks.

He still had, in fact, the most terrible and central part of the Sahara Desert to cross. A route on which there were no large oases, substantial villages or resting places at all. Although he did not know it, Timbuctoo was further from him than was Tripoli, which he had left six months before. But Laing, as always, was happiest when on the move to the destination which lured him onwards. Before leaving he wrote: 'I must say I am very desirous to reach this wonderful capital.'

*

For the first two weeks after leaving In Salah the caravan was in such a state of apprehension and suspense about the possibility of attack that its hesitant move forward was always on the brink of going into reverse. The main danger, it seemed, was not so much the Tuareg as a particularly bellicose and fierce tribe of Moors. On one occasion a lone rider on a fast camel reported the Moors were very close.

I had much difficulty in prevailing upon the merchants to proceed, and nothing short of my determination to do so alone prevented the return of the caravan. . . . My situation was not the most enviable, exposed as I was to the animadversions of the whole caravan for subjecting them and their property to such hazard, when by a little patience in waiting [at In Salah] till the road became good they might have all gone in safety.

To return, having come so far and endured so much, even a comparatively few miles, and perhaps only for a few weeks, must have been anathema to Laing. Just when his situation must have seemed impossible, a party of twenty friendly nomads took the whole caravan under its protection, including the Christian whose wealth and fame had spread before him.

We are now in the Latitude of 23° N. and proceeding at the rate of twenty miles per day over a desert of sand as flat as a bowling green.

I have little time at present to say more than that my prospects are bright and expectations sanguine. I do not calculate upon the most trifling future difficulty between me and my return to England.

Laing's optimism was as unfounded as his fortitude was magnificent. But his feelings were no doubt dictated by the fact that he thought he was at long last nearing the goal which had been his objective for so long. Behind him stretched nearly a thousand miles of wilderness which, despite every chance to the contrary, he had somehow succeeded in crossing. He seems to have believed that Timbuctoo was almost within his grasp.

For five days the strange riders guarded the caravan. They watched; and they waited. On the fifth night Babani persuaded Laing to let them have some gunpowder; it was done, although Laing objected. He told Laing that there was no need to keep his gun loaded as now there was no danger.

They were Tuareg.

*

An official French expedition to reach Timbuctoo had meanwhile been mounted with some secrecy. It had, however, hardly begun its journey inland from the West Coast when its leader, Beaufort, died of fever. Beaufort seems to have been the semi-official nomination for the French Prize; little is known of his projected mission except that he was granted 20,000 francs subsidy, whereas Caillié had only requested 6,000. After this the French Government seems momentarily to have lost interest in making contact with Timbuctoo. René Caillié, who had heard of the Beaufort fiasco, asked the British Governor of Sierra Leone for 6,000 francs to enable him to undertake the journey to Timbuctoo. The Governor declined, referring to Laing. 'He said it would be unfair to attempt to snatch the glory of first arriving at Timbuctoo, and on this ground he rejected my proposal.'

Caillié had been working for an English firm in Freetown, as he had given up all hope of gaining support from the French authorities in Senegal. The Governor of Sierra Leone had been impressed with Caillié and, although he had no intention of financing for him an expedition to Timbuctoo, he had created a post for him as superintendent of an indigo factory, with a good salary. Caillié had lingered in Freetown, still hoping for support, but none had come.

The refusal of the French governors had distressed me, but that of the English governor did not affect me at all; I felt myself the more free: I thanked heaven that I was now able to break off my engagement with foreigners, to whom I was indebted for their generous hospitality, but who might perhaps in return have laid claim to the glory of a discovery, with which I hoped to do honour to France. The sacrifice was so much the easier because I had saved nearly 2,000 francs, and this treasure seemed to me to be sufficient to carry me all over the world. Lastly, there was a hope which tranquillized my mind as to the fate of my poor sister; I had just heard of the premium offered by the Geographical Society of Paris to the first European who could reach Timbuctoo,* and I said to myself: 'Dead or alive, it shall be mine, and my sister shall receive it.'

These hopes, these visions of glory, of patriotism and of fraternal affection left me no rest, and I had nothing like peace till the evening before I left Sierra Leone. Not having been able any where to obtain the necessary assistance for a journey to Timbuctoo, I determined to undertake it entirely at my own expense.

Having resigned his employment, Caillié began preparations for his journey. He sought out various articles which he would want. He became friendly with the local Mandingo natives and spread it about among them that he was not really French at all: he was, he said, an Arab who had been born in Egypt.†

Far away to the south, Clapperton's expedition had by now delved deep into the continent and had entered the Yoruba country, eight hundred miles from Timbuctoo. Clapperton was, in fact, about as far south of Timbuctoo as Laing was north of it. Three of the English, including Pearce, had already died of sickness. Clapperton and Lander were hospitably entertained by the king, who claimed to rule over all of the vast area between the Niger and Dahomey.‡ Clapperton, asking for safe conduct to proceed further, distributed some of the presents with which his expedition was well supplied, including any number of umbrellas.

Clapperton intrigued his hosts with two evening firework

---

*At least eighteen months after the announcement of the Prize.

†The Mandingoes were the main Negro population of Mali and the Western Sudan from the Senegal to Ghana: their empire had collapsed by 1680: without political entity, many were under domination of the Fulani.

‡Modern Western Nigeria.

displays. Unfortunately one of the rockets was badly prepared and ran along the ground, setting fire to the grass. The king, who had been sitting on his veranda to watch the display, was not disconcerted, and did everything he could to delay the departure of the expedition—so much was he enjoying the stay of the remarkable white-skinned people. He suggested that Clapperton should accept a wife from him; that if the food was not sufficient or pleasant, then Clapperton had only to complain. . . . It was six weeks before Clapperton and his party could escape. Now they were headed for Kano and Sokoto, and then for Timbuctoo.

*

The Tuareg struck on the sixth day after they had joined Laing's caravan, at about five o'clock in the morning. They were armed with guns, swords, spears and daggers. They fell on Laing's part of the caravan, leaving the remainder unmolested. They surrounded Laing's tents and his piles of unloaded baggage. They fired into the tents and then rushed at them, slashing and cutting at the cords and canvas.

Laing, who had been asleep, received a ball in the side, which was the first he knew of the attack. They were in his tent before he could arm himself. He was immediately cut by a tremendous sword stroke on the thigh. Jumping up, he received a cut on the cheek and ear and one on the right arm—with which he was presumably attempting to defend himself—above the wrist. This third stroke broke his arm and he fell to the ground again; there he received more strokes of the sword and sabre, most on his head or on his hands, and the last one being across his neck. Meanwhile Laing's camel driver had been slashed on the head with a sabre; one of the West African sailors had died after five cuts, the other was shot in the leg but he crawled on his hands and knees to Babani's tent; the Jewish interpreter was cut down and slaughtered by two Tuaregs; only Laing's West African servant, who had fled the camp, escaped unhurt.

Laing was robbed of virtually all his money. As the dawn came up, the Tuareg, soon far away into the desert, left a scene of chaos and terror behind them. The worst fears of the merchants had come true as far as Laing was concerned, but they themselves appear to have suffered no loss. As Laing's blood drained away they hastily struck camp and prepared to move away in case the wild Tuareg might return.

It was soon evident that Laing's wounds were too serious for him to keep pace with the fleeing caravan. Gradually it drew away from him, taking Babani and the two surviving West Africans with it. (One source says he was so weak he had to be tied to the camel.) Laing and his wounded camel driver did not catch up with the caravan until long after it had halted again. Next day Laing started with the caravan, but once again they would not wait for him. All Babani would do for him was to leave a guide to show the way. So it continued every day. Laing, who 'suffered much' from his wounds, did not reach the caravan till late at night—exhausted, sick and utterly disillusioned at last with the wretched Babani. At the next well, two days were spent; this was the first chance Laing had to rest and to tend his terrible wounds since the attack. Then there was another period of nineteen days' hard travelling. They then arrived at the village and watering-place of Sidi el Muktar. There Laing and the caravan rested. They were about two hundred miles north of Timbuctoo.

Since the attack, Laing had covered over four hundred miles, a nightmarish ride for a man who was very close to death. There are few, if any, comparable feats in the history of African exploration.

Sidi Mohammed was a loyal friend to Laing. He seems to have taken pity on him; he cared for him with all the hospitality for which the desert was so unjustly famous. He supplied Laing's party with rice, beef and other foods. After six days the caravan moved on towards Timbuctoo. Laing, with the three surviving members of the Timbuctoo Mission, and with Babani, remained behind at Sidi el Muktar.*

---

*There has been some argument about the identity of this place; this is probably fruitless, as it has not existed for over a century. It had been named after a chief, possibly of mixed Berbers, in the eighteenth century, who had first settled there and had enjoyed great influence over the Tuareg. The man who helped Laing was Muktar's son, and the head of the family, Sidi Mohammed. Laing sometimes confused the name of the place and of the present head of the family: the latter had at least nine sons, one of whom was el Backay, Barth's

After another three weeks of rest, Laing felt sufficiently recovered to continue. Sidi Mohammed begged him to return to Tripoli the way he had come. He explained that the Timbuctoo area was in a state of ferment and that for a Christian to appear there at the moment would mean almost certain death. Laing would not consider the suggestion. He would remain faithful to what his father had always called his lack of common sense, but what he himself believed was his destiny. Babani, however, insisted that he remained longer as the wound on Laing's hand was still unhealed. But four days later Babani died, suddenly. And then, to complete Laing's miseries, a plague struck the village.* The two West Africans died of it. Laing was deeply distressed at the death of his faithful servant, Jack. 'I n'er shall look upon his like again.' Sidi Mohammed, to whose kindness Laing very probably owed his life, then died. And Laing himself did not escape the plague. 'For nine days I lay in a very helpless and dangerous state.' But he survived—a tribute to his remarkable tenacity and toughness. Sidi Mohammed had refused all offer of others to take Laing into Timbuctoo. As all his efforts to persuade Laing to return had proved useless, he eventually decided to take him in and out of the town himself. Now that he was dead, Laing was dependent on his eldest son. But Laing had no money left at all, and the son was less hospitable and generous than the father.

Laing wrote to Warrington, so far away, ten months after he had left Tripoli:

I drop you a line, by an uncertain conveyance, to acquaint you that I am recovering from very severe wounds far beyond any calculation. . . . I have suffered much, but the detail must be reserved till another period, when I shall a tale unfold of base treachery and war that will surprise you: some imputation is attached to the old Sheikh [Babani], but as he is no more I shall not accuse him: he

protector in 1853; the eldest was named Muktar, another source of confusion (this man's son was Barth's enemy in 1854). Dubois (1897) says the place was near Mabruk, about 240 miles north-east of Timbuctoo, which seems probable. Barth said it was 'half a day's journey from the well Bel Mehan'. In any event, it was evacuated after Laing's stay and most of the family moved south to the banks of the Niger, east of Timbuctoo.

*Laing described it as 'a dreadful malady somewhat similar to yellow fever in its symptoms'.

died very suddenly about a month since, and there are some here who look upon his demise as a visitation: be that as it may, he has by this time answered for all. . . . When I write from Timbuctoo I shall detail precisely how I was betrayed and nearly murdered in my sleep; in the meantime I shall acquaint you with the number and nature of my wounds, in all amounting to twenty-four, eighteen of which are exceedingly severe. To begin from the top: I have five sabre cuts on the crown of the head and three on the left temple, all fractures from which much bone has come away; one on my left cheek which fractured the jaw bone and has divided the ear, forming a very unsightly wound; one over the right temple and a dreadful gash on the back of the neck, which slightly scratched the windpipe; a musket ball in the hip, which made its way through my back, slightly grazing the backbone; five sabre cuts on my right arm and hand, three of the fingers broken, the hand cut three-fourths across, and the wrist bones cut through; three cuts on the left arm, the bone of which has been broken but is again uniting; one slight wound on the right leg and two with one dreadful gash on the left, to say nothing of a cut across the fingers of my left hand, now healed up. I am nevertheless doing well, and hope yet to return to England with much important geographical information. The map indeed requires much correction, and please God I shall yet do much, in addition to what I have already done, towards putting it right.

I shall feel obliged by your sending a copy of this to Lord Bathurst, as I write with my left hand with much pain and difficulty.*

May God bless you all. I dare not yet trust myself with my feelings, for which reason I have not attempted a line to my dearest Emma. I shall make the trial at Timbuctoo; and in the meantime remember me with the kindest love and beg her to think nothing of my misfortunes, for all will yet be well.

Laing's wounds were such that he would be fearfully scarred and disfigured for the remainder of his life. This may have been in his mind when he felt unable to address himself to his bride. But he must have had a change of heart after writing this, for a letter for Emma did eventually arrive at Tripoli.

Since March, Warrington had been extremely anxious about Laing. He had heard from Hatita, now back in

---

*All Laing's letters after the attack were written with the left hand in a spidery, nervy scrawl, even more than seven months after the attack. This supports one Arab account that he lost his right hand in the attack; if so, it was something of which he was loath to admit.

4*

Ghadames, that rumours there said that Laing had been attacked by Tuareg. The Pasha said that he also had heard of these rumours, but he was unable to confirm them. Later the Pasha was able to give assurances that he had heard that Laing, who had been attacked, was alive and proceeding on his journey. The letter to Emma was the first information which arrived from Laing himself; in the letter Laing merely said, of his wounds: 'I write with only a thumb and finger, having a very severe cut on my forefinger.' This so encouraged Warrington that he sent off a despatch to the Colonial Office immediately, advising that an earlier report he had sent was to be discounted and that Laing was safe and well: 'It is very satisfactory to learn that the wound he has received is of no consequence.'

Laing meanwhile was endeavouring to persuade someone to take him to Timbuctoo. He had been nearly four months at el Muktar's. Eventually the eldest son of Sidi Mohammed, young Muktar, agreed to arrange a passage to Timbuctoo for a 'thousand dollars', which Laing, being penniless, would pay in kind: i.e. with most of his remaining articles.

With a mind sadly depressed with sickness, sorrow and disappointment, I lift an unwilling pen to acquaint you that I am no further on my journey than when I last addressed you, having been detained here on the most frivolous pretences, and in the most annoying manner; in fact, in such a way that I have for some time past regarded my situation as that of a captive. . . . I am now the only surviving member of the Mission and my situation far from agreeable. . . . I have now obtained permission to proceed to Timbuctoo, but it is at the expense of everything I have got, but I had no alternative, and I consented because I am well aware that if I do not visit it the world will ever remain in ignorance of the place, as I make no vain glorious assertion when I say that it will never be visited by Christian man after me. With Timbuctoo my research must for the present cease, as I have no funds to carry me further. It is therefore my intention, as soon as I possess myself of such information as I desire, to mount a fleet camel and return to Tripoli. I hope Clapperton has succeeded in settling the point of the Niger's termination.

I shall be in Ghadames, please God, early in November, when I expect to be greeted by a courier from Tripoli; send me plenty of news, papers, a little tea and sugar, and some sort of a tin teapot;

also half a dozen pair of stockings and about four hundred dollars, for I am now without a stiver.*

I am recovering rapidly, but am subject to dreadful pains in my head arising from the severity of my wounds. Love to my dearest Emma, whom may Heaven bless.

Laing sent this letter off with his last remaining servant, the camel driver. This man did reach Tripoli, and was thus able to give a first-hand account of the Tuareg attack; shortly after his departure, Laing discovered that he had taken with him one of his best and most valuable pistols.

For the last stage in his great journey, Laing was to be under the care of Babani's nephew, who had gone on with the caravan to Timbuctoo, and whom Sidi Mohammed's son had recalled to Muktar's.

Gordon Laing set out for Timbuctoo late in July or early in August, 1826. Even now everyone begged him to return the way he had come. But Laing, either unaware of danger or unaffected by it, considered such pleadings were irritations. It was explained to him that the city had come under the province of a new ruler—Sultan Bello, of Sokoto; and that this meant inevitably that the place would be in an unsettled state.† Laing did not care. He had come too far, much too far, to go back now—when he was so close to success at last.

The little party proceeded on the journey for several days. Laing was without money, having only the letters of introduction from Tripoli to support him, without interpreter, and with what must have been only an extremely rudimentary knowledge of local languages, hideously scarred, just recovered from an almost fatal epidemic, and having had almost all his possessions and wealth stripped from him by the natives of the country through which he had passed. He was sustained through all these adversities by the firm belief that he was on the brink of an achievement which would bring him lasting fame.

*

---

*A popular expression of the time; a *stuiver* was a small Dutch coin.

†When Clapperton was in Sokoto, however, in the same year, he was told that the Timbuctoo area 'is under the authority of the Tuareg'.

While Laing was languishing at el Muktar's, recovering from his wounds, Clapperton had reached the Niger. He was in the area where Mungo Park was supposed to have perished, and he was shown the exact place where the incident was said to have occurred. Lander recorded:

We had all along been buoyed up with the hope of being able to obtain the journal and papers of the late Mungo Park at Busa, but, to our great mortification and disappointment, we discovered that they had been either destroyed or conveyed, no one could tell whither, many years before. The inhabitants were exceedingly reserved on the subject of the fatal catastrophe.

Clapperton and Lander were well received by the local chief. Clapperton wrote in his diary:

This morning, when I was with the sultan, his breakfast was brought in, which I was asked to partake of. It consisted of a large grilled water-rat with the skin on, some very fine boiled rice, with dried fish stewed in palm oil, and fried or stewed alligators' eggs.

Receiving a fine horse as a present from the chief, Clapperton crossed the Niger and left Busa for Kano. They entered the great trading city of Kano at five o'clock in the evening on July 20, 1826, just as Laing was preparing to leave el Muktar's. Clapperton was welcomed by the merchants he had known on his previous visits. On his first day there he was told of the great difficulties to trade brought about by the unsettled state of the desert to the north. 'The Tuareg have not allowed a caravan to pass, except those of the merchants of Ghadames, for these many years past.'

Clapperton did not delay in Kano. He was determined to push on as fast as he could. After only four or five days he departed for the North-West, for Sokoto and Timbuctoo.* He left Lander at Kano to guard their belongings, explaining that it was unnecessary to take all their baggage so far out of the way—Clapperton intending to go on to Chad and Tripoli. Meeting with some difficulties at first, he was soon back at

---

*Exactly how long he stayed in Kano is unclear. Lander says they arrived there on 'Thursday the 20th of July', and that Clapperton left on 'Thursday the 24th of July.' Clapperton's journal gives the same dates. This must be explained by the fact that at this time Clapperton discovered 'he had made a mistake in the month of May, having given it only thirty days instead of thirty-one'. He would therefore have had to adjust his calendar, which would have caused the confusion.

Kano, but then he departed again, with safe conducts as far as Sokoto. He seems to have kept Lander from his confidence about his intentions after Sokoto, but there was little reason in going to that place, which he had also stayed at on his previous expedition, except to fulfil Lord Bathurst's instruction to go on to Timbuctoo.

Kano was a busy trading city in which many African races mingled; it was the terminus for many great desert caravans. Lander was, therefore, in reasonable safety. Apart from 'severe fits of the ague', Clapperton's progress was uneventful. He found much of the country like 'the most pleasant parts of England'—with which he must not have been very familiar.

*

Early in August, 1826, Gordon Laing arrived at the far side of the desert. He was the first Christian to have crossed the mid-Sahara from north to south, an achievement which should have secured him lasting fame.

Laing entered Timbuctoo on August 13, 1826. He was the first non-African to do so, of his own will, in modern times. He had travelled some 2,650 miles since leaving Tripoli, on a journey which had taken him a year and one month; his life had been in danger every mile, and he had nearly lost it; he had also suffered from disease, privations of every kind, humiliations, frequent frustration, and disappointments that would have sent most men home months before; but he had achieved what was to him and his own generation the most difficult feat in the world. He had suffered as much and for longer, for instance, as Scott of the Antarctic was to do, or Hillary and Tenzing, in the next century; and his feat was of as much or greater value.* The journeys of Livingstone and Stanley were much more valuable contributions than was that of Laing—although the essence of such a journey was that its result could not be predicted; but how much more demanding was the effort of Laing only he could tell. Laing believed that through his achievement he would never be forgotten; that he had chiselled his name indelibly on posterity's stone.

*The journey of Captain Robert Falcon Scott and his companions from McMurdo Sound to the South Pole, 1911, was about 1,100 miles in just over two months.

When Gordon Laing arrived at Timbuctoo it must have seemed to him the final and most cruel twist of the rack on which fate seemed determined to sacrifice him. What he saw was a place of less intrinsic interest even than Ghadames, and not much more prosperous than In Salah. Laing must have been astounded that this sordid slaving mart, with little to commend it apart from its mosques, was the great golden metropolis which had been the spur to all his efforts. It was, moreover, going through one of the many periods of near anarchy which it had experienced since the collapse of the Moorish conquest two hundred years before. The local Sheikh was nominally under the protection of the Fulani Sultan of Sokoto, but in reality the desert Tuareg held the power.

Laing was naturally reticent about all this in his despatch. He did not want to lessen the impact of the journal he was writing; it was his intention that this, when published, would be the last word on Timbuctoo. Nor did he want, without full explanation, to risk lessening the importance of his achievement in reaching the place. He was, therefore, uninformative, but encouraging, when he wrote to Warrington his only letter from Timbuctoo, dated September 21, 1826. It was the first known letter ever to be written by a Christian from Timbuctoo: the last in an obscure file of disintegrated notes and letters from Laing in the Public Record Office:

A very short epistle must serve to apprise you, as well as my dearest Emma, of my arrival at and departure from the great capital of Central Africa. . . . I have no time to give you my account of Timbuctoo, but shall briefly state that in every respect except in size (which does not exceed four miles in circumference) it has completely met my expectations. Kabara is only five miles distant, and is a neat town, situated on the very margin of the river. I have been busily employed during my stay searching the records in the town, which are abundant, and in acquiring information of every kind.*

May God bless you all. My dear Emma must excuse my [not] writing. I have begun a hundred letters to her, but have been

---

*It is probable that Laing had come across the seventeenth-century history of the Songhai people, the *Tarik es Sudan*, and was thus the first European to see that important work – although whether he would have understood much of it is doubtful. A new translation was published in 1964 (Paris).

unable to get through one; she is ever uppermost in my thoughts, and I look forward with delight to the hour of our meeting, which, please God, is now at no great distance.

Little is known of Laing's stay in Timbuctoo, except that it was short and tense. It seems that on his arrival he immediately reverted to European dress—a gesture which would certainly have been typical of him. He told the chiefs that he was the representative of the English king, which does not seem to have impressed them. With his smattering of Arabic and his broad, forthright Scottish accent, he endeavoured to communicate with them. The inhabitants were hospitable and anxious for Laing's safety. Bello, the Sultan of Sokoto, had heard of Laing's approach to the city, over which he claimed dominion. He had written to the Sheikh of Jenne advising him that on no account was the Christian to be allowed to enter.* The Sheikh of Jenne, who was the Sultan's prefect for the large area in which Timbuctoo lay, wrote to the Timbuctoo Sheikh—a comparatively minor figure in the hierarchy: 'I have just received a letter from Bello, full of wholesome advice, by which I am instructed to prevent Europeans from visiting the Musulman country of the Sudan.' Laing wrote that the local Sheikh 'trembles for my safety and strongly urges my immediate departure'.

Various reports of Laing's activities in Timbuctoo eventually reached Tripoli. He was in desperate need of money, and at first his efforts to obtain some were unsuccessful. But after he produced the Pasha's letter of credit he was able to borrow a little. Owing to the cosmopolitan nature of the Moors in Timbuctoo, who had probably seen Christians in their own country, and of the ruling class, who were of mixed Moorish descent, Laing had considerable freedom to come and go in the city as he wished. But when he went to see the river port of Kabara, he did so at night, on horseback, and alone—as Tuareg were always roaming around the environs of Timbuctoo.

The dignitaries of Timbuctoo did all they could to persuade Laing to return to the care of Muktar, and from there back to

---

*Bello said, not without justification, that he had heard Christians had caused 'abuses and corruptions' in Egypt and Andalusia 'and other countries in former times'. At this time Clapperton was still on his way to Bello's capital, Sokoto.

In Salah, Ghadames and Tripoli. Laing, however, wanted to go south-west, up the Niger, towards Ramako, from where he no doubt hoped to reach an area with which he was familiar, the hinterland of Sierra Leone. This would entail going through country hostile to him, and under Bello's influence. An enormous detour, via Arouan, north of Timbuctoo, would be necessary, on the famous Timbuctoo-Morocco caravan route. He could then go south to the river at Sansanding. It was eventually agreed that this was the route Laing should take.* It was his own doing, and it was, as his father would have agreed, devoid of all common sense.

After five and a half weeks in the town, Laing joined a small north-going caravan on the afternoon of September 22, under the protection of Sheikh Labeida, a religious fanatic, who controlled the route between Timbuctoo and Arouan. Because of the dangers of the route, about which he had received so much warning, it seems likely that Laing left behind in Timbuctoo two parcels, sealed with red wax, containing his precious journal—with instructions that if he should perish the parcels should be returned to Tripoli. He took with him a few personal papers and belongings. He had with him in his personal party an Arab boy and a Negro who had been a slave of Babani's. He had only two camels: one bearing himself, the other his possessions. The Negro had been with Babani, and then Laing (who had freed him from slavery), all the way from Tripoli. It was this man who arrived in Tripoli two years later with the only first-hand account of what happened after Laing left Timbuctoo.

*

The caravan had reached about thirty miles north of Timbuctoo by the end of the third day. During this time they had not been able to replenish their water, but had travelled without incident. On the third night Labeida and some of his men fell upon Laing, the Arab boy and the freed slave while they slept. Laing was killed by many strokes of the sword and decapitated. The boy was also killed, and the freed slave

*Alternatively it is possible that at the last minute Laing decided to go north to Morocco, and that he was not, therefore, taking a detour to the West Coast.

wounded; the latter, who may have feigned death, survived and was taken by an Arab back to Timbuctoo.

So died perhaps the most courageous explorer ever to land in Africa.

Labeida rifled Laing's possessions and took what little there was left of value or interest.

The bodies were left beneath a tree, where they were later buried by a passing Arab. The caravan moved off across the silent sands which stretched away without visible end; it continued on its way to Arouan.

*

At this time, of course, Warrington had not received Laing's letter from Timbuctoo. The last he had heard from Laing was that the explorer intended to return to Tripoli, via Ghadames. Early in November he therefore sent off two couriers to Ghadames with the items Laing had requested. Emma immediately wrote a letter to be delivered to her husband at Ghadames, or to await him there. The courier had, however, already left; Warrington presumably took care of the letter, and it has thus survived. It was written six weeks after Laing's death.

I have this moment, by the Consul's desire, taken the duplicate of a letter which he has already sent, and by that letter I see I have been kept in perfect ignorance of all the dreadful, cruel reports in circulation about you. I do not know whether so doing was cruelty or kindness. Why let me deceive myself with the hopes of your speedy return? The month I first expected you to return is passed away, and, disappointed and sickened, I looked forward to the next, but to be disappointed again. At last the dreadful truth was revealed to me, and without being at all prepared for it the blow was most severe. I heard of your wounds, of your sickness. The chill of death appeared to pass over me; not a word, not a complaint could I utter, not a tear would fall from my eyes to relieve the agonizing oppression of my heart. I spent the whole night in a state of stupefaction, not understanding anything I heard. The morning dawned; the first object that presented itself to my eyes was your dear picture which hung from my neck; at the sight, my recollection returned to me, and I wept over it almost heart broken.

Warrington later wrote, in a letter, of Emma's strain at this time:

After the departure of poor Laing from Tuat [In Salah], all communication for a considerable time ceased . . . the anxiety and suspense his poor wife laboured under. . . . Watchful days and sleepless nights impaired as fine a constitution ever formed by nature. . . .

Emma finished her heart-stricken letter with a dedication of her love.

Oh, my beloved, dearest Laing; alas, alas, what have you been exposed to? What danger? What suffering? To have saved you one pang I would with joy have shed every drop of blood that warms this heart. Had I been with you in that fearful moment, my arms which would have encircled you might for some time have shielded you from the swords of those Daemons; and at last we might have fallen pierced by the same weapon. . . . Alas, Laing, how cruel, how sad, has been our fate. Are we destined to endure more misery, or will a kind providence at length pity our unhappiness and restore us to each other? Will you, my own idolized husband, return to your Emma's fond arms? Will you come and repose on her faithful bosom? Will you restore happiness to her torn heart? . . . Never for a moment, my beloved Laing, have you been absent from my thoughts. You have always been present to my imagination, waking and sleeping. You will find your Emma the same in heart and soul as when you last embraced her, entirely and forever devoted to her Laing. God of heaven protect and bless you dearer to me than life. . . . Adieu, my best beloved; may heaven soon restore you to the arms of your ever adoring, devoted wife.*

But the man who had gone into the desert was never to return.

*

As rumours of Laing's death reached Tripoli, Warrington became increasingly apprehensive. Unwisely, he communicated his anxieties to Clapperton (who fortunately never received them). Warrington had always naïvely believed that if his son-in-law could only meet with Clapperton, who seems to have been a personal hero of his, then he would be safe.

---

*This should dispose of a French version which tried to prove that Emma was really in love with Consul Rousseau's son, and that Warrington, furious, had married her to Laing. (*Annales Tripolitaines*, L. C. Feraud: Paris, 1927.)

We are in the greatest state of alarm and suspense. . . . He has been attacked between Tuat and Muktar's and dreadfully wounded in about fourteen places. For God's sake, Clapperton, put in action every engine to afford him relief and assistance and gain information of him, as, independent of his being my son-in-law, his virtuous goodness and undaunted bravery calls for every feeling that ought to arise, and God knows I venerate his name and feel proud of him. He may be with you and I think it is probable. We have written some hundred of letters to him* . . . God bless you, dear Clapperton . . . fervent prayers for the safety of you as well as for poor Laing.†

Convinced that the Pasha's influence stretched as far as Timbuctoo, Warrington grew suspicious of the latter's integrity in the matter. Living within the narrow confines of Tripoli, with all its intrigue, he was naturally prone to extreme distrustfulness, and seems to have had elements of a persecution complex. It was an easy step for him to see the French Consul, whom he hated, and who understood the Arabs so much better than himself, as the force behind Laing's disappearance.

It was not until March, 1827, that the Pasha was able to procure a written report from Ghadames of Laing's death. This Warrington forwarded to London, with the opinion that it was probably correct, and adding a long indictment of the Pasha for having failed to protect Laing. He accused the Pasha's Chief Minister, D'Ghies, of having received Laing's papers. He thus began a long and ugly episode between Britain and France about the dead man's journal. Laing's journal was widely believed—no doubt correctly—to be a document of great geographical importance, and of obvious value to any power with ambitions in West and North Africa, which meant mainly Britain and France. Through his somewhat mindless despatches, Warrington was able to sow the seeds of his own suspicion in the minds of officials in Whitehall and Downing Street, who knew little of Africa and had never been there. He deliberately mentioned Clapperton several times in the context of the Pasha and Laing, and thus also initiated suspicions about the fate of that explorer also.

Throughout 1827 conflicting reports as to Laing reached

*Laing received no letters after Ghadames, a year before his murder.
†Letter, 24.7.27: Foreign Office Papers (P.R.O., F.O. 76.26).

Tripoli as caravans from the south arrived at Ghadames. News in the desert travelled slowly, at the speed of the caravans, but because the population was so sparse and the centres at such vast distances from each other the net was cast wide. Reports that Clapperton had entered Sokoto even reached Tripoli.* Sometimes reports were categoric that Laing was on his way south-west, up the Niger River. Hope lingered on that he would yet appear on the West Coast. British suspicions were therefore inflamed when *L'Etoile*, of Paris, as early as May, gave a long account of Laing's expedition and reported his death as fact. It was generally accepted that the article had been written by D'Ghies.

Warrington persisted in his inquiries about Laing with creditable vigour and energy. He eventually decided to send an Arab traveller to Timbuctoo to trace the explorer. But his suspicions were still so violent that he had a frigate detained in the port until the Arab left, as he feared the Pasha would stop him. Nine months later, in August, 1828, he had not returned; but in that month Laing's faithful freed slave arrived at Tripoli and the worst fears of Warrington and Emma were confirmed at last.†

Emma Laing married one of Warrington's Vice-Consuls, at Tripoli, on April 13, 1829, one of the witnesses to the wedding being another Vice-Consul at Tripoli, the same Joseph Dupuis who had shown such kindness to the American, Robert Adams, at Mogador, eighteen years earlier. Warrington performed the ceremony himself. But Emma's health was broken and the couple went to Italy in an attempt to improve her condition. It was too late. Her short life ended at Pisa, less than six months later. She died of consumption, of which that pallor which the distressed Laing had noticed in her portrait, four years before, had been the earliest sign.

*

*Owing to the unsettled state of that part of Africa, Clapperton had been unable to get his despatches out.

†This man was twice carefully interviewed by Warrington, and the records survive; only one is mentioned in *Missions to the Niger*; the other, in the Colonial Office Papers, has never before been used. He admitted that on his arrival in Tripoli he had gone straight to D'Ghies, who had received and clothed him.

Clapperton, meanwhile, had at last reached Sokoto, on October 20, 1826—less than a month after Laing's death. Sokoto, a walled city, was at that time one of the most populous native cities in the interior of Africa: the capital of the Fulani, whose power spread from near Chad almost to the West Coast. In a message to Lander, Clapperton said that Sultan Bello 'appeared glad to see me, and welcomed me to his country with the utmost cordiality'. Bearing in mind the Sultan's recent supposed hostility to Laing, this may seem strange; but having a Christian traveller under close watch in his own capital was not the same thing as a Christian mixing with the merchants and Sheikhs on the periphery of his domain.

The effect of bouts of virtually unmedicated dysentery and fever on Clapperton's strong constitution were beginning to tell.

It is most violently hot here. I fancy the weather has already made some impression on my health, for I feel now and then a little feverish and unwell. I sincerely wish it may not increase upon me. Heaven knows I have had enough of sickness since I first set my foot on African soil.

This was not Clapperton's only trouble. The Sultan was not going to let him continue his journey. He was at war with the Sheikh of Bornu, near Chad, to which Clapperton wished to return after visiting Timbuctoo, and the Sultan had no reason to let Clapperton travel among his enemies. Sick and depressed, Clapperton languished in Sokoto, hoping that his luck might change. About Timbuctoo he was able to learn little. 'Timbuctoo produces no gold, it being only the great market where all the [caravans] from the north and east meet those of the south and west; that few [Moors] now come from Fez and Morocco owing, he says, to the Arabs . . . cutting off the caravans.' Clapperton seems to have lost his will. When the Sultan suggested he should return by way of Timbuctoo, he showed no interest. He claimed that

the way to Timbuctoo was almost impassable, for [travellers] who had arrived here a short while ago had with the greatest difficulty been allowed to come here with nothing but a staff and a shirt, and had been twelve months on the road owing to the war; and that, were I to go, all the country would hear of me, and his enemies would have me and all my baggage before I had been two months on the road.

How Clapperton must have regretted his hastiness and impulse in setting off so soon on an African expedition when he had not fully recuperated from the previous one. Unlike Laing, he had already achieved success and fame as an explorer. The fire which had burned in Laing was extinguished in Clapperton. Laing, in a similar position, would not have allowed events to dictate inactivity and to undermine determination for so long.

Bello was suspicious of Lander's presence at Kano with so much valuable baggage. He inveigled Lander to come up from Kano with the baggage. When Lander arrived, Bello seized the presents which Clapperton had intended for the Sheikh of Bornu. According to Lander, Clapperton never smiled again. More and more Lander, the modest Cornish servant, seems to have taken control.

Monday, 25th.—Being Christmas Day, I gave my servant Richard one sovereign, out of six I have left, as a Christmas gift; for he is well deserving, and has never once shown a want of courage or enterprise unworthy of an Englishman.

On Wednesday, January 17, 1827, Clapperton noted, briefly, in his journal.

A small [caravan] of Arabs arrived today from Timbuctoo, one of whom had seen Major Laing, who, he said, had lost his hand in an attack which the Tuareg had made on him and his servants during the night, and that his servants, a Jew and a Christian, had got severely wounded.

Between that date and March 11 Clapperton made only eighteen more entries in his journal. At about midday on April 10 he called Lander to his bedside. He said: 'Richard, I shall shortly be no more. I feel myself dying.' He gave instructions to Lander, telling him how to contact Warrington. He begged him to take care of his journal, but to leave all his other effects behind. Hugh Clapperton died of dysentery, malaria and general debility on the morning of April 13, nearly six months after he had arrived at Sokoto.

Lander supervised the burial with typical and meticulous loyalty.

Saddling my camel, the body was placed on the animal's back, and, throwing a British flag over it, I requested the men to proceed. Having passed through the dismal streets of Sokoto, we travelled almost unobserved, at a solemn pace, and halted near Jungavie, a small village built on a rising ground about five miles south-east of the city. The body was then taken from the camel's back and placed in a shed whilst the slaves were employed in digging the grave. Their task being speedily accomplished, the corpse was borne to the brink of the pit and I planted the flag close to it; then, uncovering my head and opening a prayer-book, amidst showers of tears, I read the impressive funeral service of the Church of England over the remains of my valued master—the English flag waving slowly and mournfully over them at the same moment. Not a single soul listened to this peculiarly distressing ceremony, for the slaves were quarrelling with each other the whole of the time it lasted.

Lander was now alone among a strange people, hundreds of miles from help, in a country in which the only European to have travelled previously was his late master. But he was able to prove that Clapperton's high opinion of him was justified. He returned to Kano and, the journey to Tripoli proving impossible, he managed to reach the West Coast, after a seven months' journey, visiting on the way the graves of some of the English who had perished so early in the expedition and of whom he was the only survivor. But he had not been able to trace the course of the Niger below Busa, and thus the termination of that river remained as uncertain as ever.

Almost at the coast, Lander was shown a shirt with the name 'Thomas Park' written inside it. This had belonged to Mungo Park's son, who had died only three days before. Thomas Park had been granted three years' leave of absence from the Navy to go to Africa to confirm the death of a father he had hardly known; there were persistent rumours of a white man living with the natives somewhere in the interior. He wanted to discover the exact spot where, and the manner in which, his father had died, or if he was dead at all. Lander learnt that Thomas Park had decided his only chance of success was to adopt the customs of the natives. He had thus taken no precautions regarding his health, had covered his body in clay and oil, ate the food of the natives without reservation, and exposed himself to the full glare of the sun and the damp of the night with scarcely any clothing. He had never been in Africa before. He had died two days after leaving the coast.

If Thomas Park had delayed three days, he would have met Lander. And Lander was carrying with him the first reliable news of the circumstances and place of Mungo Park's death.

Lander waited to be picked up by a British ship at a Portuguese slaving port. This was a horrifying place in which human sacrifices were commonplace. Lander was forced to take part in a fetish ceremony. A ship eventually came and on his way home he met Dixon Denham—himself shortly to die—to whom he was able to inform the details of Clapperton's death.*

Richard Lander arrived in England, with Clapperton's papers, in April, 1828. By that month René Caillié was on his great, and at that time unknown, adventure. Could the young Frenchman, with no official backing, succeed where professional explorers like Laing and Clapperton had failed? Could he get to Timbuctoo and get back alive? There were, at that particular time, no expeditions striving for 'The great African capital'. All efforts—Belzoni, Laing, Beaucourt, Clapperton—had met with disaster. Now was Caillié's chance.

---

*Denham had been appointed Governor of Sierra Leone, but died a few days after taking up his post, aged 42.

5 . The Frenchman,

RENÉ CAILLIÉ could now speak some Arabic. He had studied the Koran. He understood the customs of Arabs and African natives. He told those whom he met that he had been born in Egypt, of Arabian parents; that he had been carried away to France, in his infancy, by French soldiers who had invaded Egypt; that his master had brought him to Senegal, where he had then been given his liberty. His ambition was to return to Egypt, to seek his family.

Not surprisingly, this unlikely story was not believed. But Caillié insisted on its truth, and eventually it was believed by the Moslems in Freetown. Satisfied, he embarked at Freetown on March 22, 1827, aged 26. He was dressed in his Arab clothes. He had converted his 2,000 francs savings into silver, gold and merchandise, including silk handkerchiefs, knives, beads and tobacco—all of which fitted into one bundle. Medical and other items had been given to him by his English friends. And, unlike Laing, he remembered to take paper and writing materials. René Caillié forgot nothing.

Caillié had decided to go to a river called the Rio Nunez, which was half-way between Sierra Leone and Senegal, and where he was not known.* He arrived there nine days later, exactly a fortnight before Clapperton's death at Sokoto. Typically, he soon met a Frenchman who agreed to help him. This man owned a 'factory' up the river, from which caravans set out for the interior almost daily. There Caillié met with a small caravan which was going to Timbuctoo. The Frenchman explained Caillié's story to them and they agreed to accompany Caillié. The caravan consisted of five Moslem natives—Mandingoes—their three slaves, Caillié, his guide Ibrahim, the guide's wife, and a bearer for Caillié.

*Just south of the southern border of today's Portuguese Guinea; the small settlement near its estuary was later named Victoria; now in the Republic of Guinea.

Caillié bade farewell to his helper knowing that it might be the last of his countrymen that he would ever see.

They made some remarks upon the difficulties and fatigue which I should have to endure and which I might not have strength to sustain; but, upon my reply that I was determined to bear everything, that I might return to my country, they fixed a day for our departure. . . . I shed tears at parting from my generous friend; my regret at leaving him, however, sincere as it was, could not damp the joy which I felt in undertaking a journey upon which my mind had been bent for so many years.

They had only travelled two hours when they came to the graves of Major Peddie and his companions of the unsuccessful Niger mission of 1816.

I was seized with an involuntary shudder at the thought that the same fate perhaps awaited me. . . . The heat was beginning to be painful; our porters were fatigued, and we halted near a pretty rivulet, with the limpid and delicious water of which we quenched our thirst. We had then travelled nearly ten miles to the east. We kindled a fire; the Negro slaves went in quest of wood and my guide's wife prepared to cook our dinner.

So Caillié proceeded for many weeks, travelling across country in a south-easterly direction. They came to the country of the Fulani, strict Moslems, who were naturally suspicious of Caillié's comparatively fair complexion— although he had acquired in his years in Africa a swarthy complexion, about as dark as that of a Moor. Ibrahim always repeated the story he had been told, although it seems he thought little of it himself. Caillié seems to have varied the story; for sometimes he speaks of his explanation of returning to seek his family in Egypt, and sometimes of a pilgrimage to Mecca. It seems that there was often considerable difficulty in persuading local chiefs of his genuineness. Sometimes he was called before them for a palaver, when he was carefully questioned. Caillié would play his usual tune upon their sympathies. There was something about Caillié which won them round. By the time he left the village the inhabitants would often be under the spell of his unfailing charm. Of one village he wrote:

The Fulani; who had been told that I was an Arab, showed a sort of veneration for me, and were never weary of looking at me and pitying me: they came and sat by me, taking my legs upon their knees and rubbing them to relieve my fatigue. One of them went and fetched some leaves to make a bed.

Caillié took only the briefest notes of his journey. To be seen doing so would have risked rousing suspicions, and he says that he invariably 'retired to the woods to write and arrange my notes'. Nevertheless, he jotted down the names of many villages, the direction in which he was travelling, and scenic and other details. He knew that to be awarded the Prize he would have to write a full account of the journey.

It was the time of the annual fast of Ramadan, strictly observed by Moslems. This required that no food was to be eaten till night time, and even then only of the sparsest kind. Fortunately for the Frenchman, the Moslems with whom Caillié were travelling were not strict in their observance.

Caillié, as was the custom with most strangers travelling in Africa, soon acquired the reputation of a healer. His fame went before him, and he was continually being asked to examine babies and treat complaints, a task for which he did not care. Some of the requests were unusual.

A Mandingo asked me for medicine to cure impotence in his own person; his wife, he said, complained of him and was even guilty of infidelity. He added that a little boy who was running about was her son by one of her lovers. 'But,' said he, with a sigh. 'I cannot blame her since I cannot do as much for her.' As ginger grew in the environs, I advised him to eat plenty.

On May 24 Ibrahim, having reached his home country, left Caillié. Before doing so, he put him into the care of another guide, Lamfia. Caillié had parted with the old caravan and continued in a party of eight persons, still travelling in a south-easterly direction. The size of the caravan varied as they progressed. Carrying his umbrella, with Lamfia's wife to cook for him and the porter to carry his bundle and leather valise, 'Abd-allahi' (Caillié's assumed name), continued further into an area where no white man had been before.* Lamfia proved to be more suspicious than had Ibrahim.

*In his expeditions from Sierra Leone, Laing had been about 300 miles to the west; Mungo Park had passed further north.

I had seated myself for a few moments behind a bush in order to make some notes when I saw the wife of Lamfia advancing towards me. I immediately hid my paper and took up my trousers, which were drying at the fire. She returned to her husband, who asked her whether I was writing. 'No,' replied she, 'he is putting on his clothes.' I was near enough to hear this conversation, which indicated that they suspected me. I therefore became doubly cautious and showed a greater assiduity in the study of the Koran. When, on the road, I sometimes withdrew a little from my companions, I saw them looking at me and endeavouring to discover what I was about; but I always took care to hold in my hand a leaf of the Koran, on which I laid my notepaper.

By the beginning of June Caillié had reached the edge of the desert, as he writes of travelling 'over a fine plain of sand' four miles across. But for the most part the land was stony bush and gravel. Caillié had walked all the way. 'My feet were very painful,' he wrote, 'for my sandals galled me.' But Caillié seldom mentioned his difficulties, and for hundreds of miles he noted little except place-names and what he was given to eat (cakes of flour and honey, rice, etc., which 'Lamfia and his wife mixed with their dirty hands'.) No explorer of West Africa recorded the joys and tribulations of his table more faithfully.

On June 11 Caillié reached the Niger, at Kouroussa. 'I seated myself for a moment to contemplate this mysterious river, respecting which the learned of Europe are so anxious to gain information.' This occasion coincided with a severe attack of fever.

The heat was excessive and a storm came on. The atmosphere was heavy and obscured by clouds. I was attacked with a fever and, notwithstanding the heat, I had shivering fits, from which I suffered greatly. . . . On June 13 we crossed the river in canoes. I was obliged to remain exposed to the sun the whole morning; for the banks of the river are very open. Along the left bank but one tree was visible. . . . A great number of people were going across, and they were all disputing, some about the fare that was demanded, some about who should go first. They all talked at once and made a most terrible uproar.

Although he knew Timbuctoo was on the north bank of the river, the native way to reach the city was via Kankan and

Jenne, both on the south side. Caillié plodded on, attached, with his three servants, to another small caravan. At first Caillié was 'so ill that I experienced great difficulty in walking'. Then on one day they covered over twenty miles, a fantastic feat of endurance in the circumstances; 'We might be said to have run rather than walked.' Caillié must have been stronger than he appeared, but some of his distances must have been exaggerated (he referred to the English mile, having become familiar with the distance while in Sierra Leone). In this area the natives were rich, being not far from the gold mines of Bouré, with which they traded, and which were still being worked. They bartered rice and food for the gold; which they then exchanged on the coast for firearms and slaves.

The heat was excessive and my guide insisted on my using my umbrella to shade me from the scorching rays of the sun. He himself took the precaution of letting it down whenever we approached any inhabited place.

Caillié suspected that Lamfia had stolen some of his paper and beads. He agreed to take the dispute before a local chief. There was little doubt about who would win the argument.

I endeavoured to interest the natives in my behalf, pointing out to them my critical situation, alone and almost destitute in a strange country, and, to crown my misfortunes, speaking the language but imperfectly. Many appeared to pity me.

A new guide was found and Caillié struggled on, into the fertile and wooded area inhabited by non-Muslim Fulani. He had obtained an introduction, transmitted by his guide, from the chief of the territory through which he had just passed to the chief of this new area. Caillié's presence, and the object of his journey, were explained once more. The new chief 'seemed very well disposed towards me', and Caillié trudged on unmolested, and apparently untroubled apart from his fatigue and bouts of fever. Continual crossings of tributaries of the Niger were necessary, and these held up the caravan from time to time, but, nevertheless, he made good progress.

Caillié now entered the territory of the Bambara: a people

who had direct contact with Timbuctoo. He passed safely through the important town of Kankan,* which had about 6,000 inhabitants. There he saw natives strutting in tattered British Army red coats—brought up from the coast—that had very probably been worn also at Waterloo.

Seven weeks after leaving the Niger, Caillié limped into the small village of Tiémé, on August 3. He was uncertain as to how far he was from Timbuctoo, but he had in fact completed less than half the distance. He had, by his own estimation, tramped about 530 miles from the River Nunez.

He now succumbed to the sickness that he had been fighting for so long. An old negress took him into her hut and fed him. Caillié, shivering and feverish, was cared for by the old woman and her husband. A caravan was going to Jenne, the next stopping place on the way to Timbuctoo, but Caillié could not join it. He was lame in one foot and could hardly walk. Then came the rains, incessant and drenching. He decided to rest and to remain for a time in the village, the chief of which was hospitable to him. At first his foot got worse and he could not walk. It was covered in sores, and swollen. The old negress dressed it with leaves. For a month he lay in the hut, 'on the damp ground'. By mid-November his foot was almost better, but then he suddenly began to feel violent pains in his jaw; he concluded he had scurvy.

I soon experienced all the horrors of that dreadful disease. The roof of my mouth became quite bare, a part of the bones exfoliated and fell away, and my teeth seemed ready to drop out of their sockets. I feared that my brain would be affected by the agonizing pains I felt in my head, and I was more than a fortnight without sleep. To crown my misery, the sore in my foot broke out afresh and all hope of my departure vanished. . . . Alone, in the interior of a wild country, stretched on the damp ground, with no pillow but the leather bag which contained my luggage, with no medicine and no attendant but [the old Negress]. This good creature brought me twice a day a little rice-water, which she forced me to drink, for I could eat nothing. I was soon reduced to a skeleton. . . . Suffering

---

*In the Guinea of today. Kankan is still an important centre, and Kouroussa still one of the great crossing-places of the Niger, which is bridged there by rail and road. Caillié was, of course, the first white man ever to make that crossing. Tiémé (below) is in the Ivory Coast; in 1937 the French erected a monument there to Caillié.

had deprived me of all energy. One thought alone absorbed my mind
—that of Death. I wished for it, and prayed for it to God.

After six weeks he began to recover. But by now the
stranger who was continually ill was becoming a burden to
the family who had taken him in. He had already given them
much of his merchandise, and his bundle was rapidly diminish-
ing. The rains had ended; Caillié watched with despair as
the best season for travelling advanced.

I reflected on the best means of proceeding to the Niger, where I
might hope to embark for Timbuctoo, the mysterious city which was
the object of all my curiosity. I never for a moment reproached
myself for the resolution which had brought me to these deserts,
where I had suffered so much misery.

At last, on January 9, 1829, Caillié, with a new guide, left
Tiémé for Jenne. 'I made my hostess a handsome present,
which she received with pleasure.' He had lived as a primitive
native, in a grass hut, critically sick, for more than five
months; but somehow he had survived.

Continuing as before, he entered the town of Jenne, on one
of the branches of the Niger, on March 11. Jenne, which was
in permanent communication with Timbuctoo, was little
more than two hundred miles from that city.

There were two remarkable, if not unique, aspects of
Caillié's journey to this time. In the first place he had
travelled almost all the way—some thousand miles—on foot.
In the second, he, a total stranger with a most uncommon
story, had been received, after initial wariness, almost everywhere with kindness, consideration and generosity—in total
contrast with what explorers approaching Timbuctoo from
other angles had experienced. This was a tribute not only
to the natives among whom he had passed, and to his four
successive guides, but also to the personality of a man who
could create good-will wherever he went.

Because of his standing as an Arab traveller, Caillié
received superior lodgings (still extremely primitive by
European standards) and the attention of the chief merchants.
The house he was in even had stairs, the first he had seen for
nearly twelve months. He asked to be placed under the protection of Moors, whom he heard lived in the town. To them

Caillié told a new story. He was a native of Alexandria, had been taken prisoner by the French, had escaped from them on the West Coast, and was now attempting to get home. He explained his indifferent Arabic by the fact that he had left home so young. Once more he was believed. He was taken to the Shiekh of Jenne; he was told that he could remain in the town until the next caravan left for Timbuctoo. Jenne was a prosperous town—'about two and a half miles in circumference'—trading in many commodities, not least the inevitable slaves.

I have seen men leading these unfortunate beings about the streets, and crying them for sale. . . . I was grieved to see such an insult to human nature. . . . The town of Jenne is full of bustle and animation; every day numerous caravans of merchants are arriving and departing with all kinds of useful productions.

Once more the feast of Ramadan arrived. Caillié had been away from the European stations on the coast for a year.

Caillié gave his precious umbrella to the Sheikh, who was 'highly pleased'. The Sheikh arranged a passage on a river craft to Timbuctoo. Caillié was close to a great achievement. But now he was alone, without a guide or native friends: the worst part of the journey had begun.

*

René Caillié left Jenne for Timbuctoo on March 23, 1828. He had spent thirteen days in the town. During this time he had cleverly ingratiated himself with the Sheikh, who had written a letter of introduction for him to his agent in Timbuctoo. Unknown to Caillié, the Sheikh of Jenne was a more powerful man than the Sheikh of Timbuctoo.

The craft on which he was to make the journey was loaded with rice, millet, cotton, 'vegetable butter', and other products of the neighbourhood; Timbuctoo, situated in the desert, had to import nearly all its foodstuffs. The boat was large enough to take many passengers as well, and a party of slaves, with their charges, were being taken on it to the slave-market at Timbuctoo. Caillié was disconcerted to find that almost immediately he was ranked with the slaves. These

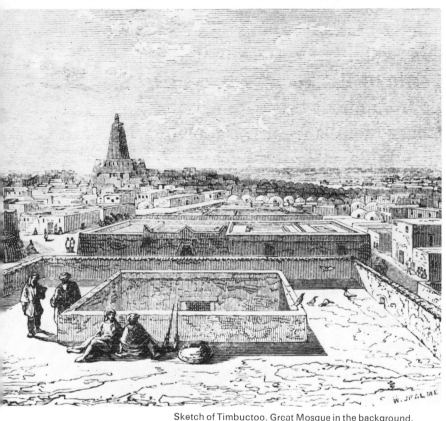

Sketch of Timbuctoo. Great Mosque in the background,
Niger at high level on the right

The Sahara north of Timbuctoo

MUNGO PARK
Timbuctoo was 'the great object of my search'

CAPTAIN LYON
It would never be possible for any man to pass through Africa unless in every respect he qualified himself to appear as a Mohammedan'

HUGH
CLAPPERTON
'The weather has
already made some
impression on my
health for I feel now
and then a little
feverish and unwell—
the way to Timbuctoo
is almost impassable'

DIXON
DENHAM
'We were determined
to travel in our real
character as Britons
and Christians and to
wear our English dress
—the buttons on our
waistcoats caused the
greatest astonishment'

GORDON LAING
'If I do not visit it the world will ever remain in ignorance of the place, as I make no vainglorious assertion when I say that it will never be visited by Christian man after me'

Laing's house in Timbuctoo

Laing's own map of the route of the Timbuctoo Mission to Ghadames, 'across the desert during privations and exposure to a degree of heat which I am inclined to believe few European constitutions could stand'

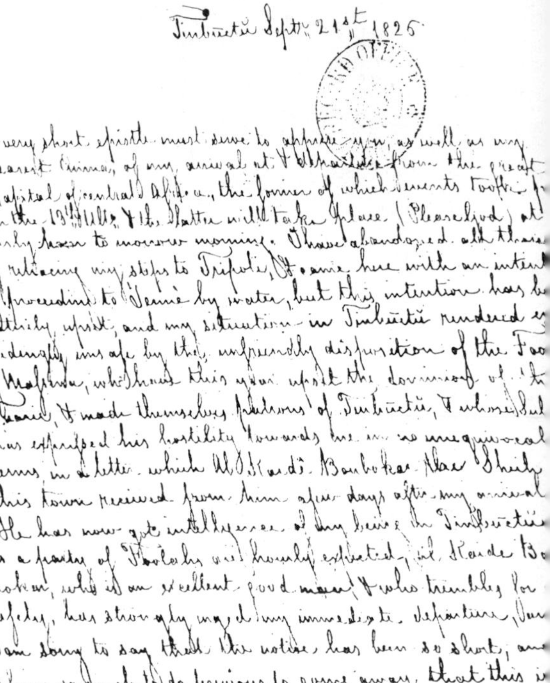

Timbuctu Septr 21st 1826

My dear Consul

A very short epistle must serve to apprize you, as well as my dearest Emma, of my arrival at & departure from the great Capital of central Africa, the former of which events took place on the 13th Ulto & the latter will take place (Please God) at early hour to morrow morning. I have abandoned all thoughts of retracing my steps to Tripoli, & came here with an intention of proceeding to Jenne by water, but this intention has been utterly upset, and my situation in Timbuctu rendered exceedingly unsafe by the unfriendly disposition of the Foo[illegible] of Massina, who have this year upset the dominion of the Tuaric, & made themselves patrons of Timbuctu, & whose Sul[illegible] has expressed his hostility towards me in no unequivocal terms in a letter which Al Kaidi Boubokar the Sheik[illegible] this town received from him a few days after my arrival. He has now got intelligence of my being in Timbuctu, & as a party of Foolahs are hourly expected, Al Kaidi Bo[illegible]bokar, who is an excellent good man, & who trembles for [illegible] safety, has strongly urged my immediate departure, & I am sorry to say that the notice has been so short, and I have so much to do previous to going away, that this is the only communication I shall for the present be able to make. My destination is Sego, whither I hope to arrive in fifteen [illegible] that the road is a vile one, [illegible] I am, and, but my trust is God [illegible] up amidst the severest trials, [illegible] numerous dangers to which I h[illegible] time to give you any account of [illegible] briefly state that in every respect [illegible] not exceed four miles in circumference [illegible] my expectations – Kabra is only [illegible] town, situated on the [illegible] I have been busily employed [illegible] records in the town, which are abundant

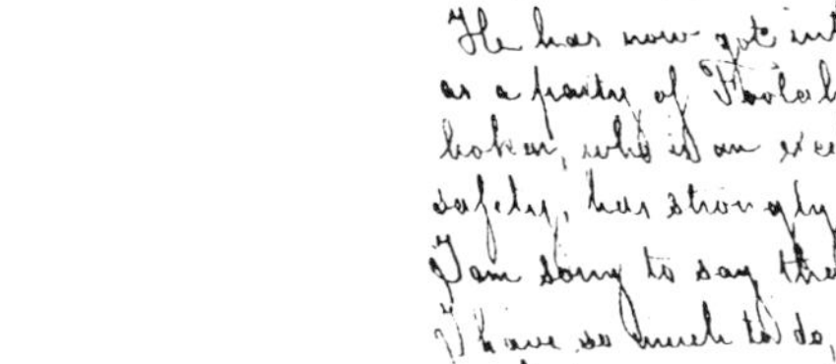

[illegible]esala December 19th 1825 –

[illegible] at length been able to accomplish [illegible] a quiet home to myself in [illegible] the house in which I am quartered, [illegible] the multitude of curious and [illegible] who have really intruded upon

Laing s last letter to reach Europe, the first by a Christian from Timbuctoo

Inset: Laing's handwriting before the attack

RENÉ CAILLIÉ
'Dead or alive, the prize for
the first European to reach
Timbuctoo shall be mine'

Caillié's sketch of Timbuctoo.
'I had formed a totally
different idea of its grandeur
and wealth'

The first photograph of Arouan,
probably the most remote of all the
larger Saharan towns : according to
Caillié, 'A detestable place'

HEINRICH BARTH
'Stubborn, humourless, loyal, and
immensely tough both physically and
mentally'

COLONEL FLATTERS
'He had an imposing
appearance but he was really
tired, depressed and
fatalistic'

The French Official Inquiry of 1910   exhumation of
Laing's remains

The French Inquiry : examination of Laing's remains at the
military post, Timbuctoo

(*left*)
A lady of Timbuctoo, drawn in the late nineteenth century

(*right*)
Tuareg in Timbuctoo, about 1911

(*below*)
The Citroen Expedition crossing the Sahara to Timbuctoo in 1923

Romanticized view of Timbuctoo, early twentieth century

were all Bambaras, both men and women. He was expected to live with them and eat with them; being Ramadan, there was little to eat, and Caillié, as a Moslem, was expected not to eat at all during the day.

After this frugal repast the slaves were freed from their chains, and I was gratified in witnessing the pleasure which these poor creatures experienced during their temporary release from bondage. They appeared very happy. They tried to walk, but it was with difficulty that they could move a few steps, for the chains which they had worn since they left Jenne had wounded their feet.

The vessel was about sixty tons and up to a hundred feet long. It appeared to Caillié 'very fragile'. It had a deck covered in mats, on which the cargo was loaded and on which the slaves slept. It was propelled by poles being pushed on the river bed; or, where the river was too deep, by paddles. The master stood at the stern and endeavoured to steer by means of another long pole, in which he experienced 'a good deal of trouble'.

The proprietor of the boat did not travel with Caillié. He was on a faster craft in the convoy, and expected to reach Timbuctoo before him. Caillié was put in the care of the Negro whose task it was to look after the cargo: 'A duty which he performed very negligently, for, after leaving Jenne, he gave me nothing but rice boiled in water, the food of the slaves.' Caillié detested the journey. The heat was insufferable; there was little shade; and 'the immense monotonous plains on all sides fatigue the eye of the traveller'. At night he had to sleep on deck with the slaves, wrapped in a sheep-skin, while the crew and other passengers rested below. After a week he became sick. He was numb and vomited continually. While he was ill he was allowed into the cabin, but this also he found 'very inconvenient', for it was occupied by one of the crew and his female slave. 'They allowed me so little room that I could not lie straight; my head touched my knees.' Even the slaves, following their master's example, behaved with 'the grossest insolence' to Caillié. Soon the crew began bullying him for money, and he was obliged to give out a number of loans, which he seems surprised to have discovered were not repaid.

5

As they progressed downstream, Caillié noted islands and landmarks; as is the privilege of explorers, he solemnly named them as he passed: 'Henry Island—in honour of His Royal Highness the Duke of Bordeaux; Maria-Theresa Island—in honour of Her Royal Highness the Dauphiness.' He noted carefully that, were a fort built on one of the islands, 'navigation would be under the control of the possessor'.

For three weeks they followed the Niger, travelling north and west. They began to approach the edge of the desert. And they entered the country where the Tuareg roamed. This was the most difficult part of the voyage. For the nomads, watching from their horses and camels on the north bank, were liable to obstruct and plunder any craft heading for Kabara—the port of Timbuctoo. They demanded tribute of all cargo-laden vessels.

As they entered this country, the boats from Jenne and elsewhere were assembled into flotillas, under command of the oldest of the masters. This chief had to arrange with the Tuareg the amount of duty to be unloaded from each boat. This done, the Tuareg would take away into the desert sacks of produce that comprised a considerable percentage of the total cargo. The proprietors and boatmen accepted this piracy with an air of inevitability which surprised Caillié. He had never seen the Tuareg before.

From now on Caillié had to remain below deck during the day. The crew explained that if any Tuareg should see his light skin they would conclude he was a Moor, and thus wealthy: the tribute would then be increased.

Wishing to see without being seen, I made several holes in the matting that covered that part of the canoe in which I was concealed. In this place the heat was so excessive that it gave me a violent headache.

A Tuareg went on board the boat of the head of the convoy. He ordered that each boat should unload one bag of millet for the Tuaregs' supper. 'The order was obeyed without hesitation.' During the whole of that night lightning flashed from the east; the heat was stifling; but there was no rain. Next morning Tuareg boarded the boats before they continued.

Others followed the convoy on horseback on the bank. The
river became very wide and deep. The Frenchman watched
it all

through the holes which I had made in the mats of my prison. We
were continually harassed by troops of these banditti. Some were
in small canoes, others mounted on fine horses, galloping along
the shore, and by the most horrid yells instigating their companions in the canoes to board us. This tumult was insufferable.
Every evening our boats were required to give them rice and millet
for their supper.

The time came for the final contribution. Argument and
bargaining over all this took a whole day. To Caillié the
frustration was excruciating. 'I was almost within sight of
Timbuctoo and durst not show my face.' The Tuareg came on
board to inspect the cargo; the crew wrapped up Caillié in a
large woollen blanket, in which he pretended to be sleeping.
The next morning, April 19, the convoy moved off at five
o'clock. They sighted Kabara soon after midday. Caillié was
allowed to reappear on deck and breathe clean air again. It
was nearly a month since he had embarked, and exactly one
year since he had left the French factory on the Rio Nunez.
In that year he had travelled about 1,500 miles, and of those
he had walked nearly 1,000 miles—one of the most remarkable feats in the history of exploration.*

*

Caillié found Kabara to be a busy little port, plagued by
Tuareg, who roamed about the streets confiscating anything
which took their fancy, and by mosquitoes. His description
of the position of the town is confused; during his visit the
Niger appears to have been at as low an ebb as it was flooded
during the time of Adams, eighteen years before.

The proprietor of the boat had gone ahead with the letter
from the Sheikh of Jenne. The Sheikh's agent, Sidi-Abdallahi,
had his slaves waiting for Caillié at Kabara. He was told to
accompany them to Timbuctoo.

*An average of about five and a half miles per day, not counting the months
in Tiémé.

After the ride to Timbuctoo, across the sandy plain, during which he received attentions from the suspicious Tuareg, Caillié sighted Timbuctoo for the first time. For a man who had suffered so much from disease and privation, and who had journeyed so far, just for that silent scene ahead, it must have been a sublime moment. But Caillié's joy and pride were mixed with a sudden and unexpected sense of anti-climax. Timbuctoo was laid out, dun-coloured and on the edge of the desert, which stretched to the horizon beyond, with its three mosques pointing to the sky: but it could be seen even from a distance to be no great and fabulous metropolis.

I looked around and found that the sight before me did not answer my expectations. I had formed a totally different idea of the grandeur and wealth of Timbuctoo.

Had all his efforts been only for this? The terrible irony of his position began to dawn upon him.

The city presented, at first view, nothing but a mass of ill-looking houses built of earth. Nothing was seen in all directions but immense plains of quicksand of a yellowish-white colour. The sky was pale red as far as the horizon: all nature wore a dreary aspect, and the most profound silence prevailed; not even the warbling of a bird was to be heard. Still, though I cannot account for the impression, there was something imposing in the aspect of a great city raised in the midst of sands, and the difficulties surmounted by its founders cannot fail to excite admiration.

Caillié had never seen a desert town, or an oasis, before.

Sidi-Abdallahi received him in the friendliest manner. This remarkable young Frenchman seems to have had no difficulty at all in persuading his host and others in the town of the reason for his journey. Because of his supposed experiences under the Christians as a slave, he was considered of great interest. And his devoutness and his obviously genuine wish to take up his father's religion once more impressed all who met him. René Caillié became virtually a guest of the town. His position for gathering information regarding Timbuctoo was to be bettered by no one until almost the next century.

Now he was able to live again in what was, compared to his recent experiences, comparative comfort. Blandly complaining that the first house he was lodged in was uncomfortable

owing to the fact that he had to share it with the same Negro
and his girl slave as on the boat, he was provided with a small
house for himself. He had his own wooden key and resident
slaves, who waited on him and prepared two good meals a
day of rice and beef or mutton. But the heat was suffocating
and he could not fully refresh himself after the experiences of
the journey: 'The nights bring with them an oppressive calm-
ness of the atmosphere, and if by chance there is a breath of
air, it is felt like a burning vapour and seems almost to scorch
the lungs. I was continually ill at Timbuctoo.' He soon discovered that his house was opposite the house in which
Gordon Laing had been lodged, 'the street only intervening
between them'.

Caillié's first impressions of Timbuctoo were confirmed.
On his first morning in the city, he went for a walk through
the streets.

I found it neither so large nor so populous as I had expected.
Its commerce is not so considerable as fame has reported. There
was not, as at Jenne, a concourse of strangers from all parts of the
Sudan. I saw in the streets of Timbuctoo only the camels which had
arrived from Kabara laden with the merchandise of the flotilla, a
few groups of the inhabitants sitting on mats conversing together,
and Moors lying asleep in the shade before their doors. In a word,
everything had a dull appearance. I was surprised at the inactivity,
I may even say indolence, displayed in the city . . . in comparison
with Jenne the market is a desert. It is very unusual to see any other
merchandise except what is brought by the vessels, and a few
articles from Europe, such as glass wares, amber, paper, etc.*
. . . Timbuctoo and its environs present the most monotonous and
barren scene I ever beheld.

Caillié requested an audience of 'the king' of Timbuctoo,
and this was easily arranged. Caillié entered the Sheikh's
house and was brought before the Sheikh, who was seated on
a beautiful mat or carpet, reclining on a cushion. Sidi-
Abdallahi related his story and the Sheikh (to whom Caillié
refers throughout as 'le roi') then questioned him in Arabic.
He asked about the Christians and the manner in which they
had treated him. He did not refer to Laing. Caillié correctly
judged that the Sheikh, unlike the Moorish merchants in the

*Traded by the Fulani and others from the coast.

town, was of negroid blood. He was dressed in Moorish style but the material seemed to be of European manufacture. 'His shoes were of Morocco, shaped like our morning slippers.'

Caillié gained a good impression of the inhabitants of the town. They had tea, which they drank out of tea services from Morocco. After the three hundred years since the visit of Leo Africanus, the people were still 'of a gentle and cheerful disposition', despite the anarchy which had reigned around them for so many generations. The women, unlike those in areas he had passed through, were not beaten. 'The people of Timbuctoo have some idea of the dignity of human nature'. The women were not veiled and were allowed to go out when they pleased and see anyone. 'I saw some women who might be considered pretty.' The Moors paid more attention to their female slaves than to their wives, and even these were 'neatly dressed', wore shoes and head-dress, and had their hair 'beautifully platted'. They anointed the head and whole body with butter. He found the slaves were treated with some consideration until their sale; when these wretched people were sold and sent off to Tripoli, Morocco and other parts, they were miserable at going away again, even if they had not been long in the town.

They always leave that place with regret, though they are ignorant of the fate that awaits them elsewhere. . . . I saw slaves affectionately bidding each other adieu. The conformity of their melancholy condition excites among them a feeling of sympathy and mutual interest. At parting, they recommended good behaviour to each other; but the Moors frequently hurry their departure and interrupt these affecting scenes.

One of Caillié's few contributions to contemporary knowledge was his account of the post-abolition slave trade, which was one of Timbuctoo's sole claims to economic importance at that time.

The female slaves of rich masters have gold ornaments about their necks. A few days after my arrival I fell in with a Negro who was parading about the streets two women whom I recollected to have been fellow-passengers with me on the boat. These women were not young, but their master, to give them the appearance of an age better suited to the market, had dressed them well. They wore fine white loin-cloths, large gold ear-rings, and each had two or three necklaces of the same metal. When I passed them, they looked at me and smiled. They did not appear in the least mortified at being exhibited in the streets for sale, but manifested an indifference which I could easily enough account for by the state of degradation to which they had been reduced.

Apart from the visiting Moors, Caillié estimated the population as between ten and twelve thousand, all of whom were engaged in eking out a precarious living from trade. The economy of the town was entirely dependent on the whim of the Tuareg who prowled around the environs.

This mysterious city, which has been our object of curiosity for so many ages, and of whose population, civilization and trade with the Sudan such exaggerated notions have prevailed, is situated in an immense plain of white sand, having no vegetation but stunted trees and shrub.

Even firewood was scarce, being brought from the neighbourhood of Kabara. Caillié remarked that should the connection with Kabara be at any time cut, the city would be reduced to famine. To prepare for such an event, the city—as ever with places threatened by siege—had stockpiled 'every kind of provision' in special warehouses. Caravans from Kabara, and boats on the river, had instructions not to defy the Tuareg for fear of provoking them to cut off the city: their every demand was to be met. Caillié now realized the source of the boatmen's resignation.

Not content with looking around the town, the Tuareg often came into the town itself. Caillié saw them sitting in the courtyard of Sidi-Abdallahi's house demanding what they called presents, 'but what might be more properly called forced contributions'.

When the chief of the Tuareg arrives, with his suite, at Timbuctoo, it is a general calamity, and yet everyone overwhelms him with attention and sends presents to him and his followers. He sometimes remains there two months, being maintained there all that time at the expense of the inhabitants and the king.

Caillié must have noted the dried-up river bed just south of the town, for he said: 'I am inclined to think that formerly the river flowed close to Timbuctoo.' The academics used Caillié's account as final condemnation of Adams, but here was in fact his vindication. Caillié humbly 'hazarded the opinion' that the Niger emptied itself into the Gulf of Benin. The Africans, he pointed out, used 'the Nile as a generic term rather than as a reference to a particular river'.

Caillié said that 'all the Negroes' of Timbuctoo could read the Koran, and implied that most of them could write: he thus seemed to directly contradict what Adams had said. But what was not appreciated was that Caillié mixed with the sophisticated Moor merchants and gained a false impression of the Negro aristocracy; Adams and Caillié saw little at close quarters of the way of life experienced by the other. Caillié visited the mosque frequently. It was usually deserted, and thus a good place for him to make his notes. But on one occasion he was approached by a middle-aged Moor, who stepped up to him gravely and slipped a handful of cowrie shells (used as money) into his pocket. Caillié noted, phlegmatically: 'I was much surprised at this delicate way of giving alms.' Thus the expertise of Caillié's deception was such that the Moors were financing the infidel in their midst.

Caillié found the great mosque, of which Leo Africanus had written, in bad repair. Several buttresses had been raised against the walls to support them. From the top of the tower he had an extensive view; from there he was able to contemplate on the town below which he had come so far to see. 'I could not help contemplating with astonishment the extraordinary city before me, created solely by the wants of commerce, and destitute of every resource except what its accidental position as a place of exchange affords.'

He had first heard of Laing's death from some merchants in Jenne; it was confirmed in Timbuctoo. He heard of the attack by Tuareg, and of Laing's arrival in the city 'almost destitute'.

On his arrival at Timbuctoo, Major Laing healed his wounds by the aid of an ointment which he brought with him from England. His recovery was slow; but he was made very comfortable, owing to the letters of recommendation which he had brought from Tripoli. . . . Laing had never laid aside his European dress, and used to give out that he had been sent by his master, the King of

England, for the purpose of making himself acquainted with Timbuctoo and the wonders it contains. It would appear that the traveller had openly taken a plan of Timbuctoo.

Caillié's informant said that Laing's plan had been carefully copied by the Moors—presumably without his knowing. He had been taunted about his religion, and told to repeat that Mahomet was the true prophet of God. He had always refused to do so, had not been physically ill-treated, and was left to 'think and pray in his way'. He had eaten little; he had lived entirely on eggs, bread and poultry, not eating the native dishes.

Often, when seated before my door, I thought of the fate of that unfortunate traveller. . . . I could not repress a feeling of apprehension lest, should I be discovered, I might be doomed to a fate more horrible than death—to slavery. But I determined to act with caution and to afford no ground for suspicion.

Caillié was so successful in this that when he asked to join a caravan for Morocco his host begged him to stay. Caillié was particularly anxious to return to France by way of Morocco in order to convince the authorities that he had genuinely been to Timbuctoo. He feared that if he returned to the West Coast it would be said that he had not got so far and had merely been living in the bush. It was with great difficulty that he persuaded Sidi-Abdallahi to let him leave, so much was the latter enjoying his company. But Caillié insisted. His host provided him with a stock of provisions to last him till he reached Arouan: paid all expenses to that place: wrote to his agent at Arouan, asking him to look after Caillié during the halt of the caravan there: and refused to accept anything in return. His farewells were so pressing and warm that Caillié was almost detained too long.

To rejoin the caravan, which had already proceeded to a considerable distance, I was obliged, as well as three slaves who had also remained behind, to run a whole mile through the sand. This effort fatigued me so much that, on reaching the caravan, I fell down in a state of insensibility. I was lifted up and placed on a loaded camel, where I sat among the packages. . . . We directed our route to the north over a sandy soil, almost moving, quite level, and completely barren.

5*

Thus René Caillié—the Arab boy who was a Frenchman—set out for Europe, in his attempt to succeed where Gordon Laing had failed. To achieve fame, and financial reward, he had to return in safety: for only a few people on the West Coast of Africa knew what he was attempting to do, and no one in the world, apart from himself, had the remotest idea as to where he was or that he had stayed for two weeks, as an honoured guest, in the most mysterious city in the world.

*

Timbuctoo was soon out of sight and nothing but desert stretched ahead for nine hundred miles. On the whole route to Morocco there were only twenty-two wells, some of which were five days apart, and several of which could be expected to be dried up. Caillié was the first European to travel this route, apart from Laing.

The oldest caravan conductors go first, to lead the way. A sand-hill, a rock, a difference of colour in the sand, a few tufts of herbage are infallible marks which enable them to recognize their situation.

The further northward we proceeded the more barren the country became. The plain had the precise appearance of the ocean; perhaps such as the bed of a sea would have if left by the water. In fact, the winds form in the sands undulating furrows like the waves of the sea. . . . The heat was insupportable.

Progress was very slow, the camels proceeding at leisurely human walking pace.

After four days the caravan reached the place where Gordon Laing had been murdered. It was early in the morning, just before sunrise, as the Moors pointed out the spot. Caillié said he was able to see the remains of a camp there, but after that he looked away 'from this scene of horror'. The caravan halted at a well not far away and breakfasted.

Already Caillié was finding the journey more rigorous than anything he had encountered so far; being, as he said, 'unaccustomed to riding on camels', he was sore and perpetually exhausted. Luckily, perhaps, he was ignorant of the terrors of the desert which were still to come.

On the next day they arrived at Arouan. Caillié found it a detestable place—the worst he was ever in: dirty, hot, surrounded by an arid wilderness, with no resources whatever of its own. The warm and brackish water of this place caused 'a violent derangement of the stomach', which remained with Caillié for the remainder of the journey. He appears to have had no appetite at all after leaving Timbuctoo, and crossed the desert on morsels of camel flesh and native food. He remained there nine days, during which time caravans came from various places on the Niger. At Arouan they assembled for the great and terrible desert-crossing to Morocco. The townspeople were extremely suspicious of Caillié throughout this time. It was said that he was a Christian. Because of this he appeared more zealous than hitherto, and made frequent visits to the mosque.

Before the caravans left Arouan a violent gale struck the town. Roofs were torn off and sand blown at the doors with such force that it was impossible to keep them closed. Everyone lay on the ground with their heads enveloped in their robes.

At half past seven on May 19 the caravan began to move out of Arouan, to the north-east. It consisted of 1,400 camels laden with gold, ivory, gum, cloth and ostrich feathers: 'a perfect tumult of men and beasts.' There were also many slaves being taken for sale in Morocco, some of whom Caillié recognized as having made with him the journey from Jenne, via Timbuctoo. After six miles they came to the last wells before the largest section of the desert crossing. Men and camels drank till they were bloated. All people of the entire, enormous caravan then prostrated themselves on the sand, invoking the prophet. Then they slowly moved away, towards the shimmering horizon and the next well, which was over two hundred miles away.

In imitation of the devout Moslems, I fell on my knees, but it was to pray to the God of the Christians: with my eyes turned to the north, towards my country, my relations and my friends, I besought the Almighty. . . . A boundless horizon was already expanded before us, and we could distinguish nothing but an immense plain of shining sand, and over it a burning sky.

The nightmare which followed was worse than anything Caillié had imagined.

*

The sands stretched away in seemingly endless desolation. The caravan, which had looked so formidable at Arouan, seemed suddenly as puny and vulnerable as a lone bird in a vast sky. The sun beat down mercilessly on all below.

Within two days Caillié was experiencing torments of thirst. Nothing mattered to him any more—not his success in reaching Timbuctoo, not the glory he hoped to bring to France, not the money he would give to his sister, not the fear of being murdered like Laing—only to quench the maddening thirst. Caillié wrote:

> I thought of nothing but water—rivers, streams, rivulets, were the only ideas that presented themselves to my mind during this burning fever.

The tiny ration of water issued at the end of each night's march did little to satisfy Caillié's craving. He tried to buy a skin of water with all the possessions he had left, but it was no use. He was told that no one would sell water—at any price; he readily believed it. During the day's rest he toured the tents of rich merchants, begging even to 'obtain a few drops of water out of charity'. It was a dangerous activity; he had already been told that to beg for water was severely frowned upon—as all were rationed. No one was privileged. Even the Moors, who sometimes had to walk beside the camels, were under the same regulation and received no water except when it was distributed to the whole caravan.

At this time they were also tormented by whirlwinds of sand, which advanced across the desert like great pillars. One of these passed right across the day-camp of the caravan, flattening tents and hurling humans around like straws. Men were thrown one upon another 'in the utmost confusion', and could see nothing beyond a foot away. 'The sand wrapped us in darkness like a thick fog.' Men groaned and shrieked, and others recommended themselves to heaven, crying out: 'There is no God but God, and Mahomet is his prophet.' Through the shouts and prayers and roaring of the wind Caillié could hear the moaning of the terrified camels, who had not eaten for four days. When the storm abruptly left them and the caravan wearily prepared to move off, it was seen that the exhausted camels could hardly walk. Without requiring any direction, they patiently moved off towards the north, gently shaking their heads as if in disbelief. Progress was painfully, infuriatingly slow; but despite all temptation to do so, the remaining water was not consumed in greater rations in case the wells ahead were dry. At last, seven days from Arouan, the caravan reached the wells of Telig.

At the smell of water the camels became unmanageable and could not be driven off by the whip. The first water which was drawn up was black and muddy, and thick with sand, but the camels fought for it furiously. Caillié thrust his head down among the camels and drank with them.

The village at Telig had perished in a sand-storm some time previously. Caillié saw the ruins of the houses.* But not far away—about half a day's journey—were the salt-mines of Taoudeni, perhaps the most terrible industrial workings in the history of man. Caillié was the first European to obtain an account of this place, although he was too exhausted to visit it. There Negro slaves were taken to work the salt-mines, three or four feet deep. There was nothing at Taoudeni at all—just the salt caked beneath the sand. The slaves lived and worked in the tunnels and trenches, a portion of their output being allowed to themselves. There was no shade, not a tree, not a shrub, not a living thing apart from the slaves and their overseers. Taoudeni being virtually uninhabitable, in the depths of the worst of the Sahara, its existence depended on the arrival of caravans which came with food supplies and left with salt. Few men lived there long, and when a caravan was late, or was attacked by Tuareg, and when the water-skins had been eaten, and leather and wooden implements, and cannibalism and other means of survival no longer sufficed, all died.

The caravan to Taoudeni came once a year. There men did not live—if they could, they merely survived from day to day.†

---

*Telig has long since been re-established as a stopping-place for caravans.

†Before the Second World War a Paris newspaper sent a mission to Taoudeni. It found conditions even worse than Caillié had reported over a century before. An American author reached these important and extensive mines in the nineteen-fifties and found nothing changed: slaves worked for themselves two days out of seven; the only free men, receiving a small wage, were there to pay off debts; the houses were built of salt and

After Telig the wells were at more frequent intervals and, although Caillié could eat practically nothing, there was more food owing to the slaughtering of camels which could go no further. But Caillié's troubles did not decrease: they only changed. For the hardships of the journey, with the resulting tenseness and even hysteria, were having their effect on the Moors also. It seems they needed something or someone on which to vent their emotions. Caillié, the only passenger on the caravan, with his lighter skin, was the obvious target. They teased him, threw stones at him and thrust things at his face. They insulted him in the worst way they could think of: 'He is like a Christian,' they said. Caillié was not the man to answer or fight back, and in any case he was in no position to do so. He took it all with his customary stoicism.

The caravan continued, covering usually between four and ten miles a day. Gradually it ate away at the enormous mileage it had to cover in order to justify its expense, its suffering and its very departure. Days mounted to weeks, and weeks became months. Caillié had nothing left but his filthy clothing, a few English coins, a little gold which he had managed to bring all the way from the Upper Niger, and his bag, with a padlock, which contained his notes. He became increasingly taunted by mirages, which appeared before him in the shape of vast sheets of water which disappeared as he approached them. He was unnerved by serpents which came out of their holes at night—according to him sometimes six feet long—and which appalled the Moors quite as much as they did himself. He was haunted by the skeletons which lay on the trackless route. He was thrown from his camel and suffered such pain that he was unable to walk, but happily was allowed to ride all the time—the only person in the caravan so privileged, owing to the state of the camels; a situation more typical of Caillié than those in which he had been hitherto in the caravan, and one can only guess whether the fall was not entirely fortuitous. Although he now suffered more invective than ever owing to his favoured position, he was no doubt able to bear it with greater ease.

carcasses; living conditions were foul; and the only females in the place were two old women. All life depended, as it had for centuries, on the arrival of the caravans (in one of which the American travelled). R. Maugham heard of brutality and slavery there while at Timbuctoo in 1959.

At last, by the end of June, the caravan began to leave the desert behind.

By the third week of July they had reached the Tafilet area. Here there were many villages, a slightly higher standard of living, and—glorious to Caillié's eyes—vegetation, including palm trees, 'beautiful and majestic'. Caillié, who had disappeared from society fifteen months before, saw the trees as signals of the approaching end of his ordeal. At Tafilet Caillié was shown an English copper compass which he believed had been Laing's; a Moor from Tafilet, in the caravan, had a sextant—also probably Laing's. They entered the stony, barren wastelands on Tafilet's northern fringe, then penetrated the passes of the Atlas Mountains. The land became populated, and Caillié found himself called upon once more as a man of medicine, a task which revolted him. 'My medical reputation drew upon me most unpleasant avocations: the mothers brought to me in crowds children in so disgusting a state that I could not look at them without horror; in vain did I avert my eyes. Caillié was also called upon to supply magic charms for unmarried daughters, which he did with pleasure, but in secrecy from the devout Moors. At each village he was pestered by mothers for his charms; in this way he was able to obtain a few delicacies for his swollen stomach, which he accepted in payment—taking care to explain that the charms would not work for twenty days, by which time he hoped to be far distant.

In this area his authenticity was questioned again, for here were men who had travelled to Egypt and who could question his story in detail. Caillié had the greatest difficulty in convincing them of his genuineness, but he was sufficiently convincing as a liar to pass even this, his most severe test. Soon he was once more gratefully accepting alms, tactfully passed to him by sympathetic and God-fearing Moors. Swollen, weak and half-dead from his exertions, he entered Fez on August 12, 1828, nearly three months after leaving Timbuctoo.

*

Fez was a populous and important city of Morocco, and Caillié was able to mingle in the crowded streets with comparative safety. He slipped away from the remnants of the caravan, camped on the outskirts of the city, and hired a mule and guide to take him to Meknes, which was almost half-way to the coast. Travelling with him were two young women, whose good looks and delicacy caused him much pleasure after so many sordid experiences. To Caillié's delight, once they had left the city they removed their veils, showing 'but little solicitude to conceal their fair complexions and pretty faces; one of them rode on my mule behind me, and I presume that my attentions were agreeable to her as she offered me a slice of melon and a bit of bread, which I accepted with pleasure'. This was a pleasant contrast to his recent mode of travel, but at Meknes Caillié found no hospitality, and left the town on foot, carrying his bag. He walked only a few miles when he realized he would never complete the journey on foot—Rabat being about a hundred miles away—and he returned to Meknes. He still had his English silver coins and his gold, with which, at this late stage in his journey, he was exceedingly, and perhaps curiously, disinclined to part. In Meknes he hired an ass and guide to take him to Rabat. He was so weak that he had to be lifted on to the animal. Nevertheless, averaging about twenty miles a day, he reached Rabat in five days' travelling —an astonishing feat at any time.

Caillié knew that there was a French Consul at Rabat, but, to his bitter disappointment, there was not a Frenchman. The Consul was a Jewish merchant, to whom Caillié revealed his secret. This man was naturally in fear of compromising himself, and seems to have done little for Caillié. Although there were other Europeans in the town, and Caillié met at least one Englishman to whom he revealed himself, and although a Portuguese ship bound for Gibraltar was in the port, Caillié was unable to break free from his predicament. At night he slept at a cemetery, and in the day he stood at street corners, in his rags, begging for water, and going to the mosques for meals from charity. After fifteen days of this melancholy existence, Caillié hired an ass and guide to take him to Tangier. It was evident that the Jewish merchant was going to do nothing for him. He proceeded up the coast, much of the way staggering on foot as his beast was already overloaded with merchandise and could barely move, sometimes on the loose sand of the seashore. Occasionally he saw vessels cruising down the coast, and longed for one 'to bear me from this frightful country'. In five days René Caillié reached Tangier. At that city lived the Consul-Generals and representatives of the European powers to Morocco.

He had covered some 2,800 miles of mostly unexplored territory in eighteen months. He had done so with little money and without influence or support.

*

The French Consul-General at Tangier was so startled by Caillié's story that he asked him to leave his house as soon as he had heard it and had provided him with breakfast. He was terrified of detection, and Caillié, who had so briefly enjoyed speaking in his own language and the civilized company, was obliged to wander around the busy streets of the city, sitting in doorways and sleeping in the open for two nights. During the day he loitered in the street of the Consul's residence, waiting for an opportunity to return to it. On one occasion, when he presented himself at the door, a maid screamed; the Consul appeared and, although recognizing him, shouted: 'Turn out this dog of a beggar.' The next day he managed to get into the house and have another interview, which he hoped would be decisive. As a Frenchman in need, he demanded assistance in returning to his country. Although the Consul reaffirmed the difficulties, Caillié's insistence seems to have had some effect. That night he returned in the dark with his bag, and remained in the Consul's home, where he was given a room and clothes. He had completed one of the most amazing, successful and daring travels in disguise known to history.

After returning thanks to Almighty God, I lay down upon a good bed, rejoicing in my escape from the society of men debased by ignorance and fanaticism. Though all my wants were relieved, I found it impossible to close my eyes the whole night, so much was I agitated by the remembrance of the perils I had passed through.

. . . It would be difficult to describe my sensations on casting off for ever my Arab costume. . . . I believed myself in a dream, and asked if it was true that I might soon be restored to my country, or whether this enchanting hope was but a delusion.

Caillié did not have to wait long for an answer. In reply to repeated and desperate calls from the Consul-General, a sloop arrived at Tangier from the French station off Cadiz. On September 27, a little before sunset, he embarked, dressed as a sailor, and in a high fever. After a voyage of ten days, during which he was treated as a hero, Caillié arrived at Toulon. For any man who had been away from home so long, and who had endured so much, it would have been a deeply satisfying moment, but for a man as deeply patriotic as René Caillié it was sublimely transcendent.

*

Quarantine regulations were strictly applied in Europe at the time, and Caillié was obliged to linger in isolation at Toulon. But he had written to the Geographical Society from Tangier, as had the Consul-General. These letters had been received with some excitement by M. Jomard, its most distinguished member and the foremost expert on African exploration in France. Jomard was so delighted at the news of Caillié's achievement that he acted with unusual speed for a man of science. 'I attentively compared the two letters, and found the result so comfortable, in the most established notions of science, that I determined to publish on that very day the news of the journey to Timbuctoo.' This was done, with all Jomard's authority behind the announcement, before the great man had met the traveller or even questioned him by letter. Jomard had therefore precipitously put his own great reputation at stake.

Jomard, like Caillié, was a fervent patriot. He was determined that the news should be true so that the glory of the first detailed account of Timbuctoo should belong to France. He sent some money to Caillié at Toulon, and when the latter arrived in Paris Jomard became his adviser, protector and patron.

Jomard quickly satisfied himself of Caillié's authenticity,

but other members of the Society were more critical. It was felt that Caillié could have remained a little way in the interior with a native family for a year, have met a Moor who had been to Timbuctoo, the Sudan and Morocco, and then easily contrived to reappear at Tangier. They suggested, in fact, that most of his story was a clever hoax. A Special Committee was formed to investigate Caillié's claim. It consisted of six members, of whom Jomard was chairman. Its report was prompt and brief. 'The committee is struck with the tone of simplicity and sincerity which reigns throughout his narrative . . .' Caillié's charm and Jomard's authority were such that they had been able to overcome all doubt in the Society itself. Only eleven weeks after Caillié's arrival in France the award of 10,000 francs was made to him. Jomard was particularly proud of the speed at which it had been done. René Caillié was one of the most celebrated men in France. The reward was formally presented, with much clapping and cheering, by the Society in full session. Caillié was made a Chevalier of the Legion of Honour by King Charles X, a rare honour at that time. Best of all, he was awarded a pension of 6,000 francs.

In a number of respects the terms of the Prize had been broken in order to award it to Caillié; the most important was that he had not submitted a written account of Timbuctoo and his journey. One reason for this was that he was determined to do the task himself, without the aid of a 'ghost writer'. As controversy about his claims mounted, he set himself to this task. It was important that he should hurry: not only to establish his integrity, but also as a contribution to the Anglo-French dialogue on Timbuctoo, which had now reached its most bitter pitch. For the English were as determined that Caillié should be a fraud as Jomard was that he should be genuine.

News of Caillié's appearance had reached London as soon as it had Paris. On the day of Caillié's departure from Tangier the British Consul there had despatched the following:

A Frenchman, who it seems has been at Timbuctoo, arrived here clothed in the dress of a Moorish beggar, and has sailed for France. . . . Great secrecy has been observed by the French Consulacy here.*

*Despatch, 28.10.28: Foreign Office Papers (P.R.O., F.O.76.26).

The British Consul at Tangier, as all other British officials in North and West Africa, had been alerted to listen for any information about Gordon Laing or Timbuctoo. The efforts which the British Government had made, throughout 1828, on Laing's behalf were much to their credit. Warships had cruised up and down the West Coast for many months, waiting for word of him, unaware that Warrington was already satisfied as to the explorer's death.

In 1829 no attempts to reach Timbuctoo were being attempted or planned. Nearly all the British explorers concerned were dead. The Frenchman was busily composing his book. But 1829 was the most active year in the extraordinary story of international rivalry over Timbuctoo. Between Britain and France it assumed the proportions of a serious international incident; and other countries—the United States, Sweden, Denmark and Holland—were involved. For the Sultanate of Tripoli it meant a year of hovering on the brink of war with one, or, sometimes, several, European powers. And it was all because of the energy of one Englishman, remote from the European capitals with which postal contact was many weeks away, and his utter absorption in the question of the papers of Gordon Laing.

*

Warrington was now convinced that Laing's journal had survived his death; that it had been brought out of the desert by Arabs; and that they had sold it to the French Consul at Tripoli. For several years he devoted all his efforts to proving his case, pursuing his victims with almost demoniac energy and persistance. He had little, if any, private wealth, but he offered $1,000 reward for the recovery of the papers. His numerous letters to London on the subject had begun to sway the views of the Foreign and Colonial Offices by 1829, and the Government was beginning to accept his view.*

Warrington's two main targets were Baron Rousseau, the French Consul, and Hassuna D'Ghies, the Pasha's prime

---

*Warrington's position was complicated by the fact that he had recently blundered his country into an exchange with Sweden and Denmark, over the tributes which those countries paid to Tripoli, which had resulted in the British Government having to apologize.

minister. Rousseau's expertise with the Arabs had already irritated Warrington, as we have seen; but it now appeared that he had a consuming ambition to be accepted as an expert in Paris, by the academicians, rather than by his rivals in North Africa. Warrington was not above intercepting Rousseau's mail in order to prove this point. And Rousseau's researches into Warrington had revealed that his wife was a bastard daughter of the King. D'Ghies was one of the most educated and cultured Arabs in North Africa. He had been educated in France and had spent much time in that country. The fact that he and Rousseau became friendly could hardly have been more natural, but Warrington always believed it was a sinister relationship devoted to the warping of all British aims.

Warrington was quite unable to express his suspicions and discoveries in an unbiased way, or to distinguish fact from hearsay; for this reason his charges have usually been dismissed by scholars, and even the Government of the day found it difficult to support him, so wild did his argument become. On one occasion the Foreign Office was obliged to inform him:

> The documents sent home by you in support of the charge which you preferred against the French Consul Rousseau were insufficient to prove him guilty of having abstracted the papers in question; and I am now instructed to remark to you that the very imperfect state of those documents, and of such as you continue to transmit to this office, must render them completely useless.*

Nothing could be more blunt than that. But it was not enough to deter a man as obsessed with righteousness and indignation as Hanmer Warrington. It was eventually realized in London that through all Warrington's wild accusations the germ of a genuine case existed. Warrington's insinuations that Laing had been murdered by D'Ghies's agents, in league with France, could be dismissed as a symptom of his chronic Francophobia; but French participation could not be so easily dismissed. The sudden and unexpected appearance of Caillié had made relations between the two Foreign Offices even worse.

---

*Letter, 2.3.30: Foreign Office Papers (P.R.O., F.O.76.26).

Warrington had four strong points in his case. The first was that Moslems had the greatest respect for the written word, more so perhaps than any other people. The importance which Laing would have attached to his journal would have been noted; its deliberate destruction was, therefore, highly unlikely. Secondly, there was the fact that Rousseau was always anxious to publish new material relating to Africa, that he seems to have been supplied on other occasions by the agents of D'Ghies, and that he or D'Ghies announced Laing's death in the French press before Warrington had been able to confirm it. An English doctor living in Tripoli, the American Consul and the Dutch Consul (who was Warrington's ally throughout) all later testified that they had heard Rousseau talk, in 1828, of a book he was writing about Timbuctoo, the first volume of which had already been delivered to the publishers; but such a book never appeared. The bearer of Laing's last letter, from Timbuctoo (whom Warrington naturally saw as a possible bearer of the journal also), and Laing's freed slave, who had come to Tripoli and had been able to give a first-hand account of the explorer's death, had both spent nearly all their time in Tripoli with D'Ghies or Rousseau, despite the furious protestations of the British Consul; Warrington's efforts to get Laing's servant safely to Malta were unsuccessful ('he must know every particular of the horrid murder, and also respecting the papers'). Thirdly, there was the fact that D'Ghies was very heavily in debt in Paris. The fourth aspect—and it was the most important—was the evidence brought back by the Arab whom the Pasha and Warrington had sent to Timbuctoo to investigate.

This man returned in June, 1829, after an absence of more than a year and a half. He reported that Laing had left his journal at Timbuctoo with instructions for its despatch to Tripoli if anything had happened to him. Warrington recalled that a letter Laing had sent while recuperating at el Muktar's had definitely stated that he would send his journal from Timbuctoo; such, indeed, had been his instructions from Lord Bathurst. But it may have been that Laing was too preoccupied and anxious during his stay in the city to work on the journal as he would have liked; he was a perfectionist, and he had lost the use of his right hand (possibly the hand itself). By leaving the journal at Timbuctoo he would give himself the chance of working on it again, and also, he would have hoped, preserved it from the dangers of the route he knew he was embarking on. Everything known about Gordon Laing indicates that this is just what he would have done. Alternatively, he might well have taken some papers with him and left others at Timbuctoo in the hope that some at least would survive.

The report of Warrington's Arab investigator must be taken very seriously, as so much else that he found in tracing Laing's last journey—all the way from Ghadames—agrees with what came to be known independently of him. He was formally interviewed by Warrington, with questions and answers carefully recorded; the interpreting was done by one of Warrington's sons, who also witnessed and signed each recorded statement. The answers, after more than a century and a half, still have the ring of spontaneity and truthfulness which must have impressed Warrington at the time.

The investigator indicated that people had discussed Laing with him, his journal and his fate, freely in Timbuctoo. He was told that Fez merchants had warned Laing of the dangers of going with Labeida's small caravan to Arouan. And thus he took 'only a few books and trifling things with him'. He had left his papers in two parcels sealed with red wax at Timbuctoo; if he reached Sansanding safely, he would send for them; if not, they were to be taken back to Tripoli by the same man who had been commissioned to take his letters. The investigator had, in fact, passed this messenger, on the way out, between Tuat and el Muktar's (he said he had only Laing's last letters with him on arrival at Tripoli). The investigator's inquiries on his return journey led him to believe that the two parcels had changed hands at Ghadames, where they had been taken over by agents of D'Ghies. They had then been brought to Tripoli perhaps a year since.

On hearing this, the outraged Warrington struck his flag from the Consulate. This indicated that there could be no more intercourse between Britain and Tripoli until the affair had been settled to British satisfaction—i.e. until the papers had been produced. It was a serious gesture, particularly so for a small country when the complainant was the most powerful and feared nation in the world.

After this several witnesses in Tripoli came forward to further implicate D'Ghies, not only with the loss of the journal but also with Laing's murder. A Ghadames merchant who had been in Timbuctoo with Laing told Warrington in a written deposition that 'two packages sealed up' were left in the city by Laing in the care of the man who eventually brought back the explorer's last letters. The Pasha hurried his own inquiries and also came to the conclusion that D'Ghies was guilty—an opinion which had little weight, for the displeasure of the British was of greater importance to him than the reputation of his chief minister. Throughout 1829 H.M.S. *Pelarus* was on 'Laing duty', continually in and out of Tripoli. It was said that D'Ghies had given Laing's two parcels to Rousseau for a reduction of forty per cent in loans he had with the Consul and in France. The messenger who had delivered Laing's last letters left Ghadames for Timbuctoo in suspicious haste. D'Ghies's brother admitted the guilt of the chief minister to the Pasha. D'Ghies took refuge in the American Consulate. Warrington was disgusted. He wrote off to the Foreign Office:

> M. Rousseau has not only defrauded the English Government of the journals and manuscripts of Major Laing, but he has stolen also letters to his wife, to me and my family. It is really too horrid to continue.*

A week later he was able to send back to London a document in which the Pasha stated his belief that D'Ghies and Rousseau were responsible for Laing's murder. The Union Jack was hoisted again at the Consulate. Rousseau fled the country on an American ship and settled in the United States. The French press, aware of the controversy, began pointing an accusatory finger at him, and his flight did nothing to lessen suspicions in London. A strong official note of protest —on the strength of the Pasha's statement—was passed to the French Government. The latter promised to mount an impressive commission into the whole affair. The French Government, clearly embarrassed, acted well throughout; in

---

*But in his last letter Laing had explained that he had not written to Emma.

December they even forwarded information of Laing's death which had been received at their Consulate in Tunis. The French Geographical Society attempted to lower the temperature by conferring its Gold Medal on Laing posthumously.*

D'Ghies had also boarded an American warship in Tripoli, U.S.S. *Fairfield* (Captain F. A. Parker)—according, it seems, to the Pasha's wish. This brought an inevitable strong protest from Warrington to John Coxe, the U.S. Consul; he said that D'Ghies had been 'proved guilty of fraud and theft', and suggested that he was also guilty of the murder of Laing. He ended by saying that the matter would have to be settled between the British and American Governments. It was a typical example of Warrington's thoughtless diatribes, and the American Consul seems to have enjoyed composing his reply:

I received your communication of yesterday, which continual occupation and fatigue have prevented my answering before the present moment. You assert that D'Ghies has been proved guilty of fraud and theft (and suspicion of murder, etc.); but you have totally omitted to inform me before what Court of Competent Jurisdiction his fraud and theft (and suspicion of murder) have been proved. D'Ghies has repeatedly assured me that in his case you alone are the accuser, judge and jury. . . . You allude to the death of Major Laing, and I can assure you, sir, that I regret as much as any one the untimely fate of that worthy man and persevering traveller. His name belongs to all civilized nations, and the loss of such a man is particularly to be lamented by the friends of science throughout. Such are my feelings with respect to him, but strong as they are, they cannot for an instant stand in the way to prevent my maintaining the honour of my flag.

The last paragraph of your letter would be a frightful menace to some, but it is not so to me.†

The *Fairfield* took D'Ghies to Spain. Both Coxe and Captain Parker were under the impression that D'Ghies would go straight to England, where he would present himself for trial by English jury: 'his confidence in their justice is perfectly firm.' But D'Ghies lingered in Majorca.

*The medal was sent to Emma in Tripoli.
†Letter, 11.8.29: Foreign Office Papers (P.R.O., F.O.76.26).

The Foreign Office considered his delay in coming to London —where they had offered him every facility to prove his innocence—condemnatory. It was not until D'Ghies was virtually a social outcast, with little if any hope of returning to Tripoli, that he moved to London. By then the French Commission, having seen none of the major parties involved, had submitted its report. It found that Rousseau was fully vindicated of the accusations brought against him; and in its opinion D'Ghies also had not received Laing's papers. The commission had the weight of its chairman, Baron Monnier, a well-known orientalist, and an impressive membership that included two Deputies. Its report was passed to the Foreign Secretary by the French Ambassador, with a polite note. But the Foreign Office were unimpressed at the inquiries, which— predictably—had merely punctured some of Warrington's more ridiculous theories in order to undermine his kernel of fact.

Those who considered Warrington's outbursts to be the slightly ridiculous signs of an outraged father with a persecution mania had a habit of changing their opinions. Coxe was no exception. Three months after the departure of D'Ghies, when he had considered all the evidence, the American Consul generously wrote to Warrington, in November, 1829:

I have been most perfectly deceived and treacherously imposed upon in the affair of D'Ghies, of which you are aware, and which I really feel it my duty to acknowledge. . . . I can now fully declare that I am thoroughly convinced that the said D'Ghies did receive the papers of the unfortunate Major Laing, here in Tripoli.*

It was not until 1832 that D'Ghies finally arrived in London, on the U.S.S. *Delaware*, to clear his name. He stayed at 38 Piccadilly, and immediately set about finding support. His tardiness had cost him such respect as he might have enjoyed with the Foreign Office. But he had influential friends and, with their help, he compiled a monster memorandum of 227 pages, much of it consisting of the same sort of invective about Warrington as Warrington had already conveyed about him. Impressive rebuttals were few. He claimed that his brother had been forced to make his confession at the

*Letter, 20.11.29: Foreign Office Papers (P.R.O., 76.26).

point of a sword. He said he had only left Tripoli, at the request of the Pasha, in order 'to avoid the vengeance of the Consul'. He insisted that the whole matter was 'a gross mistake or suggested by political animosity', and attributed it to Warrington's 'passionate character, his ignorance of [the Arabic] language, and his prejudices against me'. He complained: 'I am the victim of Mr. Warrington's injustice. Friends, family, fortune, I have lost.'* Some of this must have been idle rhetoric, for he offered to bring several witnesses from Tripoli, paying their entire expenses himself.

M.P.s had been lobbied about the matter for some years.† Eventually a Major James Fraser was sent to Tripoli by the Government to discuss D'Ghie's charges with Warrington and to conduct an investigation. He found the Consul 'Irregular in his habits of business, indiscreet in his communications, regardless of money to a degree that is painful to witness'. Nevertheless, on December 2, 1833, he reported to the Colonial Office: 'The more I see of the affair of Laing's papers . . . the warmer is my feeling towards poor Mr. Warrington.' And a month later he concluded that 'A monstrous villainy had been committed'.

Despite the fact that D'Ghies had now persuaded his innocence to the Attorney-General and a recent Home Secretary, the Colonial Secretary refused to adjudicate in the matter, by taking any action against Warrington.‡ It was felt that D'Ghies had gained much from the exposure of Warrington's weaknesses rather than from the strength of his own case. After D'Ghies began circulating in London, there was pressure from Members of Parliament to remove the embarrassing squire from his post at Tripoli.

The situation was still in this unsatisfactory state when Hassuna D'Ghies left London for Paris. With his departure his case lapsed, but the bitterness remained.

Warrington, testy and forlorn, lived on in Tripoli, angry at the way the case had been dropped and anguished at the

---

*Memo, 1832: Foreign Office Papers (P.R.O., F.O. 76.33).

†There is an irate letter about Laing in the Hobhouse Papers (Sir John Hobhouse, Secretary for War, Ireland, etc.: British Museum Department of Manuscripts).

‡This was Lord 'Goody' Goderich, who five years previously had been a singularly unsuccessful Prime Minister.

way Laing was being forgotten. In 1833 he wrote, in a letter to London: 'Let John Bull not forget the situation of poor Laing. . . . His poor, poor bones lay whitening on the burning sands of Central Africa and none so poor to do him reverence.'

From the evidence which Warrington so tenaciously collected, and so foolishly swamped with idle conjecture and invective, it seems likely that Laing left his journal and other papers at Timbuctoo: that these were taken to Ghadames, where they came into the orbit of D'Ghies: and that they were brought to Tripoli, where they were received by the grateful and no doubt excited Rousseau, who must have soon realized his mistake in letting his enthusiasm get the better of his judgement. It is unlikely, however, that a man with such a keen interest in geographical affairs would have destroyed the papers to avoid detection, even though on examination he would no doubt have learned, with disappointment, of the myth of Timbuctoo. The much slimmer evidence of a French inquiry of 1910, based on the evidence of a nephew of the murder, said that the papers had been burnt after the murder. It is just possible that the Laing journal survives, perhaps in America, and that it will appear one day. If it does, it will surely be worthy of a place with the greatest records of human endeavour and courage.

*

The rivalry that had always accompanied French and British aspirations in Africa was now fatally poisoned. The worst of nationalism began to take the place of the simple patriotism that had inspired a man like Caillié. Some remained aloof, in both capitals, from the petty bickering, slanders and accusations: others began to see exploration purely as a means of out-doing the foe. Even scholars such as Jomard, and John Barrow,* who had encouraged the British naval explorers like Lyon and Clapperton, wrote in stiff and cold terms to each other about the Laing papers. Jomard's contacts at St. Louis, on the West Coast, told him that travellers had reported that Laing had his papers with him and that they had survived and could easily be recovered.

---

*Second Secretary at the Admiralty; author of *Mutiny on the Bounty*.

But even the most splenetic Anglophobes could not question that Laing had been in Timbuctoo. In London, it was suggested by some particularly suspicious and ingenious Francophobes that Caillié had drawn his information about Timbuctoo from Laing's notes, which he had received from Rousseau; for Caillié's book appeared, at public expense, in Paris in 1830, and was published in English in the same year. It was immediately seen to be a rambling and disappointing account, much padded and infuriatingly detailed about trivial matters and lacking in detail at just those places where detail was needed—such as of Timbuctoo. It was also, quite obviously to the unbiased reader, honest; despite this, it was still suggested in London that it was a hoax. Caillié was no scholar, and his ignorance and his inconsistencies laid him open to the same sort of attack from the English as Adams received from the Geographical Society of Paris. In future years Caillié's assertions, such as that most of the houses were built of brick, were seen more and more to be unreliable. Jomard declared that Caillié's data made Timbuctoo's position 17° 50' N., 6° 0'. W.*

In the same year Caillié married a governess who had been the victim of a bigamist. He adopted her son and they left Paris to settle at Mauzé, where he had been a youth. He bought a farm near to where his crippled sister was now living. It was a small place and Caillié was a famous man. He was not a good farmer; he had been the victim of an unscrupulous sale of poor land; but his newly acquired private means enabled him to live like a landlord and squire. He interested himself in local affairs. Without much delay he became the father of four children, in addition to his stepchild.

Within a few years René Caillié began to long for Africa—the continent he had so detested when he had left it. He wrote continuously to Jomard, begging for his support. But, although the public thought of Caillié as a great explorer, the

---

*Whereas it is about 220 miles away at 16·49N, 2·59W (*Times*). Park had placed it nearer at 16° 27'N, 0° 0'. Clapperton's estimate was 15° 0'N, 0° 50'W. Jomard's and Clapperton's positions were about 400 miles apart: Timbuctoo lay almost mid-way between them. The wild margin of error is indicated by Timbuctoo's distance from the coast of about 860 miles.

scholars did not: to them he was a highly successful adventurer. What Caillié could see, and they could not, was that his experience was now unequalled; and such was the lack of information about West Africa that after the death of Richard Lander, in 1834, Caillié was the most important living traveller of that area. He was given the honorary title of Consul to the Bambara on the assumption that he would be allowed to take up the position if and when it became practicable. (Forty years earlier, in 1794, William Pitt, also impressed by stories of the gold mines, had appointed a nominal British Consul to the area.) To tempt the authorities, Caillié concentrated on the commercial aspects. He suggested that he should investigate a scheme for exporting Bouré gold. But it was no use; all his ideas were rejected.

On April 4, 1838, he wrote to Jomard: 'My age can be no bar. When Mungo Park undertook his second expedition he was probably over forty.'* It was very probably the last letter he ever wrote. Like Emma Laing, Caillié probably suffered from the scourge of the age, consumption. Less than two weeks after writing the letter he suffered one of the recurrent attacks of fever he had been subject to since his great journey. He died on May 17, 1838, ten years after he had set out across the Sahara from Timbuctoo. He was thirty-eight.

Although he was buried with every honour, and a statue erected in his memory, Caillié did not take with him the legend of Timbuctoo. It remained, and it was a subject of as great an interest as it had ever been. No one could be absolutely certain about the place except the one man who had claimed to, and he was now dead. Could it really be that something men had held in wonder for many centuries hardly existed at all except in the shape of a few primitive dwellings? That the whole thing was an utter myth? It seemed unlikely. No matter what Caillié had said, most people found it impossible to accept. The quest for Timbuctoo—a quest with a more exciting ending—would go on.

There were also voices raised in dissent. The *Quarterly Review* had reported on Laing's death:

---

*He was, in fact, 32, as Caillié would have well known.

We trust that there will be an end to the sacrifice of valuable lives, in procreating discoveries on this wretched continent, of which we know enough to be satisfied that it contains little at all worthy of being known; a continent that has been the grave of Europeans, the seat of slavery, and the theatre of such crimes and miseries as human nature shudders to think of; where eternal war rages among the numberless petty chiefs for no other motive than to seize the innocent families of the original natives and sell them into perpetual slavery. The products for commercial purposes are few, and mostly confined to the sea-coasts; two-thirds of the interior being a naked and unhospitable desert, over which are scattered bands of ruthless robbers.

In 1829 a nineteen-year-old student of Trinity College, Cambridge, won the Chancellor's Prize for Poetry at the University with his poem *Timbuctoo*. With it Alfred Tennyson displayed precocious talent, contemporary clichés and some of the power which was to gain him, half a century later, acknowledgement as the greatest living poet in the language. Its romanticism, however, was tempered by unusual common sense about his subject. After comparing Timbuctoo with the legends of Atlantis and Eldorado, he wrote:

> Wide Afric, doth thy sun
> Lighten, thy hills unfold a city as fair
> As those which starred the night o' the elder world?
> Or is the rumour of thy Timbuctoo
> A dream as frail as those of ancient time?
> . . . the time is well-nigh come
> When I must render up this glorious home
> To keen Discovery: soon your brilliant towers
> Shall darken with the waving of her wand;
> Darken, and shrink and shiver into huts,
> Black specks amid a waste of dreary sand,
> Low-built, mud-wall'd, barbarian settlements.*

But the world at large was still inclined to take a more romantic, a more poetic, view on the intriguing subject of the desert metropolis than was the poet: his great friend, A. H. Hallam, for instance. Hallam had also entered the competition; although unsuccessful, he had his poem printed privately: 'it received so much more praise than I can flatter

---

*This prediction was published just before Caillié's book.

myself it deserves, from several persons whose taste and judgment I respect, that I take the liberty of publishing it'; notwithstanding this show of modesty, Hallam had, in fact, already had the poem printed at his own expense as a pamphlet before its appearance in his *Poems* of 1830. It was very much more in keeping with the public mood than was Tennyson's austere prediction: a longing for some wonderful, almost heavenly, paradise on earth:

> Thou fairy City, which the desert mound
>   Encompasseth, thou alien from the mass
>   Of human guilt, I would not wish thee found!
> Perchance thou art too pure. . . .
>   . . .
>   Thy Palaces and pleasure-domes to me
>   Are matter of strange thought: for sure thou art
>   A splendour in the wild: and age to thee
> Did visible guardians of the Earth's great heart
>   Bring their choice tributes, willed from many a mine,
>   Diamond, and jasper, porphyry, and the art
> Of figured chrysolite: nor silver shine
>   There wanted, nor the mightier power of gold:
>   So wert thou reared of yore, City divine!
> And who are they of blisses manifold,
>   That dwell within thee? . . .

It was left to one great explorer, the greatest of all in the quest for Timbuctoo, to give an account, incontrovertible to even the most convinced romantics, of that city divine and those who dwelled within.

6 . The German

RENÉ CAILLIÉ'S book did little to stop the Timbuctoo Rush. It encouraged it. For on the continent of Europe, particularly in Germany, the book was considered lacking in authority: in Britain it was considered a fake. Timbuctoo was still regarded as an essential link in the mystery of the Niger, as well as of great interest in its own right. When Clapperton's servant, Richard Lander, reached London with his master's journal, he was received with the greatest interest and respect. Lander negotiated an agreement with the Government whereby he and his brother John would attempt to reach the scene of Mungo Park's death on the Niger, and from there continue the Scottish explorer's journey to the sea. They left Portsmouth on January 9, 1830, and reached Busa, on the Niger, five months later. The only relics of Park's expedition the Landers found were his logarithm tables, the hymn-book of his brother-in-law, both carefully preserved, a tailor's bill and an invitation to a dinner party in the Strand. The Landers' expedition set off in two native canoes, with enough provisions for a month—including two sheep. Surviving rapids and capture by the Ibos, they heard within two months 'the welcome sound of the surf on the beach'. They took the first ship they could and returned to Europe—via Rio de Janeiro. After 2,500 years since the river had been recorded by Herodotus, the problem of its termination had been solved by the sons of a Cornish publican.*

The magnet of Timbuctoo remained.

John Davidson was the son of a wealthy military tailor of

---

*Richard Lander returned to Africa with an expedition under Macgregor Laird, an indefatigable Liverpool merchant who made several attempts to capture the Niger trade (also a sponsor of the first ship to cross the Atlantic entirely under steam). The party was attacked by natives in 1834 and Lander received a wound from which he died, aged 29. His brother John got a position in the customs service, through the Royal Geographical Society; he died of an illness contracted in Africa, in 1839, aged 33.

Cork Street, London. Trained as a pharmacist, he became a director of the leading chemists of the city, Savory & Moore. Not satisfied with this comfortable position at a youthful age, he studied at St. George's Hospital and at Edinburgh University with the intention of becoming a doctor. He was still only thirty when he abandoned this and set off on a series of expensive and ambitious travels. He travelled all over the Middle East and in America, collecting a great deal of unimportant geographical information. His industry, if not his scientific contributions, was rewarded by election to a fellowship of the Royal Society. It was with this learned institution that Davidson gained some fame by unveiling an Egyptian mummy to a startled audience.

John Davidson decided that a visit to Timbuctoo would set the seal on his achievements. He wrote to his friends in the nobility, seeking their support and obtaining letters of introduction from them to 'the king of Timbuctoo'. He also gained the interest of Lord Palmerston, Foreign Secretary. In the rooms of the Royal Society Davidson met Antoine D'Abbodie, a French citizen. This man told him that he intended to beat Davidson to Timbuctoo. It was his plan to travel as a grandee, 'with his servants in hose and doublets'. Davidson took this challenge more seriously than it deserved, and he hurried his departure. He had already enlisted the services of a freed slave, recently arrived in London from the West Indies. This man, Edward Donellan, claimed to have been born in Timbuctoo, but to have left it when two years old. To test his authenticity, he had been taken to the London museums; he had recognized hippopotami and other African animals, and had given an account of their behaviour. Convinced of Donellan's honesty, Davidson embarked with him at Falmouth on September 3, 1834. The cost of the expedition was to be met by himself.

At Tangier the British Consul, Willshire (who had welcomed Riley from slavery years before), begged him to give up the project. There was tribal warfare on the edge of the Sahara, and for a stranger to travel there at that time was virtual suicide. Davidson was not interested. He saw danger elsewhere: 'I must beware of the French, for I foresee they will be intriguing against me.'

When he arrived at the Sultan's court in Morocco, Davidson found that his medical knowledge was only too well appreciated. He became the most sought after man of medicine in Fez. Within a few weeks he had treated 1,200 patients. His popularity was such that he found it extremely difficult to depart. 'My position is far from enviable; the jealousy and *amour propre* of these people is beyond all belief. I am charged with favouring one whose large arm requires two splints to support the fractured bone, or looking down upon another as puny because I give him but two pills, whilst others less deserving than himself take three.' At length he pleaded that his medicine-chest was empty, and left for the desert in November, 1836.

Felt very poorly: had a touch of the lumbago. Weather variable. Thirst excessive.

It was not what he had expected. He was distressed by the filthiness of the people and by the cruelty shown to slaves. For some petty offence girls were 'stripped and flogged with some plaited cow-hide over the legs and back: after hanging for half an hour, they were let down, when others were brought in to suffer a similar punishment'. He was appalled by the sandstorms ('all the fortitude of man fails'). He reached Wadi-Nun, near the West Coast. It was one of the terminals for the south-going caravans; Adams and Riley had both been there. For nearly six months John Davidson lingered at Wadi-Nun. He became increasingly depressed. At last the nature of his quest was made clear to him. 'My mind is made up to the certainty that I shall leave my bones in the Sudan.'

Owing to the influence of Palmerston, a naval vessel, H.M.S. *Scorpion*, was meant to supply Davidson at Wadi-Nun and to carry his despatches. But it did not succeed in contacting him owing to bad weather and heavy seas. Davidson's letters and most of his journal did get back; they contained little of interest. He meticulously recorded changes in the barometer every few hours.

The merchants of Tafilet had heard of Davidson and his intentions, of which they were suspicious. Tafilet, as another great terminal of desert caravans, was in rivalry with Wadi-Nun. It was rumoured that Davidson was going to open up to European influence the route from Wadi-Nun to Timbuctoo.

One of the last letters to reach Davidson was from the Royal Geographical Society. It begged him 'not to endanger unnecessarily your life even with the hope of accomplishing your journey to Timbuctoo; for however desirable it may be to reach that place, it is not worth risking life to obtain it'. But Davidson and his pride had gone too far to turn back. Although fighting was still continuing in the interior, he left for Taoudeni and the Sahara. In order to speed his progress, he had offered to lend to a caravan 'an enormous sum', enough to buy all the current salt stock at Taoudeni; it could be paid back to him after the salt had been sold at Timbuctoo. But in the end there were only Edward Donellan, himself and a few Moors in his caravan. Davidson's wealth was by now a by-word in North Africa. He was attacked and robbed in December, but allowed to proceed. A few days later, in December, 1836, still some four hundred miles from Taoudeni (which itself was the same distance from Timbuctoo), he was attacked again. He was shot dead and his remaining wealth taken. He was five days short of his thirty-ninth birthday.

All reports of the murder which arrived at the various Consuls on the coast said that it had been arranged from Tafilet. Edward Donellan, never to be heard of again, had continued with the caravan to Timbuctoo.

*

John Davidson was the last of the independent amateurs. Although the British Government continued to send ill-equipped explorers—an astronomer who could not speak Arabic, a soldier who could hardly write his own name—they were very much the exception. The whole attitude of getting to Timbuctoo was changing. Critical comments in the press, like the article on Laing's death in the *Quarterly Review*, had swayed public opinion. And they were not without effect on the Government. The feeling was that the lives of enough adventurers, gallant but unsuitable, had already been lost.

The death roll of British Servicemen alone who had died in the attempt to solve the Niger-Timbuctoo mystery was now over 150. Soldiers, naval officers and dilettantes would no longer receive official support. That was the feeling. And it was now shared by the new Foreign Secretary, Lord Palmerston. For 'Pam' had never been entirely enthusiastic about the Davidson mission, although he had given it his support.

There was one explorer who seemed to respond to this mood. His name was James Richardson. No one could have been in greater contrast to Clapperton, Laing, Caillié and Davidson. His attitude was stated thus:

> I am very much of the opinion that in African travel we should take especial care not to attempt too much at once; that we should proceed very slowly, feeling our way, securing ourselves against surprise, and reducing and confining our explorations to the record of matters of fact as far as possible. . . . African travel can only be successfully prosecuted piecemeal, bit by bit, here a little and there a little, now an island, now a line of coast, now an inland province, now a patch of desert.

This was the new style. It was widely agreed to be sensible and practical. But it was not a style which was likely to appeal to potential explorers among his own countrymen—or, indeed, to Frenchmen. So when James Richardson set off to study 'a patch of desert' he did so alone; and he did so undecided as to whether he would make an attempt on Timbuctoo—he would wait and see how he got on.

Richardson's sober attitude to the most exciting activity of his day was no accident. He had been born in Lincolnshire in 1806, and had been brought up for the church. When he had arrived in North Africa, after a period as a journalist in Malta, his two ambitions were to propagate Christianity and to help abolish the slave trade. But as well as these pious sentiments, which he frequently expressed, he also believed in the benefits of trade—particularly the benefits that would accrue to his own country from trade with Africa. Supported by a bible society, he arrived in Tripoli in 1845. Warrington, dejected and depressed since his personal tragedy and mentally played out since the unsatisfactory end of the exhausting D'Ghies affair, met him at the ship. Warrington's introduction was: 'Ah! I don't believe our Government cares one straw about the suppression of the slave trade, but, Richardson, I believe in you, so let's be off.'

The Pasha made his customary protestations about the difficulties of travel in the desert, but, apparently resigned to the infinite capacity of Englishmen to seek suicide in the Sahara, he gave his support. His sceptical view of English sanity must have been fortified when he learned that Warrington, of all people, assured Richardson that the road south was 'as safe as the road from London to Paris'.

As for the Consul's well-intentioned but tactless help, Richardson had this to say: 'I am obliged to Colonel Warrington not so much for facilitating my progress in the interior as for increasing my difficulties a hundred-fold.'

Richardson travelled with a caravan to Ghadames, where he remained three months. He then went on to Ghat, about six hundred miles south of Tripoli. This was a fine achievement. Richardson concentrated on establishing friendly relations with the inhabitants, in which he had some success. In Ghat Richardson met Hatita, the Sheikh who had helped Lyon, Clapperton and Laing. He now styled himself 'Consul of the English', for which he suggested he should receive a regular annual payment. The character of slavery in Ghat, which much shocked Richardson, was that the master had most of the slave's labour free, but that a small proportion was left to the slave in order to support himself: the same, in fact, as existed at the salt mines of Taoudeni a hundred years later. About Timbuctoo he received a great deal of conflicting advice. The famous city lay 1,600 miles away to the south-west. He decided to heed those who argued that to attempt the journey meant certain death. But he gathered some information about the place from travellers. He described how the river rose close to the city, but nevertheless said that: 'In comparing Caillié's description with that given by the American sailor, Robert Adams, I find Caillié's information agrees the better with what I have collected myself.' He added that:

The city is about four times larger than Tripoli. . . . The grand desideratum of merchants is the acquisition and accumulation of gold. . . . The neighbouring country is flat and sandy, stretching in plains. . . . The Moroccan merchants live in style and luxury at

Timbuctoo. . . . These details are not very interesting, and I should not have mentioned them but for the general anxiety there still exists to obtain correct and recent information of this celebrated city.

Richardson returned to Tripoli with a caravan of slaves, as Lyon had nearly thirty years before. At their first sight of the sea many of the slaves 'cowered down and, sinking, hid their faces under their tattered clothes'. Richardson reported that 'Many slaves are flogged to death *en route* from Ghat to Tripoli. The females are subjected to the most obscene insults and torments by the Arab and Moorish slave-drivers; whilst the youngest females are violated by their brutal masters'. But the most shocking assertion that Richardson made on his return was: 'Three-fourths of the slave traffic of the Great Desert and Central Africa are supported by the money and goods of European merchants resident in Tunis, Tripoli, Algiers and Egypt.'

There was one big difference between the Tripoli he had left and the Tripoli to which he had now returned. Hanmer Warrington had gone at last. His service in Tripoli had extended over thirty-two years, from 1814 to 1846. During that time his independent mood and his total inability to deal with bureaucracy had steadily increased. His insubordination was legendary in Whitehall. His position could hardly have lasted so long had he not been married to the late King's daughter, and no doubt received some protection from high places. The first row of 1846 came after an inquiry, personally conducted by Warrington, which resulted in a British subject being sent to Malta to stand trial for murder. The man whom Warrington had accused was acquitted because of an almost total lack of evidence. The Foreign Secretary of the day, Lord Aberdeen, did not have the tolerance of his predecessors.* He sent a sharp reprimand. Warrington did not change his ways. He insulted the Sicilian Consul to such an extent that another reprimand was necessary—although the British Government may have been quite as interested in removing Warrington as in placating Sicily. On March 19 two of his despatches were returned:

---

*His most important achievement was the Treaty of Oregon, 1846, which fixed the 49th Parallel boundary. Prime Minister, 1852–55.

You will remodel these Despatches in conformity with your instructions, and narrate with precision the subject and object of your communication.

On April 7 a curt letter from Aberdeen asked him to retire on a pension of £900 per annum. Warrington resigned on May 4. At the same time he asked that his son Herbert should take over the position, or, if not, that he also should receive a pension, having been a Vice-Consul for seven years. The Foreign Office replied that a successor was on his way and that, on consulting their records, the Treasury had only agreed to the appointment of Herbert Warrington without pay. A list of the establishment was asked for, and this revealed that Frederick Warrington, another son, had been drawing pay as interpreter. Warrington's career of fifty-two years' service to the Crown thus ended in bitterness and petty wrangles over pensions, for Warrington continued to plead from Italy on behalf of his son.

After this another son, Henry, moved to Murzuk, where he lived as an Arab; he was murdered in 1854. Frederick also spent much time in Murzuk. Warrington's daughter, Emma Laing, had died sixteen years previously.

Richardson had been away for eight and a half months, during which time he had made no converts to Christianity and had done little or nothing for the bible society. Although he did not come back with much information, he had spent only £50. His modest expenses impressed everyone, not least Lord Palmerston, who had inherited an interest in Timbuctoo from his predecessors.

The slaves embarked for Constantinople and Arabia: Richardson embarked for London. Back in the capital, there was plenty of interest in financing him to continue his journey. But, as Warrington had foreseen, the interest in London was less in anti-slavery than in commerce. In order to get back, Richardson lent himself to this. The British Government was particularly interested in the routes of the great caravans that crossed the desert in case they could be used for capturing the trade of Central Africa. But, unlike most of his colleagues, the new Foreign Secretary was as interested in the abolition of slavery as he was in trade. Lord Palmerston, who had succeeded Aberdeen in July, 1846, gave his assent to an official expedition, striking south from Tripoli: the first official operation on that route since the tragedy of Gordon Laing. Palmerston, who had been one of the leading 'anti-slavers' of his day, and one of the most passionately sincere, saw in the expedition a chance of gaining information about the continuance of the slave trade, as well as the capture of trading agreements. For the first time the difficulty was not so much finance as personnel. Richardson was anxious that the expedition should be international. At the same time he demanded men of the same scientific approach as himself; he had no wish to risk his life with head-strong adventurers. Richardson visited Paris in 1849. He met Jomard, and even tried to interest the President of the Republic; but he had no success. Why should Frenchmen help capture lucrative markets for England? No Frenchmen were forthcoming. Richardson then went to the Prussian Ambassador in London. He might perhaps have guessed earlier that the qualities he was looking for—pedantic, meticulous scholarship, combined with the hardy athleticism of an ancient Greek—would be found in a German. The man the Ambassador recommended was probably the best-suited man in the world at that time for the task of answering the Timbuctoo question once and for all. His name was Heinrich Barth.

*

Barth might have been bred for the task. He was a brilliant Arabist, speaking and writing the language, an experienced authority on the desert. He was the kind of scholar who would return not with a slim journal consisting of vacuous conversations with chiefs and records of temperature, but with a five-volume work that would have lasting value. And he had the strength, physique and energy of a freak in a circus. A sturdy, giant-like youth of nearly six and a half feet, he was a keep-fit enthusiast. He was stubborn, humourless, unemotional, loyal, more clever than intelligent, and immensely tough both physically and mentally.

Berth was born at Hamburg in 1821, and was a graduate of Berlin University. He was an expert geographer, a knowledgeable archaeologist, and spoke and wrote fluent French, English and Italian. From Berlin he went to London in order to study Arabic. He then took a long tour around North Africa and the Mediterranean; during the course of this he met Warrington, who was impressed by him and promised to help should he ever think of travelling south into the continent. He visited many archaeological sites, and the resulting book established him in Germany as a brilliant young Egyptologist. The book was published in 1849 while Richardson was on his vain quest in Paris. Barth had returned to Berlin, where he was lecturing (on the colonial commerce of early history) at the University, when he first heard of Lord Palmerston's offer. Palmerston's only condition was that Barth should contribute £200 towards his personal expenses. Barth's sole condition was that his work should involve exploration only. Both sides quickly agreed. Barth considered it a great honour to represent England. But while letters were still being exchanged between Berlin, London and Paris (where Richardson still was), Barth's father persuaded him to give up the project as being too dangerous. 'My filial duty did not allow me to resist.' Barth withdrew from the engagement. At the Ambassador's suggestion, another German, Dr. Adolf Overweg, a geologist, was contracted to take Barth's place. But it was then decided that correspondence had gone too far to allow Barth to withdraw, which gave him an opportunity of defying his father. The result was that there were now two Germans on the expedition and one Briton. How far this was the design of the Prussian Minister in London, who played a leading part in the arrangements, is not clear; if his designs were nationalistic, he had picked the wrong man in the earnest young lecturer, whose first loyalty was to science.

Barth carried on professionalism where Richardson, whose reputation was greater than his achievement, left it. He was thorough where his predecessors had been disorderly and ill-prepared. Although his reliability has been over-praised in the past, he was a scientist—although not a very sound one— in quest of knowledge: they, at best, had been glory-seekers. As soon as he heard, from London, of the expedition, he undertook a strenuous course in physical training to get himself fit for the journey. He steeped himself in all the known literature of Central Africa and of Timbuctoo (he was the most widely read on his subject of any explorer to Timbuctoo, including even Gordon Laing), although he was not even certain that he would attempt to visit the place. Gordon Laing had prided himself in the seriousness of his preparations when sleeping on the floor at his Scottish home, but it did not occur to him to improve his physical condition, which was, in fact, poor. Heinrich Barth was the first of the modern explorers. Although less sophisticated and knowledgeable, his approach was basically the same as that of Fuchs or Hillary.

Both Barth and Richardson were the kind of men who work best on their own.

*

Richardson and his wife arrived at Tripoli on January 31, 1850. He had married just before his departure. Barth and Overweg had arrived twelve days before, as Richardson had been delayed waiting for final instructions from Lord Palmerston. While Richardson prepared for the expedition, the two Germans went off on explorations around Tripoli. This resulted in seventy detailed pages in the account which Barth was preparing. Finding a small ruin, Barth measured everything to a tenth of an inch—but was unable to give a definite opinion as to its origin ('I think it not improbable that the art may be ascribed to Roman influence').

Richardson, meanwhile, prepared the expedition. It was to be the most lavishly equipped of any that had departed from Tripoli. The new Consul made arrangements with Malta for the necessary supplies, which could not be obtained at Tripoli. The most important of these was a pre-fabricated boat, in four sections, which were to be slung in nets between camels. Various servants and drivers were signed on. At last, on March 30, the caravan, with its mass of stores and supplies, mounted and ambled out of Tripoli. With it was Frederick Warrington, who travelled south with them for a few days.

Already there was some 'atmosphere' between Richardson and Barth. The German thought Richardson was being unnecessarily tardy. The pious Richardson, who must have seemed infuriatingly phlegmatic at the prospect before them, considered the Germans too eager 'to grapple with adventure and research'. Unlike the Germans, the Englishman had, of course, travelled in the Sahara. He was also, unlike them, newly wed.

Hope and the spirit of adventure sustained my courage; but it is always sad to part with those we love, even at the call of duty. However, I at length mustered strength to bid adieu to my wife— the almost silent adieu of affection. How many things that were thought were left unsaid on either side! It will be pleasant to fill up all blanks when we talk of these days after a safe return from this arduous undertaking. . . .

Unlike Laing, Richardson was not an emotional man, but no one knew better than James Richardson how slim were the chances of return.

As on his previous journey, Richardson planned to go via Murzuk and Ghat. Because of the contacts he had already made there, he felt confident of a good welcome. Beyond that, a welcome was also assured in Bornu. For, quite unexpectedly, an emissary had arrived at Tripoli from that country with presents for the Great White Queen.*

They went to Murzuk by the arduous direct route, over a rocky, barren plateau, probably the first Europeans ever to have done so. Barth was a keen rock-climber. They reached Murzuk after a month; they called on the Pasha, who entertained them to coffee, pipes and sherbet. As the days went on Barth began again to show signs of increasing impatience. Arrangements for the continuation of the journey plagued him so much that he omitted, in a most unscientific manner, to make a full examination of Murzuk, an important desert centre and the capital of the Fezzan. By this time Richardson seems to have been struggling to maintain a more than nominal leadership of the expedition. With the arrival of Sheikh Hatita in Murzuk, departure was made; he was to provide the escort to Ghat, with a band of Tuareg. Hatita, having been associated with British expeditions since that of Lyon in 1819, thirty-one years previously, thus had a continuous experience of them larger even than Warrington or

*The gifts, in four chests, were duly delivered to Buckingham Palace in July, 1853.

any man in Africa. For the first part of this stage of the journey Barth chose to go his own route, with Overweg. He does not give a reason, and this fact is not mentioned in Richardson's account. It may be assumed, therefore, that personal relationships had deteriorated. Neither man was the sort to give way without imagining wounds to his pride; Barth was the kind of young man, by no means uncommon, who felt he had little, if anything, to learn. Overweg was dominated by Barth.

The two parties soon joined up and the combined caravan continued to progress southward, across sandy plains and through mountainous canyons, at a time of year when the heat was most intense. After four weeks they had almost reached Ghat. Then Barth became restless again. Against the urgings of Hatita, and with the disapproval of Richardson, he decided to explore the heights of the mountainous cliff at the foot of which they were travelling. Richardson wrote that Barth went off 'somewhat stiffly by himself'. At this stage Barth still had supreme confidence in his own physical powers —he believed they could overcome any dangers he might have to face. Hatita had declined to give him a guide; Overweg hesitated, but eventually followed, accompanied by a guide. At 5 p.m. Overweg reappeared, tormented with thirst and exhausted. He expressed the gloomiest apprehensions regarding Barth and, when he had recovered, led a search party just before the sun set. Hatita refused to have anything to do with the matter.

Barth was about eight miles away, lost and half-dead from thirst and exhaustion. He found strength to load his pistol and fire two rounds, for in the distance he could see the camp fires. 'I thought the sound ought to awaken the dead from their tombs, so powerfully did it reverberate from the opposite range and roll along the wadi; yet no answer.' The shots were not heard. Next morning the search was continued. Barth's footprints in the sand were found, but the trail ceased when the loose pebbles of the mountainside were reached. Barth spent another day under the full glare of the pitiless sun, suffering terribly from the tortures of thirst. It was entirely typical of Barth that, having got himself into such a situation by his own headstrong wilfulness, he saved his life by the presence of mind and coolness of nerve that enabled him to open a vein and drink his own blood. 'I sucked a little of my blood till I became senseless and fell into a sort of delirium.'

That evening, after sunset, he was discovered by a lone Tuareg. He was taken back on a camel to the tents. The Tuareg could not believe it. Even Richardson, not given to surprise, was impressed. He wrote:

Twenty-eight hours without water in the desert! Our people could scarcely at first credit that he was alive; for their saying is that no one can live more than twelve hours when lost in the desert during the heats of summer. . . . We found rum very useful in restoring his health.

This narrow escape had a profound effect on Barth. It was a lesson which helped make him a great explorer; but in his journal he merely noted, blandly:

It is, indeed, very remarkable how quickly the strength of a European is broken in these climes if, for a single day, he be prevented from taking his usual food. Nevertheless I was able to proceed the next day.

Within two days they reached Ghat, where Richardson was welcomed back. They remained there only seven days. The expedition was to take a quite different route to Bornu than that favoured by the Denham, Oudney, Clapperton mission: via the hilly oases of Aïr. This stage of the journey—which was without the services of Hatita—was worse than anything Richardson had experienced previously. They were attacked by Tuareg bands, forced to pay ransom before they could proceed, and eventually were taken captive and obliged to give up a third of their supplies and belongings before being allowed to move on: similar experiences at the hands of the Tuareg, in fact, as Laing had suffered.

At Aïr, Richardson and Overweg were content to rest, but Barth went off to the principal oases of Agades; he found the place in a state of decay, with 'famished vultures waiting for the moment to pounce'. During his absence, Richardson and Overweg took the opportunity of drinking one of the Mission's two bottles of champagne (Barth's capacity for liquor was considerable). Richardson noted:

The other bottle I have stowed away in reserve for Lake Chad, to drink the health of Her Majesty when we launch the boat, if we are fortunate enough to arrive there.

Barth returned safely, and New Year's Eve was celebrated with two ostrich eggs. Barth wrote: 'Timbuctoo, which was in the background of this novel and living picture, seemed an almost unattainable object.' What pleased Richardson most at this time was the sight of Barth reading the Bible which he had borrowed from him. Half-way through January the three men split up. Barth was to go to Kano; Richardson to Zinder; and Overweg to Chad. They were to rendezvous at Kukawa, capital of Bornu, near Lake Chad. Richardson said: 'We took leave one of the other with some emotion, for in Central Africa those travellers who part and take divergent routes can scarcely count on all meeting together again.' Indeed, they could not.

On January 14 Richardson reached the town of Zinder, which was nominally in the Moslem Negro state of Bornu. He and Barth were the first Europeans to enter Bornu from the north. Zinder was a brutal and slave-infested society. The slave trade was rampant, and Richardson was appalled by what he saw. Female slaves were classified into 'those with the breasts hanging down, those with the breast plump, those with little breasts'. A good female slave fetched the equivalent of more than £10*: a good male less than £1. The local Sultan carried out the frequent executions himself; his barbarous method was to cut open the chest and then tear out the heart. Richardson commented: 'I am told by a well-informed person that morals are much relaxed here.' After three unpleasant weeks he left, to join Overweg in the Chad area.

On February 21, 1851, he wrote in his journal:

I had numbers of other patients today; my Epsom [salts] is fast going. Thermometer at sunset 82°; weather very troublesome today, blowing hot and cold with the same breath.

It was the last entry, but it contained a hint of the tragedy that was to come. In that area the temperature can change

*At Constantinople, the end of the journey for most, the price at the same time was about £50.

thirty degrees in a day. Richardson fell ill, and he died—probably of heat-stroke made worse by injudicious use of his medicines—on March 3. He was only two weeks away from Chad.

Barth had reached Kano, where he was able to add considerably to the information gathered by Clapperton. He found the city quite as disagreeable as had the former explorer. His reason for visiting it was not entirely scientific. The expedition, on the instructions of the Government, had taken with it a great deal of merchandise, in order to pay its way, instead of cash. Having already lost a third of this to the Tuareg, Barth now had to try to dispose of much of the rest.

For all these reasons, nothing could be more disagreeable and disheartening to me, though I was not quite unprepared for it, than the information which I received the very evening of my arrival in Kano, that the price of the merchandise such as I had was very low. . . . Forbidden to leave before the governor had seen me, destitute of a single farthing in cash, called upon and pestered by numerous creditors, and laughed at on account of my poverty, my readers may fancy that my situation was far from agreeable.

He remained five weeks in Kano, during most of which he was ill with fever. He then set out for Kukawa, near the western shore of Lake Chad, where he was to meet Richardson. After six days' travelling he met an Arab who was with a small caravan from Murzuk; he had with him—to Barth's delight—a parcel of letters from Tripoli, London and Germany. But only nine days later he heard of Richardson's death. Barth was saddened by this, but would not allow it to depress him.

My way of looking at things was not quite the same as that of my late companion, and we had therefore often had little differences; but I esteemed him highly for the deep sympathy which he felt for the sufferings of the native African, and deeply lamented his death.

He noted with satisfaction, 'the excellent health which I still enjoyed'; and, 'full of confidence, I stretched myself on my mat and indulged in my simple supper'.

Richardson's belongings had gone on to Kukawa, and Barth hurried after them. It says much for the excellent nature of the people of Bornu that he recovered them all—except for Richardson's watch, to which the Sheikh had become attached.* He also managed to borrow enough money to settle his own and Richardson's debts. A month later Overweg arrived looking 'greatly fatigued'. Barth was not impressed with Overweg's researches; his memoranda he found virtually unreadable, and on one important excursion his companion had made no notes at all. Overweg had undergone a very bad time and was half-dead with fever. But Barth, still strong and as enthusiastic as ever, had curiously little sympathy ('Mr. Overweg was, in some respects, very badly off, having no clothes with him except those which he actually wore'). Overweg navigated the water of the vast lake in the boat which had been so laboriously carried across Africa, now named the 'Lord Palmerston'. Tired and sick, the geologist gradually weakened as he was fanned by cool breezes out in the water. Barth visited the interior around the lake; both men thus added much to the information of the Clapperton, Denham, Oudney mission. Kukawa was their base. During this time a formal letter reached Barth from the Foreign Office acknowledging his report of Richardson's death, appointing him leader of the expedition, asking that it should continue, and hinting that 'a westerly course in the direction of Timbuctoo' would be acceptable. Barth became Britain's emissary in trade, and his early stipulation about being involved only in scientific work was easily discarded in the press of circumstances. Barth was always meticulous in furthering Britain's interests, and conducted himself as the ambassador of that country.

Eighteen months after Barth's arrival at Kukawa, at the end of September, 1852, Overweg lost his reason 'muttering unintelligible words in which all the events of his life seemed to be confused; he jumped up repeatedly in a raging fit of madness and rushed against the trees and into the fire'. Overweg was in a village eight miles from Kukawa, which he had come to detest, and Barth left him there to return to the town. 'He said that he had something to tell me, but it was impossible for me to understand him and I can only fancy from what happened that, being aware that death was at

*Richardson's journals – eight slim volumes – reached Tripoli, and his heartbroken wife returned with them to London to supervise their publication.

hand, he wanted to recommend his family to me.' It does not seem to have occurred to Barth that Overweg might have been pleading not to be left alone.

Next day Barth learnt that his companion, aged twenty-nine, had died. Barth was alone in a strange continent, years away from any European with whom he could talk, in a climate the fatality of which had been so well proved to him. The reaction of this remarkable man was: 'I determined to set out as soon as possible on my journey towards the Niger —to new countries and new people.' In a letter, he wrote: 'Far from feeling discouraged after the death of my comrade Overweg, I find my powers redoubled. I feel as strong as a giant.'

He was still over a thousand miles from Timbuctoo.

*

There has been some doubt and confusion about Barth's intentions, which he did not fully dispel in his book. These should be put to rest by his very clear views on the subject, stated in a letter from Kukawa in reply to an emotional letter he had received begging him to abandon any idea of travelling eastwards to Zanzibar.

It has never been my intention, nor will it ever be, to 'rush on blindfold' into any situation whatever. It is true, to reach the coast of the Indian Ocean and to determine the nature of the Equatorial regions of Central Africa and, if possible, to make out the country from whence the Nile does take its origin has been from the beginning my favourite idea. But it has always been an *idea*, never my intention, and I at least have never announced such a plan . . . it was in the beginning of last year that, in a letter sent home, I expressed my intention, if *experience* should be against an Easterly or a South-Easterly road, to turn my face Westwards in order to finish my researches in that quarter. . . . I never intended nonsense and never intended to do more than possible.*

Barth was a man of such unusual calibre, both in physical resistance and in determination, that he might well have

---

*Letter: 24.7.52 (British Museum Manuscripts), to Desborough Cooley, the London geographer. Cooley's letter was of 22.1.52, not March of that year as stated on the copy in the British Museum file.

reached the east coast had he undertaken that journey over mostly unknown territory. His would have been the greatest name in African exploration. But he went instead on the long and fruitless trek to Timbuctoo, already visited by Caillié and Laing. The magnet had not lost its power.

Barth left Kukawa for Timbuctoo two and a half years after he had last seen Tripoli. He did so knowing that it must be another two years at least before he could return to the security of the British Consulate there. But Heinrich Barth had, as he said, 'a boundless confidence in myself'.

Travelling via Zinder and Sokoto, Barth reached Kabara—the port of Timbuctoo—ten months later: a tremendous journey, the stage from Sokoto, where Clapperton had died, never having been crossed before by a European. For the first time really fearful for his life, the normally nerveless Prussian crossed the short strip of desert separating port from city. He was travelling in the guise of an official emissary from Turkey. He entered Timbuctoo on September 7, 1853.

We approached the town, but its dark masses of clay not being illuminated by bright sunshine, for the sky was thickly overcast and the atmosphere filled with sand, were scarcely to be distinguished from the sand and rubbish heaped all round; and there was no opportunity for looking attentively about as a body of people were coming towards us in order to pay their compliments to the stranger and bid him welcome . . . putting my horse to a gallop, and gun in hand, I galloped up to meet them, when I was received with many salaams.

Barth then entered Timbuctoo, picking his way 'through the rubbish which has accumulated round the ruined clay wall'. He had been told of the great importance in the place of Sheikh el Backay, and had decided to put himself at this man's mercy. He was shown to el Backay's guest-house, next to the Sheikh's own, whereupon—unusually over-wrought—he collapsed immediately with fever. El Backay was out of the town, and Barth kept to himself until the Sheikh arrived two and a half weeks later. Barth revealed his secret to el Backay; at first no one else knew that there was a Christian in the town.

Barth's residence in Timbuctoo was the object, in France

and England, of some ridicule. This did not do him justice. It was a very great achievement to arrive there at all, where so many had failed before him, and his stay was much more productive than that of either Laing or Caillié (whom Barth unfairly considered 'incapable altogether'), although he was in a worse position than either of his predecessors. His most important achievement was to quote extensively from the *Tarik*, a local history, which had long been sought by European scholars. But he also gave a very full account of the town in his combined diary and memoirs. Barth suffered from two severe handicaps at Timbuctoo. He overrated the importance of el Backay, thus insulting the chief Sheikhs of Timbuctoo, and placing himself in the hands of someone not widely popular in the town. Secondly, the Fulani still claimed Timbuctoo; Barth suffered, as Laing, from their distant disapproval of a stranger in the provincial outpost, and from the timidity of the inhabitants of Timbuctoo and their reluctance to defy anyone, vulnerably placed as they were, which had been their characteristic quality for so long.

El Backay was the son of Sidi Mohammed who had cared for Laing after the Scotsman had been mangled by the Tuareg. He was described by Barth, in a letter to the Foreign Office, as 'the religious chief of Timbuctoo'. He had known Laing well: had admired him. Since the death of his elder brother seven months before, el Backay had become head of the Muktar family. It was his elder brother who had arranged Laing's journey to Timbuctoo from el Muktar's after their father's death, at the expense of nearly all Laing's remaining possessions. The elder brother had taken the family to Timbuctoo at the request of the town in order to help in a struggle against the Fulani and to gain the support of the Tuareg. Two of el Backay's brothers were among the most vociferous of Barth's critics on account of his religion being the same as that of Laing. El Backay, however, 'Never failed to express his admiration, not only of the Major's bodily strength, but of his noble and chivalrous character.'* Barth's inquiries about Laing were cursory. He met members

---

*In view of Laing's condition, the remark regarding Laing's 'bodily strength' would seem unlikely; Barth himself would have regarded it as a compliment, and was no doubt anxious to please.

of the band who had been with Laing at the end. But he discovered nothing, although the Scotsman was well remembered: none, of course, had heard of Caillié. The Muktar family, who had once controlled the caravan routes as far as Tuat, had lost their former prestige; and in Timbuctoo they had crossed the Fulani. The local chief of the latter sent a message to the Sheikh of Timbuctoo: Barth had to be expelled from the town at once. The Fulani had strengthened their hold on Timbuctoo since Laing's day, and the Tuareg were correspondingly weaker. El Backay, delighted at receiving an ambassador from England, an honour which had both surprised and impressed the townspeople, decided to defy the order. His haughty reply was: 'The stranger is in my hand. You must cut it off before you can take him.' Barth almost certainly owed his life to this man; had he been expelled, he probably would have met the same fate as had Laing. Many attempts were made by the authorities of the town to get el Backay to change his mind; there was increasing alarm about the consequences of the Fulani hearing of the delay; but the Sheik refused to be moved.

All this time Barth was virtually under house arrest. He was only able to study the town from the terrace of his house; he considered even this dangerous. The only occasions he left the house were to visit el Backay next door.

The situation became so tense that the two men, host and guest, quitted the city for the desert. Barth had stayed a month in Timbuctoo; he had seen nothing of it apart from his arrival and departure, and most of the time he had been suffering from fever or rheumatism—in fact, his health was at its worst during his time at Timbuctoo. He wrote to a relative:

What I have most suffered under latterly is the total absence of milk, which, with coffee, has been my only food for a considerable time past. Oh, if I could but once more partake of the pleasures of your table! This hope keeps up my spirits sometimes.

El Backay had a small encampment outside the city limits, and this Barth now made his headquarters; from here he visited the city from time to time, sometimes for a few hours, sometimes for several days, according to the political climate.

El Backay's brothers also accorded him some support—and difficult religious arguments. Barth had left Tripoli a man less than customarily religious for his times, but as the journey progressed he became more and more religious; he had a great deal of practice in defending his faith. But el Backay's nephew, the son of the man who had relieved Laing of most of his remaining possessions, was hostile to Barth.

Barth was able to examine the mosques, study the life of the town, and inquire after ancient documents. That his researches were not always extensive was because he had continually to care for his own safety. One day a deputation of Tuareg arrived: 'They entered into a warm dispute with me on the subject of religion.' Barth, partly through the traditional good relations the Muktar family enjoyed with the Tuareg, was able to satisfy these fierce and suspicious people —more so than any previous Christian traveller, or many of those since—and soon they were his allies. The Tuareg still enjoying command over the approaches to Timbuctoo, Barth was in a happier position. Four weeks later an armed band of Fulani entered Timbuctoo

. . . a numerous troop on horseback and on foot, among whom were ten musketeers. They marched past my house on purpose, although the direct road from Kabara did not lead that way, in order to frighten me, while I, with the intention of showing them that they had entirely failed in their object, opened the door of my house, displaying in the hall all my firearms, and my people close at hand ready to use them.

This was the prelude to further pressure from the Fulani to get Barth to go. But neither the German nor his courageous host thought it wise for him to leave yet.

Barth spent much time writing letters, all in his uniformly neat and tidy hand, with blue envelopes proudly marked 'Timbuctoo' in the top left corner. They were mostly filled, to the last centimetre of the last page, with information about place-names, tribes, produce, glossaries and similar matters. When he broke away from this, it was usually to mention his difficulties at getting away or to satisfy himself with a few critical blows at Timbuctoo. About the city he wrote practically nothing, which was strange as he had come so far to report on it. It is clear from these letters that Barth, who had

read Caillié, still found Timbuctoo an anti-climax. He
detested the place as much as Clapperton and himself had
loathed Kano. Slavery was going on there on a large scale.
The market, he thought, was better than in Kano, but, far
from being flooded with gold, there was a scarcity of coin,
salt being in common currency: even cowrie shells were
'extremely scarce' and dollars 'scarcely accepted'. Sansanding,
not Timbuctoo, was 'the great market-place of the Western
Sudan'.

You will have heard, I think, of my happy arrival in this ill-
famed place.* It is now almost three months that I stay here. . . .
Patiently am I at present awaiting my hour of departure, which I
hope may not be very far.

Certainly it would have been a great thing to go as far as that
place [Sansanding] and disclose the whole character of nature and
the life of man on this remarkable line between Sansanding and
Timbuctoo, but as well as my bodily strength, my means are
exhausted and I thank God the Almighty if He grants me but safe
return home.

Amongst other things they have smoking a capital crime, so
that even in Timbuctoo, except near the house of el Backay, a man
smoking is in great danger than in the streets of Berlin [*sic*]. The
whole town does consist of houses built of mud, for the greater part
only one storey high. . . . Certainly the mixed population of this
place for itself is not able to repulse any attacks . . . at least twice
as large when the Songhai empire was in its prime. . . . My situation
is certainly not a very pleasant one, but it may all end well.

The Songhai have some interest for history, though notwithstanding excellent historical works which they possess there are
few among them who have read them; the history of the Songhai
empire, of which I have sent lately my extracts to Europe, will, I
hope, create considerable interest in the scientific world.

Beside my other labours, I am at present busily employed in
making a complete vocabulary of the Temashirt [Tamashek] or
the language of the Imoshar [Tuareg], which I find rich and very
interesting.

*The news that Barth had safely reached Timbuctoo came from the British
Vice-Consul at Ghadames, who heard of it when a caravan arrived from Tuat;
it did not, in fact, reach London till more than four months after this letter.
Barth normally wrote excellent English, but the tensions of this time seem for
once to have effected the style, although never the incomparable presentation,
of his material, maps and sketches.

It seems not quite impossible, after all, that I shall finally leave this town, of which I am greatly tired, in a very few days. May the Merciful God grant me a safe return; my way is a long and difficult one. I shall drink a glass of water from the Niger upon your health. . . .

I must say that, I myself not trading and not inquiring therefore in a direct way, the interests of the Arab merchants have preserved my life and my liberty during my stay in this place merely with a loaded gun in my hand and a pair of loaded pistols in my girdle, else I would have fallen a sacrifice to the intrigues of hostile men long ago. . . . In a couple of days I shall leave this town which it was my warmest desire to leave many months ago.

Despite his denial of trading, Barth had sent a short note to the Foreign Office in which he said:

Full security for English trade from all sides.*

After a near-riot, Barth, some Tuareg and el Backay fled to another encampment near the town. There followed one of the biggest events in Timbuctoo for many years. A moonlight conference took place. Bland as ever, Barth noted: 'The spectacle formed by this multifarious host, thronging among the sand-hills in the pale moonlight, was highly interesting, and would have been more so to me if I could have been a tranquil observer of the scene; but as I was the chief cause of this disturbance. . . .' Messages were sent back and forth between the various parties, and eventually it was decided that Barth could be allowed to stay at the camp, but el Backay and his brothers would not allow him to re-enter the town unless the Fulani withdrew their force.

This was the end of the six months during which Barth, by now one of the most famous men in the western Sudan, had gone in and out of Timbuctoo. Although everyone was now anxious for Barth to leave the area, not least the explorer himself, it was another eight weeks before Barth was finally able to successfully extricate himself from the web of

---

*Extracts from seven letters: 27.11.53 (British Museum Manuscripts); 2.10.53 (Foreign Office Papers, Public Record Office); 15.12.53 (P.R.O.); 22.1.54 (British Museum); 26.2.54, P.S., 13.3.54 (British Museum); 15.3.54 (Public Record Office); 3.1.54 (Public Record Office). 'Well worth publication,' Barth noted hopefully at the end of one letter.

intrigue and rivalries into which he had thoughtlessly flung himself.

He would go home the only way he knew: the way he had come. It was a trail of some 2,700 miles as the crow flew, but in the end it would take him, he hoped, to Tripoli and to Europe once more.

*

Soon after Barth had left Timbuctoo, a parcel was sent after him. It contained letters dated a year and a quarter previously: from Lord John Russell (Foreign Secretary),* Lord Clarendon, the Prussian Minister in London, and from various other officials. To Barth's dismay, there were no personal letters at all—only a copy of the *Athenaeum*, fifteen months old. From the official letters Barth received encouragement, authority to negotiate trade treaties on behalf of the British Government, and the news that another British expedition, led by Dr. Edward Vogel, also a young German scholar, was to be sent into Central Africa. Vogel, at the Prussian Minister's urgent pleadings, was being sent to replace Richardson. Understandably Barth was amazed that the letters had reached him. They had followed him via the Sahara, Bornu and Sokoto. Although the outer cover of the packet had been taken off, the seal of the inner cover was still intact.

The party travelled along the north bank of the Niger for many miles. After seven weeks, Barth crossed the river in a boat; it was here that he parted with el Backay, who had been his faithful and courageous protector for so long. The Sheikh's last words were an exhortation to the guides not to argue with Barth, and to have 'regard to the rate of progress in the journey, as he knew that I was impatiently looking forward to my home'. Now that he had seen Timbuctoo and had his report of it, Barth for the first time seems to have lost much interest in his travels: all he wanted was to get back to Europe.

***

*Unknown to Barth, Russell, who had succeeded Palmerston at the Foreign Office, had resigned within forty-eight hours of writing this letter. He was succeeded by Clarendon, his great rival.

Having landed on the far side of the river, he fired two shots as a signal to his friend of his safe landing. Barth had el Backay to thank for his life, just as Laing had been so generously aided by the Sheikh's father. If there was a noble family in the Sahara, it was that of el Muktar.

Nearly two months later Barth was back in Sokoto, which he had left sixteen months previously. Seven weeks after that he was in Kano. In both Sokoto and Kano he spent only a few days. In the Hausa country he found none of the supplies which he had left for his return—owing to reports that he was dead.* Once again he was hopelessly in debt. Within two weeks of leaving Kano, Barth had one of the most extraordinary experiences of his expedition.

I saw advancing towards me a person of strange aspect; a young man of very fair complexion, dressed in a robe like the one I wore myself, and with a white turban wound thickly round his head. He was accompanied by two or three blacks, likewise on horseback. One of them I recognized as my servant Madi, whom, on setting out for Kukawa, I had left in the house as a guardian. As soon as he saw me, he told the young man that I was 'Abd el Kerim', in consequence of which Mr. Vogel (for he it was) rushed forward and, taken by surprise as both of us were, we gave each other a hearty reception from horseback. I had not the remotest idea of meeting him.

Vogel had left Tripoli on June 27, five months previously. He had been escorted as far as Murzuk by Frederick Warrington, who, according to the Consul-General in Tripoli, had been 'virtually leader and head of the mission' up to that point. Vogel had somewhat hastily reported Barth's death, word of which reached Europe soon after Christmas, 1854— to the great annoyance of the 'dead man'. Barth had written to Vogel believing he might be waiting for him at Kukawa, but Vogel had been unable to read the Arabic address, and had kept it unopened, waiting till he met someone who could read it.

The two men dismounted, 'in the midst of this inhospitable forest', and sat together on the ground. Barth had some coffee made. He learnt from Vogel that the supplies at Kukawa which he had so carefully left were all gone.

---

*His obituary had already been published in Berlin.

But the news of the want of pecuniary supplies did not cause me so much surprise as the report which I received from him that he did not possess a single bottle of wine. For, having now been for more than three years without a drop of any stimulant except coffee, and having suffered severely from frequent attacks of fever and dysentery, I had an insuperable longing for the juice of the grape.

Barth was unlikely to have been mollified by the news that Vogel was on his way to Zinder in order to check and improve on the situation of that place, which Barth had already given. Vogel was an astronomer; from him the British Government hoped to receive more exact calculations than they had received from any explorer hitherto. He was the first white man Barth had seen since the death of Overweg more than two years before, and the first person he had been able to speak to in his native tongue in that time. After only two hours together, the explorers parted.

Barth arrived at Kukawa twelve days later. He had hardly had a day of rest since leaving Timbuctoo. He was surprised to find, in his house there, two British soldiers: Corporal James F. Church and Private John Maguire, both of the Corps of Sappers and Miners. They had come out with Vogel but, having had a tremendous row with them, he had preferred not to mention them. The soldiers, it seems, had found the desert-crossing rather more rigorous than they had expected. Two had been supplied, at the request of the Foreign Office ('two capable and trustworthy sappers and miners to accompany a young German'), on the personal recommendation of Lord Raglan, Master-General of the Ordnance. They had come out with Vogel from England, but one man went sick almost immediately on arrival at Tripoli and went home. Maguire, selected from thirty-six volunteers, was a replacement from Malta. The temptation for these soldiers, more poor than intrepid, was the gratuity of up to £15 which they would receive on their return to England, as well as special pay accumulating during their absence.

Owing to the severity of his indebtedness, Barth could not get out of Kukawa for four months. But three weeks of this agonizing wait were passed pleasantly with Vogel, who had returned to Kukawa. Vogel then set out on an expedition with Maguire, to fill in some of the blank spaces Barth had left on the map, and to explore the area between Chad and the Nile. Barth had taught the soldier how to use a compass as Vogel 'could not be induced to undertake such a task, as it would have interfered greatly with the collecting of plants, which, besides making astronomical observations, was his chief object'. Neither man was ever seen again. Edward Vogel was twenty-seven. Of Maguire practically nothing is known. This poor British redcoat, who had been taught to take a bearing but could hardly write his own name, disappeared in Africa in the service of a science about which he knew little, and in a land as remote from his own as some hideous nightmare.

It had been decided that Corporal Church, who was in a rebellious mood, should return to Europe with Barth. They crossed the desert on camels in mid-summer, with temperatures of 112°. The unfortunate Church found Barth a more severe master than Vogel. They travelled back on Clapperton's and Denham's old route.

I desired Corporal Church, who felt assured that Captain Clapperton had indicated the mountain chain on the west by mistake, to ascend the slope of the chain in order to convince himself that that meritorious traveller had not been misled in such a strange manner.

Frederick Warrington was waiting for them at Murzuk. He had prepared a feast, but Barth could not eat it because he would not sit down at the same table with Church. After Murzuk, Barth had to take a little-used route owing to political disturbances; he and Church were the first Europeans to travel to Tripoli this way. The speed with which Barth made his journey from Kukawa to Tripoli—desert all the way—is an indication of his urgency; he completed it in less than four months, an extraordinary achievement.

I set out on my last march on the African soil in order to enter the town of Tripoli, and although the impression made upon my mind by the rich vegetation of the gardens which surround the town, after the long journey through the desert waste, was very great, yet infinitely greater was the effect produced upon me by the wide expanse of the sea, which, in the bright sunshine of this intermediate zone, spread out with a tint of the darkest blue. . . . It was market-day. . . . Amidst this busy scene, in the most dazzling sunshine, with the open sea and the ships on my right, I entered the snow-white walls of the town and was most kindly received by all former friends.

It was September 28, 1855. Barth had been given up for dead nearly a year before. He had been away five years, five months.

*

After his recent experiences, and particularly the crossing of the desert in summer, most men would have been glad of many weeks of rest and recuperation. But Barth delayed only four days in Tripoli. Soon he was installed in Long's Hotel, Bond Street.

Within four weeks of being in the dreaded el Hamra Hamada, the northern Sahara, he was discoursing with Palmerston in No. 10 Downing Street.* Barth was enthusiastically received in London. He was awarded the Order of the Bath by Queen Victoria—a rare and distinguished honour for a foreigner who was neither statesman nor royalty, but a worthy acknowledgement of his loyal and faithful work for England after Richardson's death. He received an honorary degree from the University of Oxford. He received the Gold Medal of the Geographical Society of Paris. He was recognized as the foremost North African traveller of his day. He stayed with the King of Prussia at his palace.

Barth brought back final and incontrovertible evidence that the Timbuctoo legend had been a myth: that the 'Timbuctoo Rush' had wasted lives: that it was a dreary and unimportant place unworthy of its fame. Barth, unwilling to belittle the impact of his own performance, did not underline this, but he was a scientist, and honest. The Caillié controversy quickly faded out; the Frenchman had been right after all. It was perhaps Barth's role as an iconoclast that first turned feelings against him.

The glory did not last long.

Barth's great work was published, in five volumes, in 1857; for its publication, Barth had received the generous

---

*It was one of Palmerston's last interviews. In six weeks the Prime Minister was dead.

grant from the Government of £4,250 (he himself described that as 'handsome'). He had also received £1,250 in publication rights from Longmans and Gotha. It was immediately translated into French and German. It was entirely typical of Barth that he should undertake the laborious task of a condensed German translation himself. On the English publication, Barth wrote to Clarendon, Foreign Secretary: 'I shall never forget the kindly interest taken in my proceedings by Your Lordship, as well as by Lord Palmerston and by so many other eminent men in this country.'

The book was full of self-congratulation, which the English were not accustomed to in their explorers; neither did they care for his condescending remarks about the work of others, most of whom had lost their lives. He was always harping on the importance of his own discoveries, which he had, in fact, overrated; the discovery of the Benue River, in Hausa, was his only major contribution, but his detailed descriptions filled in vast gaps, especially in regard to the readjustment of the slave trade. There was a streak of pomposity and conceit in Barth, and the English never really understood him. Barth felt, rightly, that the extent of his travels gave him something to be conceited about. He had no time for false modesty. Although he had returned with nothing startling, no man had accumulated so much material on that part of Africa, and no man before (and few, if any, after) had travelled so far. His information was remarkably wide and various; its standard of accuracy was not perfect, but it was high.

Barth believed his journey and personal contacts in Bornu, Hausa and Sudan had opened up Central Africa to Europe. He could not understand why the British, in his view hopelessly languid, did not do more to take advantage of his work.

He became involved in a petty row with the War Office about the extent of the gratuity which should be paid to Corporal Church: Barth, backed by the Foreign Office, having written a careful but not ungenerous recommendation, and Church having defended himself with unconcealed animosity and malice.* Two freed slaves whom Barth had brought with

---

*Despite this very acrimonious business, there is not a word of criticism of Church in Barth's book, and he makes Vogel accept at least equal responsibility for the collapse of discipline and trust in the expedition. Church received a reward and Overweg's sister a pension.

him from Chad soon tired of civilization and were returned to Tripoli at Government expense, much to the relief of the out-raged British public, unconvinced of their freedom. Barth became increasingly bitter. Even at the best of times he had never suffered fools—and he considered that the world's population was mainly compounded of fools; his apparent rudeness and his touchiness made him enemies as thick as the flies in Kano. When his friends applied for a chair at a German university, it was refused him, and he was not made a professor until just before the end of his life—having already been made president of the Berlin Geographical Society. The King of Prussia suggested he should be Consul at Damascus, but he failed to get the post. He tried to get backing for a Polar expedition, but was unable to find it.

He thought longingly of Africa and the Desert. It was the same *nostalgie*, the urge to return to something known and understood which no one else around him knew or under-stood, that had afflicted so many before him: Mungo Park, Lyon, Caillié. . . . But for Barth it was cruelly magnified, for his character knew little patience and resignation was foreign to him.

'I have been accustomed to the desert,' he wrote, 'to infinite spaces, where I have not had to worry about the trivialities that stifle men. . . . I deplore finding myself here, in chains.' It was a cry from a not ignoble heart.

7 · Epilogue

WAS the 'Timbuctoo Rush' ended at last? Whether from habit, folly, witlessness or innate conservatism, the statesmen of Britain and France continued to harbour a delight in the aura that had come to surround its name. It was, as they now knew, a town that was not only of comparatively little importance as compared to other places visited by Barth and Clapperton, but was poor and was dying: nevertheless, they coveted it with little less spirit than Portugal had done centuries before, when it was supposed to be a fabulous city of culture and gold.

In the next half century the narrow nationalism which Richardson and Barth had so deplored gained further control over Saharan activities.

French interest was stimulated by a Moroccan Jew, Mordecai Abi-Serour, who lived in Timbuctoo from 1860 to 1862, in extreme danger, and under the protection of el Backay. He accumulated a considerable fortune, which titillated the appetites of French merchants in Agadir. On his return he was sent to Paris. There he was taught how to use various instruments by the Geographical Society, who took care of him. Abi-Serour became a faithful servant to geography and science in Morocco, but he never returned to Timbuctoo.

Barth was a man with a very pronounced sense of honour and personal integrity. Although he detested nationalism, he considered that his loyalties, as far as the Western Sudan was concerned, lay with England. He was therefore incensed, on his return to London, to discover that the Royal Geographical Society had been the centre of insinuations about his travels. Rumours about reckless expenditure in the mission had been spread by men who had never seen Africa; these had led to a question in the House of Commons in June, 1854.* Having

---

*Richardson's I.O.U.s of 1850 were still arriving in London 1856.

suffered from the lack of funds for so long, this was particularly galling to Barth. Also he had often written to the Prussian Minister in London about affairs which he insisted were purely 'of a scientific character'—i.e. not concerning trade—and this had engendered much suspicion. Once one of Barth's letters to the Minister had been opened at the Royal Geographical Society. And Barth had found that it was difficult to get back some of his despatches and maps, which he had needed for his book. Throughout this matter the Foreign Office supported Barth, and wrote in the strongest terms to the Royal Geographical Society. Barth never forgot this loyalty of the Foreign Office, but relations between him and even it deteriorated. He also quarrelled with his friend, the cartographer A. H. Petermann, who had always supported him against the critical faction of the Royal Geographical Society. Barth's advice in sending out further materials to Vogel (or to recall him) and of sending presents to the various chiefs and princes he had met was adopted. And when Vogel and Maguire were reported to have been murdered it was he who first advised the Government. Reports of Vogel's death reached London first. The Royal Geographical Society thereupon suggested that Maguire should go to Timbuctoo 'in order to fix the position of that place'—an obvious snub to Barth, whose co-ordinates had been criticized.* The Government acted on this, but its message never reached Maguire; reports of his murder reached London five months later, in August, 1857†. He had been killed seven months before, while attempting to get back to Tripoli.

Barth had brought a letter from el Backay in which the Sheikh asked the British Government 'to rid our land of the French troops'. Although el Backay's fears were somewhat premature—there being rumours but no troops—his sentiments were exactly what the British Government liked to

---

*In a letter from Timbuctoo (Public Record Office, 2.10.53) Barth gave the position as 18° 30′ 3″–18°45′N., 1° 45′ W., which was wrong by about 200 miles. After consultations with Petermann, he changed this for his book to 17° 37′ N. and 3° 5′W., which was more accurate.

†Another German, Maurice von Beurmann, was sent to confirm the deaths of Vogel and Maguire and trace their journals. He was strangled, in the interior, in 1863. An expedition planned by Barth in 1861 was also unsuccessful. In all, seven expeditions went to trace Vogel, including that of the Frenchman, Biny.

hear. He promised, moreover, to gain 'a letter of immunity' for the British from the Fulani Sultan himself. The Foreign Secretary sent a formal reply, via Tripoli:

> I would have you know that the Queen of England has heard the report of Doctor Barth (named Abdel Kerim among the Arabs), who visited you at her command, in your country, to renew the friendship existing between you and us, and to make you known to her. . . . The letters you sent by him have arrived. We have read them and well understand what they contain. It has been a great pleasure to us. The hopes of the English Government have been understood by you. What we wish is to open the eyes of the Arabs of the south to commerce and all appertaining to it, and we are now aware that you have looked upon our mission with pleasure and have accepted our friendship with joy. . . . Your friend, Clarendon, Minister of the English Government.*

But el Backay was in no position to open up negotiations with the British. He was fully occupied taking care of himself. The British, for their part, were engaged in a war with Russia. As the years went on, el Backay's hopes of the English, who would doubtless have placed him in power, began to fade. Barth did what he could. Among others he wrote to, recommending the Sheikh and his family, was the French Governor of Senegal. By a remarkable chance, when his letter arrived at St. Louis, one of the family had just been arrested as a spy, for which he would have been killed. Barth's letter was enough to have him acquitted. Thus Barth's debt was to some extent repaid. El Backay himself died in 1864, still waiting for the English to come, his influence having dwindled to almost nothing.†

The following year Heinrich Barth died in Berlin: unpopular, forgotten by the public, but respected at last as the

---

*Letter discovered by a French traveller, Dubois, in Timbuctoo. There is a draft of another letter from Clarendon, written by Barth, in the Public Record Office: this is similar in many points to the above, but speaks of sending boats to Timbuctoo up the Niger. This letter may not have been sent, but when el Backay's nephew went on a mission to Tripoli he was told that a British ship would be sent up the river. Another of el Backay's nephews was trying, meanwhile, to make a treaty with the French in Algiers.

†When Dubois visited the city in 1896, two of el Backay's sons were still alive, but lived elsewhere. Only one descendant of the Muktar's lived at Timbuctoo, where he enjoyed a modest position.

leading authority in the world on his subject. He died of a stomach disorder, probably a result of his great journey, at the early age of forty-four.

*

Amazingly, and despite the wide readership of Barth's definite account, explorers and adventurers were not yet finished with Timbuctoo. And the strange lure of that place had not by any means ended its long list of deaths. A wealthy Dutchwoman, Alexandrine Tinné, departed for the city after an unhappy love affair. She penetrated from the Upper Nile, and almost reached Murzuk; she was murdered on August 1, 1869, by Tuareg, aged thirty-three. They had suspected her water container held gold or money. In 1871, Paul Seleillet, a railway enthusiast, left Algeria for Timbuctoo; he got no further than the edge of the desert. Eugene Joubert and C.-N. Dourneaux-Duperré were murdered by their guides south of Ouargla, on their way to Timbuctoo in February, 1874. In 1877, von Bary left Tripoli for Timbuctoo, via Aïr; he also was murdered.

But these were not the major travellers, who, from the time of Richardson and Barth, were increasingly the tools of national ambitions. In the Sahara the French were now becoming as active as they were on the West Coast. The well-known 'carving-up' of the African continent was soon to begin, and the French and British particularly were anxious to discover which parts of the joint were worth having on their own plates. Of the two nations, the French were the most enthusiastic. The British Government, on the other hand, found itself pressed by the expansion of its traders and merchants, and by events in Egypt; ironically, it got some of the best of the joint. On January 2, 1882, the Colonial Secretary wrote to Gladstone: 'We have already quite enough territory on the West Coast.'

*

Barth was always generous in his advice to young explorers, and three Germans soon followed him as great explorers of the Sahara; Gerhardt Rohlfs, Gustav Nachtigal and Erwin von Bary. His greatest disciple was Henri Duveyrier, who went to live among the Tuareg. It was the brilliant but starry-eyed reports of this famous French writer on the desert and its nomads which were to result in so much unnecessary bloodshed and death a few years later. In 1876 three White Fathers left Paris for Timbuctoo in order to convert the city to Christianity. They were murdered in the desert.

It was Duveyrier who advised Oskar Lenz, a young German born in Leipzig, before the latter set out for Timbuctoo. Lenz was the only white man to see Timbuctoo between Barth and the French conquest. His sponsors were the African Society of Germany, for whom he had already visited the Gabon. Their commission was to study the Atlas mountains, but Lenz was more interested in Timbuctoo. Duveyrier was no doubt partly responsible for his somewhat lighthearted departure from Morocco in 1880. He was determined to travel in as much comfort as possible, disguised as a rich Turkish doctor. He took with him across the Sahara an expensive mattress. He wrote: 'I was never able to persuade myself to give up using white sheets during my journey. I continued doing so to the end.' Despite the desperate lack of water which afflicted the caravan for long stretches of the desert, Lenz insisted on his daily shave, even if it meant cutting down on his ration of drinking water. On April 10 he reached Tindouf, the first European to do so. At Taoudeni he found the salt mines deserted, presumably due to the ever-feared non-arrival of a caravan. At Arouan he found that the Sheikh had clothes, underwear, numerous medicine bottles and books, which had belonged to Gordon Laing fifty years before.

Lenz arrived in Timbuctoo, with a salt caravan from Taoudeni, on July 1, 1880. He received the hospitality which the native people of that place had always shown to travellers. He, however, was less bothered by Fulani rulers than Laing and Barth had been. He stayed there for twenty days, during which he accumulated a mass of material, most of it trivial. He came to the conclusion that Timbuctoo's importance had been greatly exaggerated. He described the stay as 'some of the best days of my life', which was either untrue or eccentric in the extreme. On his departure, the Sheikhs came to pay him a farewell visit—apparently impressed by his indomitable cheerfulness.

Lenz decided to return a round-about way, via Sokoto, to Senegal: it was a decision which he much regretted. He was continually robbed, and had to pay ransom at many points in order to continue. He arrived in Senegal penniless and destitute. The clothing which remained to him was in rags; it was barely covered by a tattered overcoat. Lenz said to the surprised French officer in charge of the first settlement that he reached: 'The coat may be old, but it was made in Paris.'*

*

While Lenz was trudging back to civilization from Timbuctoo, one of the most appalling disasters of the Sahara was taking place.

On December 4, 1880, Lieut.-Colonel Paul Flatters had led an impressive force out of the Algerian oasis of Ouargla: eleven French engineers and soldiers, seventy-seven *tirailleurs* of the First and Third Regiments and irregular native troops, and five guides (ninety-three men in all), and over three hundred camels, with supplies for many months: all for the most powerful expedition France had sent into the desert. Its objective was to trace a suitable route for the great dream of France: the Trans-Saharan Railway—a development which would link Algeria with the South, including Timbuctoo, and which would, it was said, do for France what the railways had done for North America.

Flatters, in his late thirties, was the son of a Franco-German sculptor. He had an imposing appearance and a good reputation as a soldier. He was considered an expert on the desert. Many years before, he had wanted to lead an expedition to Timbuctoo; his application had been turned down.

---

*Lenz wrote a meticulous and lengthy account of his journey in two volumes, and entitled it *Timbuktu*, but since Caillié and Barth had exploded the myth there was little scholarly interest in it. It was translated into French two years later, but has never been translated into English. In 1885 he penetrated far up the Congo. He became a respected academic in Prague and in Vienna, where he died in 1925.

Over the years his pleasing style had become deceptive: he was in reality, tired, depressed and fatalistic. The column arrived at a remote spot named Inzelman. The last well, at Amguid, was eight days behind them; prior to that, there had been a twelve-days journey from the well at Hassi Messegnem. Despite the careful preparations, water was dangerously low. The whole idea of a railway was becoming remote. On January 29, 1881, a despatch left the expedition from Inzelman:

Tout va bien. Tout le monde est bien portant. Nous espérons revenir par l'Atlantique vers le mois de juillet ou août.

It was the last message. A party of Tuareg had been watching the progress of the expedition; they now suggested that Flatters should go forward with a party to get water from some wells ahead; he should take most of the camels with him, to bring back the water; the remainder of the expedition could wait with the unloaded supplies until the party returned with camels and water.

The mission had travelled some four hundred miles; it was thirsty; it was beginning to wilt. Flatters decided to accept the advice of the Tuareg. He thereby committed the fatal error, in the circumstances, of splitting his force.

With six other Frenchmen and thirty-one *tirailleurs* Flatters went on ahead; Lieutenant Dianous was left in command of the column. Flatters paid for his folly. He and all the Frenchmen with him were shot down or cut to pieces by a Tuareg onslaught; only a few of the native *tirailleurs* managed to escape and get back to the main column. The remaining *tirailleurs* were taken prisoner.

The few camels which remained with Dianous were loose, and they were driven away by the Tuareg. An awful decision now faced the young officer. The only thing that was certain was that they could not stay where they were, or they would all soon perish of thirst. The Tuareg hovered around, and waited. Dianous made the decision to withdraw to Ouargla—on foot.

Whether or not his decision was inevitable, it was virtually suicidal; more so, perhaps, than attempting to trick the Tuareg themselves into a trap, or to try to bring them to battle. Dianous is known to have spent a long time making his agonizing decision, and it is no wonder. On camels, and with guides, the journey had taken them nearly two and a half months: now they had neither. On February 18, 1881, the march began.*

Dianous was a better commander than Flatters. He sent out scouts to watch his flanks and the route ahead. They reported that a large force of Tuareg were riding a parallel course, although out of sight. It was obvious that the Tuareg intended to delay their attack on the French force until it was no longer able to defend itself. For the only thing Dianous had plenty of was ammunition. After about a week the column had nearly reached the next big well, but before they did so they were given a supply of dates by the Tuareg, apparently out of pity. The dates were poisoned. The men ran about in the desert raving and screaming. Dianous managed to get the column to move on. Many of the men were in agony: some were half-mad: some tried to kill themselves: one of the Frenchmen died.

Two days later the column had almost reached the wells. Then they saw a thick line of mounted Tuareg facing them. The Tuareg waited a long time, and then they charged. Dianous had his men drawn up in classical formation and, starving but still disciplined, they fired their volleys to such effect that the attack was fought off. The Tuareg had suffered heavily; their reaction was to slaughter those prisoners whom they had kept in servitude since the attack on Flatters. While this was going on in sight of the column, Dianous was killed by a sharpshooter's bullet. Not long afterwards there was only one Frenchman remaining, a sergeant. Nearly three hundred miles of desert lay between the survivors and the French post at Ouargla. They were not yet even half-way.

They ate lizards; chewed their leather belts and equipment; and by taking a zig-zag course shook off the Tuareg, who were now straying from their own territory. The dangers

---

*The furthest extent of Flatters' expedition appears to have been about 25° 6′N., 3° 5′ 5″ E., almost due South of Ouargla, in the wilderness near the Tarrili N'ajjer. De Prorock said he found the spot, between the wars, at Bir Garama, a valley in Tin Tarabin; his historical accounts are generally inaccurate. The official Commission into the disaster gave the area as Éguéré, haut Ighargar.

were thirst and hunger. Stragglers were left to die, and as day followed hellish day the column slowly thinned. The bones of a camel found lying in the sand were ground to powder and devoured. Then dead men were eaten. Then dying men were killed by those impatient for the miserable flesh. The column was over two hundred and fifty miles from Ouargla when the sergeant, almost too weak to walk, was cut down by the *tirailleurs*.

On March 28, 1881, the remnants of the Flatters Mission for the Trans-Saharan Railway staggered into the village of Hassi-Messegnem. In the following weeks a few appeared at French outposts in southern Algeria. They were half-mad, but from their garbled and sometimes incoherent accounts the story of the expedition and its fate was built.

The effect on French opinion was great and traumatic. It ended for over half a century serious exploitation of the Sahara. Once more interest was confined to the southern periphery and to Timbuctoo, but now the interest was more in territorial acquisition than in trade for its own sake.

It was in 1881 that the French conquest of large parts of West Africa began, and Timbuctoo was one of the goals. The English, who had lost their chance after Barth, were busy, under G. T. Goldie and Joseph Thomson, in acquiring the richest sectors remaining for colonization, the Lower Niger—now Nigeria. They were content to leave the desert to France.*

*

The French conquest of the Western Sudan was made from a series of forts which were built to link the Niger to the Senegal: the Senegal having long been under French influence. The foundation of this plan was carried out by a Captain J. S. Galliéni.† Galliéni gained for France what Barth had

---

*Although as late as 1890 the British had an unofficial post at Cape Juby, which they had held since the seventeenth century, but they eventually left even that to Spain. During the next twenty years the desert was more fully explored by Fernand Foureau.

†In 1914 General Galliéni was Military Commander of Paris. He is famed for the story of the mobilization of a fleet of Paris taxi-cabs which, by transporting an extra division to the front, influenced the Battle of the Marne at a critical point.

tried to get Clarendon to gain for Britain: a treaty for the exclusive rights of commerce on the Upper Niger. For this he was awarded, like Laing, Caillié and Barth, the coveted Gold Medal of the Geographical Society of Paris, although his contribution to science and exploration were not great. But the French Government, and more especially the Army, were not content with trade alone. In 1884 a gunboat was brought to the area in sections and launched on the Niger.* Germany, which acquired bases at Togoland and the Cameroons, was also showing an interest.

Lieut.-Colonel T. P. E. Bonnier was in temporary command in the Upper Niger area, but he was fully engaged in operations behind Sierra Leone. In command on the Niger itself was Naval Lieutenant Boiteux. This young man, like so many before him, was obsessed with the idea of reaching Timbuctoo—an obsession which had so often proved fatal, and was to do so again. He wanted to be the first to raise the tricolour in Timbuctoo. On his first attempt, orders from Bonnier brought him back. On his second attempt, he was at first successful.

In December, 1893, Boiteux set out with two gunboats and two barges. He steamed up to Kabara. There he negotiated with the Sheikhs and merchants of Timbuctoo, who explained that they were—as they had been for so long—only too happy to be conquered in order to escape from the oppression of the Tuareg.

The river being high at that time, Boiteux was able to get the barges up to Timbuctoo. Leaving most of his force at Kabara, he went up to the city with two guns and eighteen troops. He had forgotten the experience of Flatters, who also had split his force in face of Tuareg. A few days later the entire French force at Kabara was slaughtered by Tuareg. Boiteux and his force, who heard the firing in the distance but sallied forth too late, were on their own.

When Bonnier heard of the besieged force at Timbuctoo, he was four hundred miles away. His orders were to renew

---

*Eight years later Lieutenant Mizon sailed up the Niger and the Benue, terrorized the area and tried to claim Northern Nigeria for France. In 1889, Camille Douls was murdered 75 miles S.W. of In Salah when on a semi-official French mission to Timbuctoo.

7*

operations in Senegal; he decided to disregard them. He also divided his force, but more wisely: one column was to march along the northern bank of the river to Kabara; the other was to proceed up the Niger itself in three hundred canoes. Bonnier went with the waterborne detachment; they reached Kabara first and relieved the anxious Boiteux at Timbuctoo. A detachment was left in the town, at a fort which Boiteux had built; over the little fort flew the tricolour at last.

Bonnier then marched bravely out of the town to do battle with the Tuareg—yet another foolish blunder. That night, January 14, 1894, the force formed square, under a brilliant, star-lit sky. There was much celebrating and drinking; 'having spent the evening gaily', the majority of the force prepared to sleep in the open. Before dawn the Tuareg swooped down: fourteen Europeans and about sixty *tirailleurs* were massacred in wild scenes of confusion and panic. Only one officer escaped; at the head of about seventy survivors, he managed to reach Timbuctoo.

Four weeks later the column which had been marching up the river reached Timbuctoo safely. It had covered 813 kilometres in six and a half weeks. Its leader was an efficient, ponderous, careful officer: exactly the kind of man to deal with the Tuareg, who had gained a fearsome reputation out of all proportion to their strength owing to a succession of French officers ignoring basic military principles. His name was Major Joseph Joffre.* In an action before Timbuctoo he left a hundred and twenty Tuareg dead on the field for only one European (himself) and one Spahi wounded. In the next few days the surviving Tuareg chiefs came into the town to submit to France. Joffre's orders were to complete the occupation of Timbuctoo and its area; this he did satisfactorily. And so the 'mysterious city' became an outpost of the French Colonial Empire.

As it had for so long, this trading town of secondary

---

*Commander-in-Chief in the First World War. It was Galliéni who recommended Joffre for Chief of the General Staff in 1911. They are usually given credit together for the successful outcome of the Battle of the Marne. Joffre achieved the near impossible in writing a totally dull and boring book about his Timbuctoo adventure.

importance had claimed its usual tribute; no one place in
French West Africa claimed so many lives in its conquest.

*

It seemed at first as if French routine and order would do
something to revive the town, which had been dying for so
long. Entry to and exit from the city were no longer at the
mercy of the Tuareg. Efforts were made to restore some of
the buildings; the chief merchants refurbished their homes.
But soon *ennui*, alcohol and *cafard*, those insidious enemies of
the French colonial system, set in. The old trade with the
north dwindled away when France opened up a route connecting the Western Sudan with Senegal; soon most merchandise went that way. Only slaves and salt remained.
Timbuctoo, despite its world-wide fame, was not considered
the most desirable of postings in the service of France.

A year after the conquest, in May, 1895, the first two
White Fathers arrived. They were the first civilian Europeans to settle in the town. The White Fathers were a
militant group who went about the Sahara fully armed in the
cause of Christianity. Within a month one of the Fathers had
been converted to the life of Timbuctoo, had a young Negress
mistress and had taken to drink: the other left within seven
months. The remaining Father, August Dupuis, continued
the mission and clinic, mastered Songhoi and Tamashek, got
into trouble with the local French administration—which
considered it had prior claims to some of his female conquests
—became the greatest authority on the history of Timbuctoo,
and drank to an excess that shortly became a legend in West
Africa. It was not altogether surprising, therefore, that, when
his superiors got to hear of all this, that Father Dupuis was
recalled to Algiers. He refused to go, resigned his calling,
assumed a native name and became at first a servant of the
mission. He married a local girl, had several children and
became head of the Moslem university at the town.*

The next European civilian to visit Timbuctoo after the
arrival of the two Fathers was Felix Dubois, a journalist and

---

*Dupuis died in Timbuctoo in 1945. His wife died in 1954. A daughter lived
until recently in the same house, in the street in which Caillié stayed.

minor explorer. His book, predictably, was *Timbuctoo the Mysterious*. On May 6, 1902, a French force defeated the Tuareg in the Sahara, thus ending the power of the nomads. In 1903 the French authorities put plaques on the houses in which had stayed Laing, Caillié, Barth and Lenz. In 1909 Captain A. H. Haywood, of the Royal Artillery, obtained long leave from Sierra Leone for what he described as 'a journey of exploration'. He arrived at Timbuctoo in 1910, and his words revealed the strange hold the place still had in the imagination of men.

My feelings were those of disappointment, for I had expected a far more imposing-looking place. I had pictured to myself a town of fine Moorish buildings, minaretted palaces, and the bright appearance of an Oriental city. . . . In point of fact the general appearance of the town was very much like many others. I had seen on my journey.

He heard that Laing's papers were still in the hands of the descendants of the family which had murdered the Scotsman, but that they could not admit it for fear of French retribution; a rumour for which not an item of fact has ever been produced. The captain departed on a caravan to Gao, In Salah and Ouargla.

In the same year an official French inquiry was conducted by Bonnel de Mezières into Laing's death. Arriving at Timbuctoo, de Mezières was able to talk to direct descendants of those involved in the murder, including the eighty-two-year-old nephew of Labeida. He was taken to the place of murder, on the route to Arouan. He had excavations made under and beside a tree, and dug up bones which must have been those of Gordon Laing: medical officers at Timbuctoo confirmed that they were of a European adult. According to the old man, Labeida's only share of the booty was a golden brooch in the shape of a small cock. It was still in the family in 1910, and belonged to the assassin's grandson. Unknown to de Mezières, the brooch had been Laing's most precious possession—Emma's own charm and her parting gift.

In 1918 an air-link of the oases was proposed. An air force detachment left Ouargla in two lorries in order to organize a trial flight from In Salah to Timbuctoo. Every man in the expedition was murdered in the desert. But French aviators still dreamed of opening up the Sahara and Sudan by air. In February, 1920, the inaugural flight of a service from Algeria to Timbuctoo left Algiers. On it was the legendary General Henri Laperrine, who had consolidated the French hold over the Sahara after the Tuareg, supported by Senussi, had risen against France during the First World War. He was considered one of the greatest living experts on the desert. The plane became lost: ran out of petrol. A forced landing was made in the desert. The three men, pilot, mechanic and Laperrine, headed north, carrying cans of water. After several days the General realized his mistake and they staggered back to the aircraft, where they waited to be discovered. In the shade of the wings, the temperature was over a hundred degrees Fahrenheit. After fifteen days he died. The pilot and mechanic survived him, although mentally affected through drinking all liquids in the plane: eau d'Cologne, methylated spirits, iodine, glycerine and their own urine. The particular cruelty of the Sahara, shown again and again in history, was that only five miles to the south there was a well.

On January 7, 1923, five caterpillar-wheeled Citroen cars arrived at Timbuctoo, having crossed the desert by way of Touggourt and In Salah. Six years later the last (admitted) slave caravan crossed the desert in the opposite direction. In 1930 the African Society of London erected a plaque at the place of Laing's death; but there is still no memorial to him in his homeland, and his achievement did not, as he had hoped, 'rescue my name from oblivion'.

In 1935 the conquest of Tindouf completed the pacification of the desert. The following year Théodore Monod executed the feat of crossing the Sahara from West to East.

Despite the prestige of being a French post, Timbuctoo continued to decline. Trade with the Mediterranean fluctuated. The geographical position of Timbuctoo became, increasingly, an irrelevance. The greatest event of the year was still the annual arrival of the salt caravan from Taoudeni: eight hundred camels protected by French native troops under European officers, or by the Foreign Legion.

In 1940 the French census gave the population as 5,000. At

the height of the Songhai Empire it may have been more than 50,000.

In the nineteen-fifties some of the town was in ruins, parts of it abandoned to the encroaching sands. There were about thirty-five Europeans, mostly American missionaries and French administrators. The small air-strip near Kabara was falling into disuse. The road to Kabara again had an unenviable reputation as the haunt of brigands and a place of robbery. Slavery, both in its legalized and clandestine forms, lingered on. Prostitution was rampant, thus appearing to confirm the words of a seventeenth-century author who wrote: 'A stranger who enters Timbuctoo cannot do without women. The food and the climate provoke concupiscence and put men in condition to perform prodigious feats.'

In 1960 the independent state of Mali achieved independence. Timbuctoo returned to Mali rule after five and a half centuries and became a provincial centre. The most notable change this brought about was that inevitable, but expensive, symbol of nationhood: a national airline with enormous jet aeroplanes. The airfield at Timbuctoo was rebuilt; Russian jets flew in and out, often with tourists.

Whatever the tourists come for, it is not to visit a decaying, primitive and uncongenial town, where men have lived in the same sort of dwellings for a thousand years, or its poor and wretched inhabitants. It is to touch a legend: to gain a stub of a ticket, a stamp in a passport, with the name of one of the most famous place-names in the world. Sometimes they disgorge from a plane, in a party, and spend three hours drinking at the guest-house before continuing around the world. At other times they visit the houses of Caillié and Laing, surrounded by shrieking children, where they are told that these were the first white explorers to precede them. Although the myth of Timbuctoo is broken, the name of the mostly insignicant and sordid slaving post lives on with some strange attraction and power, while the memory of the men who broke themselves to undo one of the most widely held and persistent myths of history is utterly forgotten. Men die easily, but myths die hard.

It is the same city for which Major Houghton and Frederick Hornemann the student had set out alone: which Mungo Park and forty others had hoped to see before they all perished: for a glimpse of which Ledyard, Dr. Oudney, Ritchie and others with them had died; for which Belzoni, the Italian giant, had perished at last; for which Hugh Clapperton had gone to Africa a second time, only to be buried there by Lander; to the lure of which Gordon Laing had succumbed as if a moth to a lighted candle; to reach which had taken the supreme efforts of René Caillié, Heinrich Barth and Oscar Lenz, men of quite unusual determination and courage. When it was still a myth it had drawn from man nobility and displayed him at his best. Now, no longer a siren of death and terror, its dangers all long dead, it shows man only at his ridiculous. The quest for knowledge, for the trade which is said to bring civilization, for fulfilment of personal ambition, for national glory even, has become the quest for a luggage-label.

Chart

Circa 450 B.C.:	Herodotus places the source of the Nile in West Africa, and begins over 2,000 years of confusion.
Circa A.D. 150:	Ptolemy avoids Herodotus's error, but gives a lake (possibly Chad) as the source of the Niger, thus adding to the subsequent confusion.
Circa 800:	Songhai begin rise to power in Western Sudan, Found towns of Gao and Jenne.
Circa 1000:	Timbuctoo a summer camp of the Tuareg.
Circa 1100:	Timbuctoo becomes a permanent place of residence for Songhai, and a market owing to its position—the meeting-place of those who travel by water, on the Niger, and those who travel across the sands.
Circa 1300:	Timbuctoo has become a trading centre, its communications extending from the West Coast to the Mediterranean. Guinea gold exported to Europe via caravans starting from it.
1324:	Mandingo Emperor of neighbouring Mali stays at Timbuctoo with his famous caravan of great wealth. Founds a mosque.
1336:	Timbuctoo annexed to MALI EMPIRE, now at its peak, and starts era of prosperity. Timbuctoo starts becoming Muslim.
1353:	Ibn Batuta, Arab traveller, visits the city, and describes wealth of Mali Empire.
Circa 1350:	Spaniard may have visited Timbuctoo to work on the mosque.
1373:	Timbuctoo first appears on a European atlas, by Abraham Cresques of Majorca.
Circa 1400:	Tuareg gain domination of the city from declining Mali Empire. Mali-Songhai Wars.
1468:	SONGHAI conquer Tuareg and gain control of the city. Under Askia the Great, Timbuctoo reaches its zenith as a trading centre and place of learning. But Askia's capital remains at Gao.

1470:	A Florentine merchant, Benedetto Dei, visits the city. He has little to say about the place, except that 'much business is done there'.
Circa 1487:	Portuguese, Rodrigo Robelo, may have reached the town. For a century Portuguese try to establish a trade treaty with the mysterious city. The Portuguese writer, J. de Barras, in charge of his country's interests in West Africa, describes the town as 'three leagues north' of the Niger.
1496:	Askia makes the pilgrimage to Mecca, from where eminate rumours of the magnificence of his caravan—such as that he gives away 300,000 pieces of gold as alms.
1526:	Leo Africanus visits Timbuctoo, in a mission from the Sherif of Fez. Describes a fabulous court.
1530:	King John III of Portugal, influenced by reports of wealth, sends ten man mission to Timbuctoo: only one man—Pero Reinel—survives, and he may not have succeeded in reaching the town.
1546:	Songhai defeat Mali.
1565:	Another official Portuguese attempt to reach the city.
1570:	The Ortelius map marks Timbuctoo as the capital of a huge province of the same name.
1591:	Moroccan Army expedition to Timbuctoo. Defeats Songhai in March: sacks city in April. Timbuctoo in MOROCCAN EMPIRE.
Circa 1600:	Defeated Songhai no longer able to control Tuareg. Timbuctoo starts to decline.
1600:	Leo Africanus translated into famous English edition. Europe unaware that his information now superseded.
Circa 1650:	Ties with Morocco collapsing. Attempts of Mali to benefit from decline of Songhai and Moroccan Empires fail, after Mandingo Wars. TUAREG, plundering trade, assume real control for more than 200 years, with occasional bouts of resistance from Songhai, Moors, Mali. Elements of anarchy. Descendants of Moorish conquerors and Songhai intermarry and become ruling class of Timbuctoo. Population about 25,000.

Chart 199

1670: French sailor taken to Timbuctoo, and dies there in slavery.

1698: French explorer, André Brué, gives an account of the situation of Timbuctoo—from hearsay—accurate in several respects.

1788: 'The Association for the Promotion of the Discovery of the Interior of Africa', founded. Incorporated in the Royal Geographical Society (founded *1830*) in *1831*. Backs expeditions of Ledyard, Simon Lucas, Houghton, Hornemann, etc.

1796: Mungo Park fails to reach Timbuctoo. But 'Timbuctoo Rush' has begun.

1797: James Jackson makes plans for going to Timbuctoo, but backs down.

1799: Army Surgeon Weales applies to lead an expedition to Timbuctoo, but dies in a duel at St. Vincent. About the same time, James Watt dies on the coast while arranging a mission to Timbuctoo.

1806: Mungo Park passes Kabara, within *8* miles of Timbuctoo and engages Tuareg.

1809: James Jackson publishes account of the town.

1811: American, Robert Adams, in Timbuctoo.

1811: Heinrich Roentgen, German adventurer, leaves Mogador for Timbuctoo: never heard from again.

1814: Johann Birckhardt, a Swiss, employed by the African Association to live in the Middle East till his Arabic is perfected (he does so to such effect that he is able to rediscover the ruined city of Petra and to make the Pilgrimage to Mecca); he is then to join a caravan from Cairo to Timbuctoo. He dies in Cairo.

1824: Geographical Society of Paris offer Prize, valued at 10,000 francs, to first person to return to Europe with account of Timbuctoo.

1826: FULANI claim town. Gordon Laing visits Timbuctoo: first emissary from Europe for *300* years.

1828: Frenchman René Cailié enters the city in disguise, and returns with an account of the decline which had begun over two centuries previously.

Circa 1830:	Fulani still claiming town, but TUAREG have regained the real power.
1853:	German Heinrich Barth visits Timbuctoo: returns with further description of the town and history of the Songhai.
1880:	Oscar Lenz visits Timbuctoo, other attempts since Barth having ended in murder or failure.
1887:	French gunboat forced back from Kabara by Tuareg.
1893:	French Army enter Timbuctoo. FRENCH RULE begins.
1940:	Population at census: 5,000.
1960:	Republic of MALI granted independence. Timbuctoo returns to Mali rule after five and a half centuries.

Sources

UNPUBLISHED MATERIAL

Colonial Office Papers (Public Record Office)
Denham and Clapperton   C.O.2.13/15/16
Gordon Laing   C.O.2.13/15/16
Lander   C.O.2.18/19
Lyon and Ritchie   C.O.2.8/9

Foreign Office Papers (Public Record Office)
Barth and Vogel   F.O.101.34/36/45
Gordon Laing   F.O.27.421
    F.O.76.22/26/27/33/36
Warrington   F.O.101.13/15

Barth Papers (British Museum Dept. of MSS.)
Letters   Add MSS. 32117.ff.15–63

PUBLISHED PRIMARY MATERIAL

Narrative of Robert Adams (London, 1816; Boston, 1817).
Africanus, Leo. *The History and Description of Africa*, Vol. 3, trans. J. Pery, ed. R. Brown (Hakluyt Society, 1896).
Barth, H. *Travels in North and Central Africa* (London, Germany, New York, 1857; Amsterdam, 1858; Copenhagen, 1859; Paris, 1861).
Belzoni, G. *Fruits of Enterprise* (London, 1821).
Bovill, E. W. *Missions to the Niger*, Vol. I (Hakluyt Society, 1964). Includes Laing MSS. in Royal Society, etc. Vols. 2, 3, 4 (1966). Bornu Mission, 1822.
Biographical Dictionary of Eminent Scotsmen, Vol. 3, R. Chambers (Glasgow, 1834). Includes Laing's letter to his family.
Caillé, R. *Travels Through Central Africa to Timbuctoo* (Paris, 1830; London 1830, 1907)
Clapperton, H. *Journal of a Second Expedition into Africa* (London, 1829)
Clapperton, H., and Denham, D. *Travels and Discoveries in Northern and Central Africa* (London, Paris, Boston, 1826)
Crene, G. R., trans. and ed., *Voyages of A. Cadamasto and Other Documents on Western Africa* (Hakluyt Society, 1937)
Davidson, J. *Notes Taken During Travels in Africa* (London, privately, 1839)
Edinburgh Review, Vol. 49 (Edinburgh, 1829). Includes some of Laing's letters.
Europeans in West Africa 1450–1560, trans. and ed. J. W. Blake (Hakluyt Society, 1942)
Flatters, P., etc. *Documents Relatifs à la Mission Diridée au Sud de l'Algerie* (Paris, 1884)
Gray, W., and (?) Dochard *Travels in Western Africa* (London, 1825)
Hallett, R. *The Records of the African Association* (London, 1964)
Haywood, A. H. *Through Timbuctoo and Across the Great Sahara* (London, 1912)
Jackson, J. G. *An Account of the Empire of Morocco to Which is Added an Accurate Account of Timbuctoo* (London, 1809)

Joffre, J. J. C. *My March to Timbuctoo* (Paris, 1895; London, 1915)

Laing, A. G. *Travels in Western Africa* (London, 1825)

Lander, R. *Records of Captain Clapperton's Last Expedition* (London, 1830)

Lander, R., and Lander, J. ed. R. Huish, *Travels, etc.* (London, 1836)

Lenz, O. *Timbuktu* (Leipzig, 1884; Paris, 1886)

Lyon, G. H. *A Narrative of Travels in Northern Africa* (London. 1821)

de Mezières, B. de. *Le Major A. C. Laing* (Paris, 1912)

Mollien, G. *Travels in the Interior of Africa* (Paris; London, 1820, 1967)

Motter, T. H. V. ed., *The Writings of Arthur Hallam* (New York, 1943)

Paddock, J. *Shipwreck of the Oswego* (New York, 1818; London, 1818)

Park, M. *Journal of a Mission in the Interior of Africa* (London, 1815; Paris, 1841)

Park, M. *Travels in the Interior Districts of Africa* (London, 1799; Berlin, 1800; Paris, 1841)

Richardson, J. *Narrative of a Mission to Central Africa* (London, 1853)

Richardson, J. *Travels in the Great Desert of Sahara* (London, 1848)

Riley, J. *The Loss of the American Brig Commerce with an Account of Timbuctoo* (New York, 1817; London, 1817; Italy, 1904)

Skelle, J. *Azalai* (New York, 1956)

Tennyson, Lord. *Poems by Two Brothers* (London, 1893)

OTHER PUBLISHED WORKS

Baker, J. N. L. *A History of Geographical Discovery and Exploration* (London 1931)

Bodington, N. *The Awakening Sahara* (London, 1961)

Bonnier, G. *L'Occupation de Tombouctou* (Paris, 1826)

Bovill, E. W. *The Golden Trade of the Moors* (Oxford, 1958)

Brown, R. *The Story of Africa*, Vol, 1, Vol. 4 (London, 1892)

Burns, Sir A. *History of Nigeria* (London, 1955)

Connelly, T. W. J. *History of the Corps of Royal Sappers and Miners*, Vol. 2 (London, 1855)

Dubois, F. *Timbuctoo the Mysterious* (Paris 1897; London, 1897)

Eydeux, H.-P. *L'Exploration du Sahara* (Paris, 1938)

Gaffiet, R. *Le Major A. G. Laing à Tombouctou* (Dakar, 1931)

Gallaher, J., and Robinson, R. *Africa and the Victorians* (London, 1961)

Gautier, E. F. *Sahara* (Paris, 1928; New York, 1935)

Gibbon, L. G. *Niger: The Life of Mungo Park* (London, 1934)

Gwynn, S. *Mungo Park* (London, 1934)

Heahen, Adu, *Britain. the Sahara & the Western Sudan 1788-1861* (Oxford, 1964).

Hall, L. *Timbuctoo* (New York, 1927)

Hallett, R. *The Penetration of Africa*, vol. 1 (London, 1965)

Herrmann, P. *The World Unveiled* (Germany, 1956; London, 1958)

Howard, C. With Intro., J. H. Plumb, *West African Explorers* (Oxford, 1951). Anthology.

Kirk-Greene, A. H. M. *Barth's Travels in Nigeria* (Oxford, 1962)

Lecler, R. *World Without Mercy* (London, 1954)

Leithauser, J. C. *Worlds Beyond the Horizon* (Germany, 1953; London, 1956)

Longebardi, C. *L'Aganie d'Une Mission* (Paris, 1938)

Maugham, R. *Slaves of Timbuktu* (London, 1961). With extracts from MS. of M. Moseley.

Miner, M. *The Primitive City of Timbuctoo* (Princeton, 1953)

Murray, H. *Discoveries and Travels in Africa* (Edinburgh, 1818)
Nelson, T. *A Memoir of Oudney, Clapperton, and Laing* (Edinburgh, 1830)
Priest, C. D. *Timbuctoo*, in *National Geographical Magazine*, 1924.
de Prorek, B. K. *Mysterious Sahara* (London, 1930)
Quarterly Reveiw, Vol. 38, Vol. 39 (London, 1828, 1829)
Seabrook, W. *The White Monk of Timbuctoo* (New York; London, 1934)
Shaw, F. L. *A Tropical Dependency* (London, 1905)
Sykes, Sir F. *A History of Exploration* (London. 1934)
Terrasse, H. *Histoire du Maroc* (Casablanca, 1949)
Turnbull, F. *Sahara Unveiled* (London, 1940)
Ward, E. *Sahara Story* (London, 1962)
Welch, G. *The Unveiling of Timbuctoo* (London, 1938). The story of Caillié,
  using French biographies.
Wellard, J. *The Great Sahara* (London, 1964)
White, S. *Dan Bana* (London, 1966)

REFERENCE WORKS

Allgemaine Deutsche Biographie (Leipzig, 1875-1910)
Annual Register (London, 1798–1826)
Dictionary of National Biography (London, 1885–   )
Dictionnaire de Biographie Francaise, ed. Balteau, J. (Paris, 1933–   )
Encyclopaedia Britannica (Chicago, 1964)
Encyclopaedia of Modern History: Larousse, ed. Dunan, M. (Paris; London, 1964)
Grand Larousse Encyclopédique (Paris, 1960–   )
La Grand Larousse Encyclopédie (Paris, 1887–1902)
Neue Deutsche Biographie (Berlin, 1952–   )
Nieuw Nederlandandsch Biegrafisch Weerdenboek, Vol. 1 (Leiden, 1911)

ATLASES: from which all distances etc. in the text

Concise Oxford Altas (Oxford, 1960)
Times Atlas of the World, Vol. 4 (London, 1956)

Index